FREEDOM FROM HISTORY
and other untimely essays

FREEDOM
FROM HISTORY

and other

untimely essays

by

Frank E. Manuel

New York University Press
New York 1971

ACKNOWLEDGMENTS

Thanks are given for permission to reprint a number of the essays in this book: "From Equality to Organicism" (*Journal of the History of Ideas*, January 1956); "Henri Saint-Simon on the Role of the Scientist" (*Revue internationale de philosophie*, 1960); "In Defense of Philosophical History" (*Antioch Review*, Fall 1960); "Two Styles of Philosophical History" (*Daedalus*, Spring 1962); "Toward a Psychological History of Utopian Thought" (*Daedalus*, Spring 1965); "Thoughts on Great Societies" (*A Great Society?*, New York, Basic Books, 1968); "Newton as Autocrat of Science" (*Daedalus*, Summer 1968); "The Use and Abuse of Psychology in History" (*Daedalus*, Winter 1971).

BY THE SAME AUTHOR

The Politics of Modern Spain, 1938
American-Palestine Relations, 1949
The Age of Reason, 1951
The New World of Henri Saint-Simon, 1956
The Eighteenth Century Confronts the Gods, 1959
The Prophets of Paris, 1962
Isaac Newton, Historian, 1963
Shapes of Philosophical History, 1965
The Enlightenment (editor), 1965
Utopias and Utopian Thought (editor), 1966
French Utopias: An Anthology of Ideal Societies (with Fritzie P. Manuel), 1966
Herder's Reflections on the Philosophy of the History of Mankind (editor), 1968
A Portrait of Isaac Newton, 1968

PROLOGUE

This is my sixtieth birthday; but since the temper of the times is not conducive to the gathering of an appropriate *Festschrift* by my students, I thought I would prepare one for myself. What I have done is to assemble those essays and formal lectures prepared during the past fifteen years that for some reason seemed worth preserving—a fair sample of my work since I was levitated from the solid ground of economic, political, and diplomatic studies into the murky atmosphere of intellectual and psychological history.

A number of these historical monologues were presented *viva voce* before live audiences, and were composed with that setting in mind. This is therefore oral history in a very special sense. It follows the tradition of Herodotus, who, we are told, read his narratives in the marketplace of Athens. And hopefully it could serve the same purpose as those royal chronicles intoned for the Persian kings when they were sleepless.

While some of the pieces became points of departure for weighty volumes ornamented with the accustomed and accursed paraphernalia of footnotes, backnotes, and sidenotes, the original versions have the merit of brevity enforced by the fleeting academic hour, and perhaps the clarity of first, if fugitive impressions. A third of the essays have not been published before, and a few represent work in progress that may remain in limbo for eternity.

In retrospect, I see that there has been greater unity to my central intellectual preoccupations in recent years than I once imagined. While my interests have rarely drawn me beyond the bounds of Western culture, I have never settled down to a diligent cultivation of a single national history or a favorite century. I have been fascinated by vague rather than concrete subjects—man's attempt to find a philosophy of history for himself, the enduring but continually varying significance of the mythic in his consciousness, and his pursuit of images of the ideal city. The specific achievements of the scientist, that unique creature of our civilization, have intrigued me less than the problematic role he has played in what has generally been a society of warriors and priests. The refractory records of philosophical histories, interpretations of myth, and utopias have been "vexed," as Francis Bacon would say, to yield secrets of man's mind and sensibility in their metamorphoses through the centuries. It was inevitable that at some point I would come to grips with the major psychoanalytic attempts to wrestle with symbolic expressions of the unconscious.

An outsider might find me distressingly ambivalent toward the subjects with which I deal historically. He may discover that in one essay I extol the poetic and educative virtues of philosophers of history, in another I would all but throw them out of the guild, if not the city. Utopias remain for me inspirations of the noblest longings of man, but also sources of his cruelest deceptions. The mythic that has survived in our lives is conceived as an enrichment of human thought and feeling, and yet I am ready to contribute to its erosion by rationalist analysis. The ways of the new psychology are accepted, but hardly without a measure of skepticism. Despite long years of engagement, there are moments of doubt about history itself, as the deliberately ambiguous title bears witness.

An arrow once shot from the bow can never be recalled, the Bedouin say. No attempt has been made to gloss over inconsistencies, delete an occasional repetition, or tone down changing moods and attitudes. Anyone who has maintained himself in an unswerving, upright posture over the past two decades has probably been dead on his feet.

Washington Square   Frank E. Manuel
New York

CONTENTS

A Historian's Credo

1. Freedom from History   3
2. The Use and Abuse of Psychology in History   23
3. In Defense of Philosophical History   53

Utopias Ancient and Modern

4. The Golden Age: A Mythic Prehistory for Western
   Utopia   69
5. Pansophia, a Seventeenth-Century Dream of Science   89
6. Toward a Psychological History of Utopias   115

The Scientist in Society

7. Newton as Autocrat of Science   151
8. The Intellectual in Politics: Locke, Newton, and
   the Establishment   189
9. Henri Saint-Simon on the Role of the Scientist   205

Reflective History

10. From Equality to Organicism   221
11. Two Styles of Philosophical History   243
12. Thoughts on Great Societies   265
    Index   291

FREEDOM FROM HISTORY
and other untimely essays

A HISTORIAN'S CREDO

I

FREEDOM FROM HISTORY

Since I am a historian by birth, in preparation for this lecture I took to reading the speeches that professors had delivered under similar provocation at other times and places. Not to learn from them—perish the thought!—but rather to avoid repeating too much of what had already been said. As was to be expected, I found that their manner varied enormously, from the sonorous proclamation of Schiller at Jena that universal history must pass judgment on the whole moral world of man to the studied nonchalance of contemporary British Regius professors, who slide into their chairs without attracting notice.[1] In passing I learned that the inaugural act itself, far from being an innocuous academic exercise, could be fraught with danger. Ernest Renan, for example, delivered his address at the Collège de France on February 21, 1862, and was promptly suspended from his post. I trust you understand, Mr. President, that when I chose to talk on "Freedom from History," it was not with the prospect of being taken literally and freed from history in any professional capacity. I had multiple meanings in mind, but that one was excluded.

To outsiders, history as a branch of knowledge presents the aspect of a homogeneous totality, like any other discipline. In

Inaugural Lecture as Kenan Professor of History, New York University, March 12, 1970.

3

point of fact, however, there is not a modicum of consensus among us with respect to either the selection of essential materials or the establishment of final goals. We agree only about trivial things. Today, chronological coding is about all that unites us, the sequence of the before and the after. And should new forms like comparative history become modish, who knows but that some of our number may even withdraw interest from the chronological codes and treat events as abstractly and synchronously as the structural anthropologists.

In the face of the bewildering varieties of contemporary historiography, I have occasionally borrowed a page from Chairman Mao's little red book, "letting a hundred flowers blossom and a hundred schools of thought contend." [2] But at this solemn moment I must confess that my utterances in the past have been somewhat disingenuous; for while I recognize the existence of a great diversity of growths in the historical garden, I do not really wish all of them equally well; in fact, there are a few I would gladly see wither on the vine. Toward some I have tolerance, toward others mere forbearance; and then there are the darlings of my heart. Inaugural lectures are times for pontification; one speaks with finality, and no amount of assumed diffidence can hide the dogmatic streak that lurks in all of us. This official profession of faith will thus be a statement of where I stand in the historical spectrum. As a declaration of intent it comes rather late in life; but history being proverbially an old man's game, inaugurals and valedictories in this field tend to interpenetrate. I can wish for things I may not be very hopeful about, and plot out historical ways that have only a marginal chance of coming to fruition.

In the nineteenth century, history dominated the whole mentality of the west. Augustin Thierry predicted in 1834 that history would be the signature of the nineteenth century and would give its name to the age as philosophy had to the eighteenth. If you founded a nation, justified a legal code, explained a system of morals, illuminated the inner meaning of a religion, or advocated a world revolution, you did so on historical grounds and used the rhetoric of historical argument. Romantic nationalism made the evocation of past victories a central ingredient of political life. In theories of evolution or revolution, history was the clue to existence; and moralists required that man put his conscience into harmony with true historical development. For conservatives, the historical became the source of legitimacy; to revolutionaries, history issued infallible directives for action. As a by-product of this universal immersion in the historical, human experience achieved an extension that was even more momentous than the restoration of the remains of Greece and Rome. The recovery of vast expanses of the past in literature, art, archaeology, ethnology, religion, geology, and biology, was a great acquisition of mankind— a permanent acquisition, it was believed at the time.

Since World War I, however, the role of the historical in our thought and sensibility has undergone a radical change. Histories of all kinds of things have continued to multiply at a rate so fast that the problem of storage is becoming acute. The bonds of Europocentrism have finally been broken, a major revolution, for despite random explorations of other cultures, until well into our own time the passion for the historical was global in name only. But paradoxically, in the very midst of accumulating mountains of material, we are beginning to question the meaningfulness of history itself. At a time when literally hundreds of thousands of persons throughout the world earn their livelihood by engaging in some form of historical research, the worth of their investigations has become problematic. The men of the nineteenth century exulted in their historical intoxication; today one detects a feeling of glut, of surfeit. There is a desire to wake up fresh in the morning and to look at the world anew, to cleanse the Augean stables of their historical refuse with one mighty Herculean sweep. Antagonism to history is not limited to those who lead the wild dash toward modernity. There is a quiet disenchantment among the very persons who are the appointed historiographers of the society. I am voicing a measure of unease about history, an ill-defined discontent, a discomfort in its practice, a malaise. This dissatisfaction is perhaps related in part to a general unease with culture itself, which Freud diagnosed in his famous essay of 1930, *Civilization and its Discontents*. It may be that history is only the first of a long line of intellectual pursuits that will be summoned before the bar of utility by a technological civilization operating through anonymous Kafka-like agents, and that each in its turn will be condemned. But forms of negation are now in evidence that are especially and pointedly directed against history.

The downgrading of historical knowledge is, of course, not a uniquely twentieth-century phenomenon. Despite the overwhelming approval of history in western culture from its earliest beginnings, there was nonetheless an intermittent undercurrent of depreciation fed from diverse sources. In some respects the present-day assault on history is a composite of previous criticisms reanimated.

Perhaps the first denigrator was Aristotle, who in the *Poetics* made an invidious comparison between history, which dealt only with the particular facts of sense experience, and poetry, which treated of universal truths. History merely described what happened, while poetry, more philosophical, what might happen.[3] Christian mystics, always regarded with mistrust by institutional religion, have been a constant threat to the guardians of priestly historical tradition. In preparing for union with God, the mystics have exercised themselves in blotting out the memory of old experiences and damning up their senses against the reception of new ones. They have striven to put themselves into a state of passivity in order that they might receive the spirit directly without mediation. Those who seek to achieve similar states through chemical ingestion will in any age reject history.

At a polar extreme from the mystics, Descartes' reflections in the first part of the *Discourse on Method*, the Bible of the new rationalism, became a proof-text of the anti-historical. History was full of mythic fictions, a dazzling structure without foundation. Excessive frequentation of the ancients, the study of their politics and their childish science, deflected a man from the concerns of his own time. It was wasteful, like too much travel. "One finally becomes a stranger in one's own country. . . ." [4] The undergraduate who today interrupts any historical recollection with the cry "irrelevant!" is in this limited respect an unconscious Cartesian. Even as a repository of lessons, history was misleading for Descartes, because the examples were usually touched up and their vulgar circumstances erased. Since only the discourse of reason mattered, he condemned history as a record of transient passions and insignificant occurrences, unworthy of a philosopher's attention. When in the next century Vico set up the postulates of his new science, the grandest apologia of history in the west, he trained his guns directly on Descartes as the principal enemy.

The eighteenth-century *philosophes* were adept in dredging up historical examples to destroy Christianity, but, absorbed as they were in a new, brazen look at reality, many of them wanted to get history off mankind's back and to expunge the very memory of past cruelties and irrationalities. Followers of Rousseau posited a contradiction between original nature and history that has been periodically re-asserted by modern Adamites. Schopenhauer, an alien in the historicist early nineteenth century, picked up Descartes' theme of belittlement. "[History] never knows the particular by means of the general, but must comprehend the particular directly, and so, as it were, creeps along the ground of experience; while the true sciences move above it. . . ."[5] This type of argument wounded some historians in a tender spot and they proceeded in great haste to fabricate scientific credentials for themselves.

By far the most trenchant criticism of the uses of history in the modern period came from Friedrich Nietzsche. At a time when Ranke, the great exponent of historicism, was still alive, this man emerged from the very heart of the German philological tradition to denounce the hypertrophy of history as a disease, to explode what he conceived to be the myth of continuity, and to exalt the will of the free, creative individual untrammeled by the past. He would have man break with the historical, grasp the present in its emotive fulness and spontaneity, and come down hard upon reality with a bang. Nietzsche's abuse of history as the gray, paralyzing inhibitor of action has a contemporary resonance: "One who cannot leave himself behind on the threshold of the moment and forget the past, who cannot stand on a single point, like a goddess of victory, without fear or giddiness, will never know what happiness is. . . . Such a man . . . sees everything fly past in an eternal succession, and loses himself in the stream of becoming. At last, like the logical disciple of Heraclitus, he will hardly dare to raise his finger." [6] Nietzsche's writings abound in caricatures of his history-besotted countrymen, their bellies loaded with an enormous heap of indigestible knowledge. His description of a generation of German scholars who had history forced down their gullets would find sympathetic echoes among many of our students: "The young man is kicked through all the centuries. . . . The crowd of influences streaming on the young soul is so great, the clods of barbarism and violence flung at him so strange and overwhelming, that an assumed stupidity is his only refuge." [7]

To these old attacks the twentieth century has added new ones of great persuasiveness and power. A whole group of writers have diabolized the idea of history. In addition to the two traditional meanings of the word in most European languages—history as the past events themselves and history as conscious writing about the past—a third meaning has begun to insinuate itself into our speech. More and more, history is becoming the personification of a potent daemonic force abroad in the world, which intrudes into our individual lives and catches us up in tragically absurd adventures not of our own choosing. Its usage in this sense connotes a terrifying, intimate fate. History appears as a ruthless monster that smashes into our lives, drags us off to war, devastates nations in mass holocausts, and may yet destroy us all in a final cataclysmic historical event. In a rare period of relative peace, the century from Waterloo to Sarajevo, Europeans made their private middle-class histories with a fair degree of autonomy and cultivated their collective history confident that it would bring a cornucopia of good things. But in the period since World War I, who has not felt himself imperiled by onrushing, devouring, suffocating history? What does history hold in store for us, we ask, sweating with anxiety. In the face of this history men like Camus have arisen to pit their strength against the inhuman forces, to defy their apparent omnipotence, and to challenge their imperiousness with an existential commitment to a moral absolute of individual, personal choice. "[R]ebellion, in man, is the refusal to be treated as a thing and to be reduced to mere history. History is surely one of the limits of man. . . . But in his rebellion man in his turn fixes a limit to history." [8] For others, apprehension of history-in-the-making numbs the sensibility toward history as past. Fear of the future—doubt whether there will be a future—becomes so great that they shut *both* gates to the historical, the fore and the aft, and live only in the present.

In a more limited political sphere and in the rhetoric of contemporary class conflict, historical culture is being denounced as a manifestation of a particular phase of capitalist development. The charge is that the regurgitation of history in the universities is a bulwark for a decadent bourgeois society, which is unjust, immoral, and destructive. When nations are either engaged or prepared to engage in mass slaughter, the formal teaching of the historical exemplars of humanism is labeled a fraud. History is despised as the tool of an ugly society bereft of any emotive or philosophical authenticity. To purge and renovate that society, history has to be pulled up by the roots. There is a smell of young barbarism and book-burning in the air. Ironically, many of the elders who govern our technological-scientific-military society with its passion for advertised innovation also have little need for the past. The American industrialist who affirmed that history was bunk and the nihilist who ends discussion with a scatological exclamation or an apocalyptic threat have advanced from opposite corners to a common meeting-ground. For both, history has no reason for existence.

Traditional apologias for history are no longer pertinent. The wise justifications of Thucydides and Bolingbroke and Hume avail us nothing. The question is not what history may have done for mankind in earlier ages, but what history has done for us lately, and what it intends to do tomorrow. It may well be that history has done too much for us, that it has done more evil than good, that a curt good-riddance might be appropriate; that history, having spawned too many chimaeras, false idols, blinding fictions, having cloaked itself with glittering promises that remain unfulfilled, is a burden upon civilization that ought to be cast off. History in its present incarnations may in fact not answer to the manifest needs of the times, and if tolerated at all, may come to be looked upon as nothing more than a harmless pastime. In brief, *historia* has been deposed as *magistra vitae*, and like a forlorn *émigré* may have to compete for even an humble place in the world.

Now I, too, can think the unthinkable and conceive of a society that has virtually banished the historical. Instead of a complex existence that interweaves the three presents of St. Augustine —the present of present things, the present of past things, the present of future things—there would be total saturation with present things. A society might become possessed with the manufacture of novelty to the point where extension into the past has no meaning for it. Technological change can be so dazzling and so destructive of objects that the past loses visibility. Though we may have access to far more data about other centuries than ever before, we may have far less feeling for them as their monuments are constantly removed from sight. In a culture that has set its highest value on newness and youth, the agedness of a thing or person, with the exception of a limited number of privileged objects called antiques or antiquities, becomes a mark of increasing worthlessness. As far back as 1931, the French poet Paul Valéry foresaw an era when men would be tied to the past by no recognizable habit of mind. "History will offer them strange, almost incomprehensible tales, because nothing in their age will have had an example in the past and nothing of the past will survive into their present." [9]

But Valéry's dark prognostication is not likely to be fulfilled in the near future. Though history has been dethroned, there is every reason to believe that we shall continue to have much history-book manufacture for our time. Unfortunately, the crisis of modernity is apt to favor the proliferation of those very kinds of history that should long ago have been outgrown and to foster the development of new modes that, in my judgment, are not congruent with the deepening of a personal and humanist historical consciousness—as you see, my pontification is about to begin in earnest.

In order to define my own position, I cannot avoid reference to what I consider the negative historical identities. The popular idols of macro-history, ethnicity, contemporaneity, pragmatic history, and the many-headed idols of structure and measure are flourishing in despite of the widespread attack on history; indeed, they sometimes pose as effective answers to those who doubt its utility.

Over the past two hundred years, since Voltaire coined the phrase "philosophy of history," various schemes have been invented that arrogate to themselves the function of making the earthly sacred, solving the riddle of man's existence, and establishing the direction in which mundane events are moving—all with an absolutism and a circumstantial particularity from which orthodox sacred history itself discreetly held aloof. Unlike the heterodox *profeta* Joachim of Fiore, the medieval father of macro-historians, St. Thomas Aquinas cautiously hedged about the disposition of the world. He wrote in the *Summa:* "Till the Judgment Day some new things are always being revealed by God to the highest angels. . . ." [10] In their attempt to substitute for Christian eschatology, modern philosophies of history hypnotize us with a few gnomic phrases: world history as an alternativity of the organic and the critical spiraling toward a higher level of being, freedom from necessity, a triad of thesis, antithesis, and synthesis, a struggle of life and death, a succession of expansions and contractions, a progression toward the noösphere. These pseudo-histories primarily serve a religious purpose. Thomas Churchill, an Englishman of the turn of the eighteenth century who, like myself, was addicted to this form of literature and was the first translator of Condorcet and Herder, naively expressed the emotions that works of this character inspire. They gave him the illusion, he said, of swimming in infinite spaces of time. His sentiments recall the oceanic feeling of one of Freud's correspondents describing a religious experience.

Periods of anxiety and crisis will spur the writing of philosophies of history, as though they were guides to the perplexed and history's special province were to define the purpose of man's existence on earth or authoritatively to chart the course of future events. Men will continue to derive solace from the grand vistas of millennial history, full of hope when a better future is foretold them. Or they will thrill with horror like spectators at the Grand

Guignol when the decline of the west or the end of the human race is predicted. But such fantasies, though they may appease an enduring psychological need, are not the stuff of rationalist history.

Far more insidious than the macrosystems is ethnicity, which pretends to confer identity upon collectives by recalling to them a racial, folk, or national history of common sufferings and glorious victories. The nineteenth-century high tide of the historical coincided with the great age of ethnicity; and we cannot approach its most prolific historians without a vague feeling of embarrassment that, for all their evocative genius, they did not escape the toils of a vulgar nationalism. No other form of knowledge has the inborn tendency of history to geographic fragmentation and spiritual provincialism. The very structuring of the discipline in the university often remains rigidly national and therefore parochial. An undisguised passion for self-maximation quickly transforms the ethnic history that is initiated as benign cultural nationalism into a kind of racism. The symbiotic relationship between cultural nationalism and state history has forged so tight a grip that there is little immediate prospect of emancipation from this adolescent narcissism of the Romantics. Yet how can one refrain from a certain dismay at the ubiquity of the egocentric illusion in which, in varying degrees, historians participate? The broadening of historical culture to include new peoples and social classes and hitherto unrecognized and unfathomed areas of plain human experience is a great conquest over the constrictions of Hegelian idealism; but regression into ethnicity makes a mockery of the triumph.

It may be objected that the current fashion for ethnic history should be approached with more sympathy and understanding. Who am I to deny those collectives who were shut out of history-book making the megalomania of national history if it helps them build an identity? But while I empathize with the aspirations of ethnic groups and social classes coming into awareness of their individuality, the achievement of identity in any meaningful terms is always an unconscious psychological process; it cannot be "store-boughten"; and ethnically-based histories, hastily improvised as identity cards, spark false images and eradicate the complexities of past experience with its manifold, painful ambiguities. They create caricatures of identity. Every human collective has the inalienable right to its history, but the perspective from which it is written—the world or the tribal tent—will determine whether it inflicts more wounds than it heals. One thing is certain: there is no special "ethnic accessibility" to history, no mystic identity of subject and object, no innate gift of comprehension which would make Jews the chosen custodians of Jewish history or blacks of black history. All men must be presumed to have more or less equal access to all historical phenomena by simple reason of their humanity.

On the analogy of a man learning from his own life experience, the idol of pragmatic history promises to distill easy lessons from the past. In the sixteenth and seventeenth centuries, history as a repository of wise examples yielded a rich literature, and was the chief vehicle for the education of princes, who were thus taught to avoid the errors of their predecessors. It left them free, of course, to make mistakes on their own initiative that were infinitely more disastrous. It may well be that in an enclosed and highly stable system, historical lessons give the careful observer of traditional modes some technical advantage over the ignoramus in beating his rival. But as the Chinese historiographers knew, this holds good *only* for the period of balance and equilibrium, only until a peasant boy rises up and destroys the dynasty. After the fact, it becomes clear that in this case the applicable etiquette of Chinese political behavior was suspended. It is precisely at critical points of discontinuity, when the old modes are fractured, when examples from history are most needed, that they have least to offer. There is onceness to history, and even if one could make insightful judgments and draw appropriate conclusions from historical events, they would not yield rules of conduct for a new concatenation of circumstances. And if there were lessons to be drawn from history, they would not be heard by men deafened by the thunderous passions of the moment of action. As Hegel told his students: "In the turmoil of world affairs no universal principle, no memory of similar conditions in the past can help us—a vague memory has no power against the vitality and freedom of the present." [11] Wretched men in the throes of disaster will sometimes turn for advice to the first historical pundit who presents himself. But historians who freely proffer such advice are like those moon-cussers who, waving lanterns from craggy rocks to ships in distress, lure them to their destruction.

Contemporaneity, a latter-day faith, is the old pragmatic idol in a new disguise. There is every likelihood that professional activity will be increasingly concentrated on contemporary or recent history. The illusion is widespread that recent history is somehow more relevant than ancient history, that the ills which beset us are inherited from the more immediate past and that studying these events might lead to the discovery of sovereign remedies. Since everyone is impressed by the accelerated tempo of the times, chronologically distant examples appear bizarre; but the very recent past, it is expected, can become a platform from which to project lines of development and therefore to prognosticate. Of course, if we pursued the analogy between personal and group behavior we might arrive at a contrary conclusion, recognizing that it is often an event from our very *early* history that springs up to hit us in the face with traumatic force and that the more dangerous monsters may leap from the distant past—witness the primitive savagery of our own century.

Past history and future utopia are two ways of wrestling with the finitude of existence. The cutting off of one or the other leaves us impoverished creatures whose firefly span is shorn of much significance. And by history and utopia I mean the whole human past and the open, imaginative vision of all future possibilities, not mere presentness extended to the year 2000. Futurist history with its mixed bag of half-truths and falsehoods has become a quasi-science, a form of history that can be practiced with relative impunity because it soon is a part of yesterday and as such is hastily forgotten, buried beneath an avalanche of more recent predictions. Shrinking the whole past into the just-become past and compressing the future into an exercise in graphed extrapolation is nothing but another form of bondage to the present. These are shriveled, spurious pasts and futures, so limited in scope that they imprison us in immediacy, the closed-in space of the instantaneous, the frozen moment in a film. The growing preference for recent history as a field of study is really a copping-out from the historical.

The last idols on my little list, those of structure and measure, represent new historical ways that are gaining ground both in the American and in the French schools. Their proponents encourage the reduction of historical knowledge to measurable quantities, manipulable series, or formal structures that bring it into line with the spirit and method of the other sciences. If the physical sciences are triumphant, let us become like unto all the Gentiles and live by their law. The ambiguities and dubieties of history would then dissolve. The advocates of this type of history seek for uniformities, ransack the past for repetitions, and arrange their materials in accordance with one or another of the available codes. American specialists train themselves in the most refined statistical methods and have learned to program their data for computers. The inevitable tendency develops to ask primarily those questions that can best be answered by means of the new techniques, questions that are often trivial. Technology comes to determine the shape and the substance of the investigation. The relationship of history and quantifying techniques can be a fruitful one: I would gladly avail myself of data arranged with greater refinement than my customary scale of one, two, three, many, and very many. But for what purpose is the relationship established? *Timeo computeros et dona ferentis*—I am chary of gift-bearing computers. Scientistic history can become one of the more obvious ways of avoiding and evading human history. Will the new techniques serve history or will history be gobbled up by the new techniques? That is the question. The union of man and horse, Metternich once remarked, is clearly a beneficial one, but in that union it is important to be the man and not the horse.

If French structuralism, whose chief exponent is Claude Lévi-Strauss, should prevail, history would cease to be a separate form of knowledge and become a mere auxiliary to the sciences of man. The laborious results of the critical, historical method, ordering and verifying the documents and artifacts of the past and fixing their place in a chronological sequence, would then be inherited by the other disciplines. The historian who deliberately prepares his materials with this design of feeding scientific consumers shows the solicitude of a victim for those who are about to cannibalize him. The basic options have been set forth in the debate between Sartre and Lévi-Strauss, between the humanist phenomenological view of history on one side and, on the other, an anthropological structuralism that mocks history as a formless mass with no autonomous being. In his book *The Savage Mind*, Lévi-Strauss quipped contemptuously: "As we say of certain careers, history may lead to anything, provided you get out of it." [12] Though few historians would declare themselves structuralists in the French sense, a glance at the program of the forthcoming international congress of historical sciences in Moscow will show the degree to which academic history the world over is in fact becoming faceless, nameless, and anonymous, dehumanized and depersonalized. Beneath it all, I cannot help detecting the fear of man that permeates so many of the projects of our time.

Now you are surely asking yourselves in polite silence: If one denies that there is any pragmatic use to history, either as a storehouse of lessons or as a basis for prognostication; if one deplores a special interest in the most recent past with which there is a sort of superficial familiarity; if one rejects the emotive exhilaration whereby history can infuse a nation-state with a sense of cohesion and community and the consolations of religious feeling that may be derived from philosophical history; if one is repelled by the reductionism to which history would be subjected by codification, reification, and scientific models, what then *is* the purpose of history? In the early part of the hour I took cognizance of a desire prevalent in our society to be free from history in its double aspect as dead hand of the past and grim fate of the future. Now I have turned my back on all those who would salvage the historical by making it directly useful in any one of a number of enterprises that still enjoy public approbation in the present. What have I to offer in their stead? Surely not the restoration of history to its nineteenth-century hegemony.

Despite the forces militating against its survival, I believe that history in our age could become a powerful critical agent by affirming the very possiblity of human otherness both in the goals it sets for itself and in the works that it creates. It may have to live in denial of the values that dominate our society and in rebellion against its temper. The mind-blasting imposers of immediacy, armed with the newest electronic equipment, are the secret operatives of the anti-historical establishment. I have no prescription for mass culture, nor for those who, while mouthing shibboleths about transcending history, have fixated themselves in costumed historical postures, some comic, some tragic. I speak for a history that goes against the grain. In the face of the obsession with presentness and the omnivorous novelty-making mania, history can offer freedom from the transitory fads by recognizing a distinction between the mere apes of newness and original genius that breaks through the crust of desiccated tradition; in a world where knowledge has been forced to seek uniformities, similarities, repeatability, history can reflect an alternative world-view that stresses human particularity, specificity, individuation in form and content; in a society whose science seeks for the impersonal, the mathematical, and the paradigm of the unconscious structure, history can be one form of knowledge that stands apart and speaks out for irreducible personalization, the experience of a human being in time and place; at a moment when greatness seems drowned in anonymous institutional consciousness, history can keep alive the vision of the monumental persons of all ages; amidst the devouring rivalries of ideologies and systems, history can achieve freedom from the dogmatic in the re-creation of the "other" with total empathy.

Each act of history-writing is a personal testament and a confrontation of the self and that other. It may even be desirable candidly to present the historian as part of the picture. In his fashion, that eighteenth-century English gentleman Edward Gibbon, viewing ancient Byzantium and popping his head through the canvas from time to time, achieved in his day this kind of participation. The central fact of this personalist history will not be its relativity, which is taken for granted, but its assertion of the creative vitality of man in the multiplicity of his works.

Again I hear a skeptical question: is this German *Historismus*

with its idealization of specificity all over again—a school whose
sibilancy has always put me off? My answer is that while I do
not renounce the lineage of Vico and Herder, Ranke and Dilthey,
I believe that today historical individuation can control a variety
of materials, achieve a depth of perception, a breadth of dimension, and a subtlety in symbolic interpretation which the traditional historicists hardly dreamed of when they elevated the
specific and the particular to an independent value. History can
now lay claim to types of concreteness that Ranke would never
have recognized. For him the object of individuation was primarily the nation-state and events the overt, commonly accepted
accounts of state-actors. This exclusive emphasis upon the state
as the collective worthy of being considered a "living thing" led to
the submergence of other entities: the individual himself, the family, the religious community, the city, the social class, the intellectual or work group. We today are open to a variety of historical
experiences that elitist historians of the German School, like
Dilthey, would not have deigned to examine. We cannot deny
any class its history out of aristocratic snobbery, nor refuse any
human activity historical existence out of disdain for the ordinary
conduct of life. Sexuality, unmentionable, tabooed, in the world
of both the German historicists and the German Marxists, can,
as Sartre maintained in a brilliant polemic, be rendered historical
as "one way of living the totality of our condition—on a certain
level and within the perspective of a certain individual venture." [13]
In pondering Ranke's famous assurance in his first great work
that he simply wished to show what really happened, I have sometimes marveled at the covert arrogance of the "simply." A historian is still committed to revealing what really happened, but
that means really, really happened, on the manifold and varie-
gated levels of experience of which we have a growing awareness.
The insights of Marx on the dynamics of social change and of
Freud on individual human development can be brought together,
not in the vapid, oracular utterances of the literary Freudo-
Marxians, but in histories that depict life situations. For me,
this would involve less a commitment to the details of their systems than to the spirit of their inquiries, their radical shifts of

emphasis away from traditional causality and motivation. Perhaps the family constellation, which at once frames the psyche of the individual and is the agency through which class, ethnic, and religious consciousness is first transmitted to him, could become a new primary focus of the historical, far more sensitive to change than the state. In any event, historians can no longer hold by nice, comfortable, old-hat utilitarian theories as if nothing had happened in psychoanalysis and social thought.

There are formulas in the historical marketplace that purport to explain the intricate interplay between the individual's life history and the collective history in which it develops—Dilthey's elaborate web of connexities binding the individual to an epoch's *Weltanschauung*, Sartre's labored dialectical progression from the individual, through the group, to a historical totalization, Erikson's perceptive attempts to link individual psychoanalysis and group behavior by something less tenuous than Freud's axiomatic analogy. While some of these theories are attractive, none is conclusive. Exploration of this relationship remains the great frontier of a new humanist history; but succinct psychological macrostatements or the hypostatization of a psycho-historical process will not solve the enigma. The historian who is emancipated from a hierarchy of values, as hoary as Aristotle, that bestows inherent superiority upon the universal and the abstract, must be leery of a new enslavement to a general schema, for he has worlds of human concreteness to conquer.

One final reflection. Historical study committed to a humanizing of the past can represent for a modern secularized man an audacious challenge to the absolutism of death. We come full circle around to join Herodotus of Halicarnassus, who wrote his history "in the hope of thereby preserving from decay the remembrance of what men have done and of preventing the great and wonderful actions of the Greeks and the barbarians from losing their due meed of glory." [14] In one of his more fanciful etymologies, Vico derived *humanitas* from *humando*, burying, and taught that what men do with the dead becomes a measure of their humanity. [15] In a society that fails to grapple with death, shoves it under a plastic grass carpet with machine-like speed, historians rather than priests become the keepers of the dead. The historian can, Ezekiel-like, enter the valley of the dead and make the dry bones live again; or he can count them, catalogue them, read them as auguries, measure them, paint them up and worship them as his ancestors. Preservation that is mere cataloguing and locking in a closet is death itself. The shades must be tended, offered libations, or they will die a second, and definitive, death. If we cut short the constant remembering of the rich wholeness of the historical, we rob life itself of one of the meanings with which we in our time are free to invest it. As Ernst Cassirer, one of the twentieth-century philosophers most sensitive to the unique role of the historian, wrote in his *Essay on Man:* "[H]uman works are . . . subject to change and decay not only in a material but also in a mental sense. Even if their existence continues they are in constant danger of losing their meaning. Their reality is symbolic, not physical; and such reality never ceases to require interpretation and reinterpretation. And this is where the great task of history begins." [16]

NOTES

1. Johann Christoph Friedrich von Schiller, *Was heisst und zu welchem Ende studiert man Universalgeschichte?*, in *Werke*, ed. Ludwig Bellermann (Leipzig and Vienna, 1910?), VI, p. 183; H. R. Trevor-Roper, *History: Professional and Lay. An Inaugural Lecture delivered before the University of Oxford on 12 November 1957* (Oxford, 1957), p. 4.
2. *Quotations from Chairman Mao Tse-Tung* (Peking, 1966), pp. 302-303.
3. Aristotle, *The Poetics*, with English trans. by W. Hamilton Fyfe, Loeb Classical Library (London, New York, 1927), p. 35.
4. René Descartes, *Oeuvres et Lettres*, Pléiade ed. (Paris, 1953), p. 129.
5. Arthur Schopenhauer, *The World as Will and Idea*, trans. R. B. Haldane and J. Kemp, 2d ed. (London, 1891), III, p. 221.
6. Friedrich Nietzsche, *The Use and Abuse of History* (1874), in *The Complete Works*, ed. Dr. Oscar Levy (New York, 1964; first published 1909-1911), V, p. 8.
7. *Ibid.*, V, p. 61.
8. Albert Camus, *L'Homme révolté* (Paris, 1951), p. 307.
9. Paul Valéry, *Regards sur le monde actuel* (Paris, 1931), p. 185.

10. St. Thomas Aquinas, *Summa Theologica*, trans. Fathers of the English Dominican Province (New York, 1911), Part I, Question 106, p. 416.
11. Georg Wilhelm Friedrich Hegel, *Reason in History. A general introduction to the Philosophy of History*, trans. Robert S. Hartman (Indianapolis, 1953), p. 8.
12. Claude Lévi-Strauss, *The Savage Mind* (Chicago, 1966; original French ed., Paris, 1962), p. 262.
13. Jean-Paul Sartre, *The Problem of Method*, trans. Hazel E. Barnes (London, 1963; originally published as *Questions de Méthode*, prefatory essay of *Critique de la Raison Dialectique*), p. 62.
14. Herodotus, *The Persian Wars*, trans. George Rawlinson, Book I, in Francis R.B. Godolphin, ed., *The Greek Historians* (New York, 1942), I, p. 3.
15. Giambattista Vico, *The New Science*, trans. T.G. Bergin and M.H. Fisch (Ithaca, 1948), p. 8.
16. Ernst Cassirer, *An Essay on Man* (New Haven, 1944), pp. 184-185.

2

THE USE AND ABUSE OF
PSYCHOLOGY IN HISTORY

Almost a century ago Friedrich Nietzsche, that history-intoxi-cated son of the German philological school, delivered a tirade against the hypertrophy of history in the life of his times. In ap-propriating the title of his essay, I confess to a similar ambivalence respecting the modern uses of psychology in historical studies. After some years of history-writing I have begun to fear that I may be losing my way in the jungles of psychologism. In my pre-dicament I could of course appeal to the analytical philosophers and ask them to enlighten me about the implicit assumptions of my work; but having read their interpretations of the writings of my colleagues I am obdurately resistant. Instead, I shall seek a way out of my perplexity by hearkening to the advice of Alfred North Whitehead, who once said that when a man is lost he should not ask where *he* is, but where the *others* are. And so, advancing behind a chronological shield, I intend to locate myself by passing in critical review the experience of historians and psychologists whenever they have come into close proximity. After skimming over the eighteenth-century origin of their relationships,

The Rabbi Irving M. Levey Lecture, Princeton University, April 29, 1970, was a briefer version of this essay.

I shall concentrate on the last hundred years and even more especially on the recent period, when both disciplines have become mammoth academic enterprises, whose cohabitation, some might say, is doomed to sterility from the outset, like the improbable mating of a whale and an elephant. What my presentation lacks in depth and subtlety, I hope it may achieve in breadth. Perhaps at the end I may find a place for myself, and, who knows, others might be willing to join me even if it means standing midstream in rather shallow waters.

My level of discourse will not be hard-nosed and analytical but descriptive of the goals and achievements of those who sensed the rich potentialities of a new field of expression and proceeded to cultivate it. Men have been prospecting for a long time in this region, and I am less interested in the scientific theories they brought with them than in what they have carried back from their expeditions. Though I have not made an actual body count, I suspect that of late there has been more hortatory exposition of what might or should be done than perspective on what has in fact been going on. Commenting on the topos, on the content, of psychological history-writing may prove more illuminating than either dissecting benighted historians who enjoy the freedom of blithely going their narrative way, or issuing manifestoes on what would constitute a perfect psychological history.

In the past three centuries major attempts have been made to recover not only the written thoughts of men of other times but their thinking; not only the record of their actions but the secret purposes and hidden, even unconscious, feelings that spurred and accompanied the *res gestae*; not only the literary and artistic objects but the sensibility that was expressed and the emotions aroused in the creators as well as in their contemporary audiences. When there are Pyrrhonists about who question the veracity of recorded history in its most commonsensical usage, how must they regard an undertaking that presumes to re-create inner experiences, which do not usually manifest themselves in clear-cut fashion through specific and forthright documents! And yet this is what psychological history has self-confidently set out to do. Admittedly, this wild intention has always been a minor element in historical narrative since the first Persian chronicles, echoed in the Book of Esther, where we are told what a personage "speaks in his heart." Greek and Roman historians used a variety of devices to disclose the secret purposes and unfulfilled desires animating their protagonists; and the Renaissance historians who imitated them availed themselves of a rich psychological vocabulary in describing the wellsprings of human conduct. It is only since the early eighteenth century, however, that some historians have committed themselves to making the re-creation of inner experience the core of their work, shifting the focus from the deed to the psychic events that transpired in the doer.

I

More and more I see in Giambattista Vico, that lone Italian who lived in Naples from 1668 to 1744, the bold conceptualizer of this novel form of historical consciousness. In its exterior aspect his *Scienza Nuova* was a rather conventional theology of history with a cyclical pattern. But if we look beyond the structure, we are amazed to find that he wrote of "tre·spezie di natura," three kinds of human nature, and postulated that in each stage of a *ricorso* men had quintessentially different modes of perceiving reality, that not only the physical conditions but the feeling tone of existence was profoundly different in each one, that the very capacity for expression assumed radically different shapes: signs and emblems at one time the only way for mute humans to externalize feelings; poetry the only speech of barbaric men; and not until the rational epoch the voice of reason in prose. Every stage in the cycle was marked by its own balance between rational faculties and aggressive violence, between terror of death and a desire for convenience, between robust imagination and calculated punctiliousness. In sum, the nature of living—of thinking, feeling, and willing, the three traditional faculties—had undergone revolutions in time. And the changing quality of existence was discernible in the history of language, in literature and in laws, and in visual arts like painting.

How was it possible for Vico, a man of the early eighteenth century, to interpret that evidence, to re-capture the emotions and spirit of the age of heroic barbarism? His answer was that the cycle of history was imbedded in the human soul. Understanding of the transformations was possible because men in fact themselves lived through the whole of the cycle from primitivism to rationality in the course of their development from earliest infancy through adulthood. And all about in the world there remained vestiges of primitive mentality in savage countries and perhaps in the behavior of women.

The great French romantic historian of the next century, Jules Michelet, translated and commented on the works of Vico when they were hardly known in western culture. Michelet's voluminous history of France can be conceived as an effort to explore the changing consciousness of Frenchmen in their thousand years of national life. His dramatization of the Renaissance as a new way of perceiving the world was an innovation in the uses of psychology in history entirely in the spirit of Vico's "New Science." By mid-nineteenth century Michelet had at his disposal more refined psychological tools, some inherited from the utilitarian tradition of the Enlightenment, others derived from the works of Jean-Jacques, that great revealer of the previous age, who had made himself transparent and bared his own complex private world as a model for every man.

In the latter part of the eighteenth century the Germans had a parallel to Vico in Herder, who imagined that through the course of world history an infinite number of human aggregates would be fashioned in isolation by the physical and climatic conditions of their living-space and that each one, in a totally unique way, would forge for itself an idiosyncratic balance of sense perceptions which no other *Volk* could imitate. This *Volk*-genius was early embodied in a mythology, a religion, a poetry, in short a *Volk* culture, within the confines of which men of that *Volk* were forever fixed. In the later efflorescence of a culture, elements of reason might appear, but for all time every work of literature, art, and music was in its essence a reflection of the primitive, affective *Volk* psyche. Herder's universe pullulated with *Volk* cultures at different stages in their life-cycles; and though he made feeble efforts to establish connexities among them in an overriding concept of *Humanität,* he was the founder of a particular type of German historicism that emphasized the search for concrete psychological "specificity"—the word is his friend Goethe's —in time and place. For both Vico and Herder the nature of things was hidden in the emotional differences among human collectives.

Hegel's contribution to psychological history does not, in my judgment, lie primarily in his characterization of the stages in the history of spirit, but rather in his power to grasp and present the phenomenological fulness of crucial human relationships—for example, his insightful diagnosis of the contrarieties of the master-slave bond, and his depiction of *Entfremdung,* alienation, which was passed on to Marx and Kierkegaard and has since been inflated as the central psychological distinction of modern consciousness.

II

In the last decades of the nineteenth century, there was a substantive discontinuity in the history of psychological history, a breakthrough. Psychology began to achieve a measure of recognition as an autonomous science in the German academic world. Though it had had a long literary and philosophical past—the name itself was invented by Rudolf Goclenius of Marburg in the sixteenth century—when psychology first appeared as an independent form of knowledge at the university it underwent a crisis of adolescence. What was it? A physical science in quest of uniformities? Or did it belong to humanist studies and could it be subsumed under history? Almost simultaneously with the rise of experimental psychology, new schools of psychiatry were founded, and the unconscious itself was baptized around the eighteen-eighties. This date then becomes a convenient starting-point for taking a prospect of the more modern relationship of history and psychology.

In the German and French schools there were two early significant moves in the direction of fusing these disciplines, the older one under Wilhelm Dilthey, born in 1833, and another under Lucien Febvre, born in 1878. Dilthey's first important

writing was published in 1883, and twenty-five years later he was
still at work on a critique of historical reason, some fragments
of which appeared posthumously after World War I.[1] A professor of philosophy in Berlin, he strongly influenced Troeltsch
and Meinecke, Heidegger and a whole generation of German
academic historians of ideas. He even left his mark on Spengler,
who would have spurned any identification with him. Lucien
Febvre ultimately became a professor at the Collège de France
and one of the founders of *Annales*, a journal that was to prop-
agate his ideas. Though both Dilthey and Febvre were dedicated
to exploring the relationship of psychology and history, they
were virtually unaware of each other's existence, separated as
were their intellectual worlds by a generation gap and by the
then insuperable barrier of the Rhine. And they meant rather
different things by psychology. Both, of course, were totally
untouched by such outrageous novelties as the doctrines of their
contemporary, Sigmund Freud. As for the historical forays of
Freud himself and his immediate disciples, they rarely came
within the purview of the academic historians of any country
at this period. (Preserved Smith, of Cornell University, was one
of the exceptions.) Dilthey and Febvre represent two different
versions of an initial stage in the emergence of psychological
history in recent times.

Though Dilthey's testament remains unfinished, his essays
on the towering figures of western European thought, above all
his Schleiermacher and his young Hegel, leave no doubt about
his purposes.[2] He would have had all studies of man absorbed
into intellectual history and would have allowed no independent
status to either psychology or sociology. Rejecting the feasibility
of any connected world history in a traditional sense and scornful of the Rankean state as the primary object of historical knowledge, Dilthey was convinced that the history of man could best
be presented as a series of psychological world outlooks, more
significantly emotive than rationalist, embodied mainly in the
writings of literary, religious, and philosophical geniuses. For all
his ambition to seize the essence—in a phenomenological sense—
of entire ages and to interrelate economico-social and philo-

sophico-religious trends, he always seemed most comfortable with biographical studies of creative men in whom he saw the various psychic currents of an age criss-cross and ultimately assume a manageable structure. His heroic figures are vessels for the dominant passions, cosmic attitudes, and deep-rooted beliefs of a whole epoch. Through the study of the historical varieties of human psychic experience he found an affirmation of freedom, an emancipation from dogmatism, a humanist deliverance. Though he belittled Nietzsche, it is now easy to recognize that with a far less arresting rhetoric and with none of Nietzsche's moral fervor, Dilthey was developing a parallel conception of monumental world personages the expression of whose spiritual, form-imprinting natures was the stuff of history. Resurrecting and consorting with these overmen was virtually the sole justification for historical knowledge.

Rarely, if ever, did Dilthey descend from the heights of exalted intellectual history sprinkled with affects. In theory he was committed to relating the individual psychological natures of his heroes with the grand world outlooks which they had evolved, to lay before us the fulness of his subject's lived experience. But it is always lived experience as a closeted Wilhelmine professor of philosophy conceived it. His histories are elitist dramas of the passions of great men's souls. Dilthey studied the manuscripts of his protagonists and provided us with glimpses of their social status, of their intellectual friendships, occasionally of a great love. Their search for God is always apprehended with a deep sympathy and understanding of the intricacies of the western religious tradition. But nothing below the navel was mentionable. Economic and social reality may penetrate his narrative, but only as part of a world-view, and political revolutions are quickly transformed into abstract ideas. Incapable of grappling with total psychic breakdown, when confronted by Hölderlin's madness Dilthey dissolves into utter banality and depicts the dying poet as sitting in Tübingen, his mind "wandering, wandering." [3] If this is *Erlebnis*, it is the *Erlebnis* of soap opera. On the other hand, the nuanced description of Schleiermacher's religious experience attains universality. Dilthey was aware of the depths of the unconscious, but for him it was accessible only in the form of an artistic creation.

Dilthey has testified to the impression made upon him by Husserl's phenomenology, and in his turn Heidegger in *Sein und Zeit*, which historicized the categories of cognition, described his view of the historical world as dependent on the philosophical implications of Dilthey's writings. To the extent that pure intellectual biography is still being written and there are still attempts to present *Weltanschauungen* in literary psychological terms, Dilthey endures as a living if limited influence. Karl Jaspers, who began his career as a student of psychiatry as practiced in Germany in the first decade of the twentieth century, untouched by Freud, was less restrictive in his studies of Swedenborg, Hölderlin, Strindberg, and Van Gogh, in which he combined a phenomenological psychology with an attempt to communicate the varieties of world historical outlooks.[4] His pathographies were even intended to show the neurotic drives of his characters as allies in their creative achievements, an insight which Freudian psychohistorians have sometimes claimed as their unique discovery. But when he sought to encompass the whole psychic universe in his *Psychologie der Weltanschauungen* of 1919, a work that caused quite a stir in its day, his typologizing remained on the same intellectualist plane as Dilthey's.[5]

The French historical tradition since Michelet has been rich in the study of religious and other forms of emotional expression; but it was not until Lucien Febvre that a declaration was made on the centrality of "histoire psychologique." Febvre summoned his colleagues to devote themselves to histories of *mentalité* and *sensibilité*. I would loosely translate *mentalité* in this context as what was "thinkable" in a human collective at a given moment of time. While the Germans tended to be impressionistic in their psychological portraits, Febvre insisted on great technical, one might say positivistic, rigor.

The heritage he bequeathed is nonetheless problematic. After we have been assured in the opening of his *Luther* that the underlying preoccupation of his study was the relationship between the individual and the mass, between personal initiative and public necessity, we are left dangling. Whether or not one agrees with the conclusions of Erikson's *Luther*, published as a study in psychohistory thirty years later, it does propose answers to the initial query set by Febvre, whose "histoire psychologique" flatly refused to engage with what he dismissed as the hypothetical Luther of the youthful period. "Let us frankly abandon the effort to reconstruct Luther's early surroundings; their effect on his ideas and sentiments could never be estimated. . . . It is better even to hold out against the seductions of the psychoanalysts for whose taste no theory is too facile. . . . A Freudian Luther is so easy to imagine that one feels not the least curiosity or wish to prosecute the acquaintance when an investigator undertakes to delineate him. For, in fact, might one not with an equal facility conjure up a Lutheran Freud, and observe how completely the illustrious father of psychoanalysis exemplifies permanent traits of the German national genius, of which Luther in his day was so notable an exponent?" [6] This is the voice of a French nationalist of the twentieth century, relying on a fatuous, ad hominem argument against Freud, with whose writings he had only the most casual acquaintance.

Febvre's *Rabelais* is the work in which his particular skill in communicating what another epoch "willed, felt, and thought" established the school's prototype of *histoire psychologique*, its virtues as well as its limitations. When Febvre concentrated upon an interpretation of his subject's religious beliefs, he was able to demonstrate with a plethora of empirical evidence that Rabelais' "plaisanteries courantes" and "malices d'Eglise" could be read as proof of atheism only by committing the historical sin of sins—anachronism.[7] Febvre moved in ever extending circles to define the limits of what was thinkable and what could have been experienced in one's relationship to the supernatural in sixteenth-century Europe. Far from a herald of the new rationalism, Rabelais appears as a kind of Erasmian Christian, as do his giants. In passing, Febvre developed a character for the age in standard literary psychological terms, and he proposed the identification of the discrete elements of a collective historical psychology as the historian's primary mission. But the "mental struc-

ture" of the age is confined to the conscious level—the manifest
content of ideas and beliefs, the style of their expression, where
the line was drawn between the natural and the divine, or the
intensity in the externalizing of emotion as compared with men
of the twentieth century. In the world of the sixteenth he found
imprecision, lack of historical awareness, absorption with the
senses of smell and hearing rather than sight. This sort of workmanlike history of ideas and sensibility is still practiced in France
both in the literary and in the historical faculties, and is yielding
a steady flow of respectworthy Gargantuan dissertations on subjects like the idea of nature or of happiness in various epochs.

But Febvre pointed out one of the greatest obstacles in the
way of any attempt to define the history of sensibility in a segment of past time. In the course of a review of Johan Huizinga's
Waning of the Middle Ages, he asked skeptically whether in fact
it could ever be determined that some periods were characterized
by more love, fear, cruelty, or violence than others in their overall
feeling tone, and he cautioned against reading into other epochs
a psychology derived from contemporary sensibility. How would
it be possible, he wondered, to apply psychological models of the
comfortable twentieth century to ages that knew endemic famine,
awoke and went to sleep with the sun, suffered extremes of heat
and cold as a norm. He mocked biographies of Pharaohs that
were merely portrayals of moderns gotten up in the stage costumes
of ancient Egyptians. Cooperative research in which historians
and psychologists would be joined—and he referred to French
academic psychologists like Dr. Henri Wallon—was the only
safeguard he could propose against such follies. But though conscious of the pitfalls, Febvre held to the very end that capturing
the unique *sensibilité* of a past age was the ultimate goal of the
historian to which all his other efforts were subordinate. "It is
true that to presume to reconstitute the emotive life of a given
epoch is a task at once extraordinarily seductive and terrifyingly
difficult. But what of it? The historian does not have the right
to desert." [8] Stirring declamation, *de l'époque.*

One of Febvre's disciples, Robert Mandrou, who adheres
to the pure tradition, spent years in the detailed study of the

judicial aspects of witchcraft in seventeenth-century France, and has recently produced an exhaustive history to show the transformation in the mentality of the judges of the *Parlement* of Paris that made a belief in witchcraft, still acceptable to so sophisticated an intelligence as Jean Bodin's early in the century, virtually impossible by the end.[9] This is a classical, multifaceted diagnosis of an important change in the mentality of a ruling group and of the political, social, and scientific forces that effectuated the revolution. Mandrou is a superb craftsman, who does not presume to plumb lower depths. His methodology is positivistic and its conclusions hardly to be faulted, except for neglect of the general question—which may be the critical one for a historian with a psychological bent in 1970—of what the change signified on an unconscious psychic level. Recent American studies of white racism, perhaps an analogous phenomenon, which sometimes call themselves psychohistorical and may be pretentious and methodologically sloppy, nevertheless give an inkling of how a historian might explore collective obsessions related to excremental and oedipal fantasies.[10] Such ideas are untouchable in the purist French school of "histoire psychologique," though there has been a growing intrusion of psychoanalytic concepts in recent issues of *Annales*.

When the elaborate outside scaffolding of Michel Foucault's theoretical model is stripped away, there still remain elements of Febvre's original program in Foucalt's brilliant and well-documented definitions of seventeenth- and eighteenth-century concepts of madness and reason, and perhaps even in his attempts, in *Les mots et les choses*, to grasp the content of mental structures of various epochs.[11] His analysis is more intricate and formally constructed, if less readily demonstrable, than Febvre's approach to a historical mentality. Freud, who belatedly made the scene in France after World War II, had forced Foucalt's generation to peer into the underground recesses that were still forbidden to the previous one. Though I frequently lose Foucault along the way of his argument, I find his work the most exciting new event in French "histoire psychologique," though not as unrelated to the original master of the school as might be imagined.

III

Apart from the continuation of the Dilthey and Febvre traditions, the years between the World Wars brought novelty in two important respects. First, a number of brilliant young Frenchmen of the Ecole Normale, military class of 1905, Raymond Aron and Jean-Paul Sartre among them, in the most daring intellectual adventure since Mme. de Staël's, traveled to faraway Berlin and submitted themselves to the influence of German sociology and the phenomenological philosophy. At about the same time, the advent of Hitler and the grim exodus from Central Europe brought to America men of the generation of around 1900 who had in various ways come within the orbit of Freud's doctrines. I refer to thinkers like Herbert Marcuse and Erik Erikson, not to speak of a large contingent of psychoanalysts who made the United States the world center of Freudian thought and practice. Then, in the loose, free-wheeling intellectual atmosphere of the post-World War II period in America, a host of theories were formulated with an intimate though problematic link to Freud. Marcuse tried to amalgamate a philosophical interpretation of Freudian texts—often excerpted ruthlessly without regard to the main body of the work—with a Marxist-Hegelian world view that on the face of it is totally alien to Freud. Erikson, joining forces with Freudian ego psychologists, struck off in a truly new direction of psychological history, and in the 'sixties popularized the term psychohistory. And in the same postwar period Sartre attempted a monumental syncretism in which phenomenological philosophy, Marxist dialectical materialism and, of late, Freudian psychoanalysis—*quelle galère*—are made to lie together in existential unhappiness. His *Critique de la raison dialectique*, now a decade old, does not yet seem to have made a breach in the historical ramparts of either Europe or America.[12] In France a new generation of structuralists writes about him as if he has long since been, as they say, transcended; but the announcement of his demise is premature.

When Freud finally married the unconscious after the long flirtations conducted by other men (the *mot* is his), the ground was laid for a fundamental innovation in the employment of psychological concepts in history, though, as I have indicated, virtually no historian was aware of it at the time. The therapeutic technique devised by Freud resulted in the accumulation of literally hundreds of thousands of personal histories. Perhaps Erik Erikson exaggerated when he once said that in the twentieth century we have learned more about individual human development than in all previous ages put together; but the clinical histories have surely provided us both with new types of data and with a flood of material that are not of the same order as the literary and philosophical reflections of the past. After all, every classical analysis produces about 10,000,000 words that in some fashion reveal the inner life of a man. From now on out, human conduct can no longer be explained in terms of plain utilitarian motives, as it was by nineteenth-century writers, and even Augustinian churchmen are today willing to complicate the war of the two cities by adopting tactical suggestions on the ways of the devil from the great disbeliever.

Freud himself made a number of applications of psychoanalysis to history. Though he retained a certain diffidence, shying away from the interpretation of Descartes' famous dreams, for example,[13] at times he boldly ventured brief psychobiographical hypotheses about creative men, as in his essays on Leonardo and Dostoevsky, where paintings and novels were used as illustrative documents.[14] In this manner he could support his conceptions with objective materials that were public property and did not require disguise, as did his own self-analysis and the casehistories of his patients. Aside from his interpretations of literary documents, he invented for us a macrohistorical myth on the origin of civilization; he advanced an extravagant psychological hypothesis about the beginnings of Jewish monotheism (he once called his *Moses and Monotheism* a "historical novel"[15]); and he interspersed his writings with analogies between primitive and neurotic behavior. The identification of phylogeny and ontogeny was axiomatic with Freud. The psychological history of civilized mankind probably did not differ substantively from one period to another. Wars and revolutions, whatever their genesis, could be viewed in general terms as changing opportunities for the manifestation of aggression. From time to time there were massive social outbursts against the excesses of instinctual repression in civilized society. But history as a whole meant only the recurrent, eternal conflict of Eros and death.

While Freud's historical essays were attacked for errors in detail, his analytic method of gaining access to the unconscious opened a vast new area to historical inquiry. The followers of Freud, in imitation of the master, but often without his reticence, or at least ambivalence, proliferated psychobiographies. In the beginning their efforts were devoted almost exclusively to the pathography of literary figures—an example would be Marie Bonaparte's *Poe*, which enjoyed the imprimatur of the master in a few introductory remarks.[16] The writings of poets and novelists lent themselves to plausible readings as symbolic representations of the inner states of their authors, their deep loves and hates, their longings and terrors. Fictional incidents were analyzed as disguised materials or fantasy wish-fulfillment of neurotic drives, all by analogy to the dream-work of patients. A similar method of symbolic interpretation was extended to painters by Ernst Kris, a psychoanalyst who was trained as an art historian, and to composers by Editha and Richard Sterba.[17] Except for obiter dicta, until very recently it has not been attempted with physical scientists—though some of us may be creeping up on them, casting doubt on the autonomous development of science itself. The effect of all this on historical evidence in the traditional sense is disconcerting, and sometimes constrains the more hide-bound professionals to avert their eyes from the glass, like the eminent contemporaries of Galileo. Henceforth the plainest affirmations in memoirs, despatches, letters, and secret confessions may require intricate psychological interpretation in the light of the Freudian model. The unconscious demands a hearing and will not be silenced.

Though some psychoanalytic biographers formulated hypotheses about the nature of creativity as a universal phenomenon, in general their artistic subjects were approached as self-contained little monads sufficient unto themselves. This kind of discrete treatment was superseded, however, when political scientists and historians, trying to explain historical developments on the grand scale, applied Freudian personality theory to world-historical actors. An American professor of political science, Harold Lasswell, was one of the first to come up with a formula relating the individual and the collective, something to the effect that the great politician displaces private affects upon public objects.[18] The merit of the political studies has varied enormously—Woodrow Wilson has received a sophisticated treatment at the hands of Alexander and Juliette George and a vulgar one in William Bullitt's analysis, which Freud may or may not have approved.[19] Despite scandalous instances of overinterpretation, immense new vistas have been opened up on the behavior of the monumental figures of world history; and if one is repelled by the grossness of some analyses, one has only to look back on such pre-Freudian compilations as Augustin Cabanès' *Grands névropathes, malades immortels* to appreciate the enormous strides that have been taken.[20]

This, I believe, is the perspective from which to examine the work of Erik Erikson. With Erikson, who has written both programmatic statements and two biographical studies of politico-religious figures, the analytic method applied to history has received its most subtle exemplification.[21] Yet the basic problem raised by Lucien Febvre remains unresolved. We are obliged to ask: Is the ideal psychological model of human development in eight stages, constructed by Erikson, universally applicable? Is this not a summary of twentieth-century psychoanalytic experience, whose relevance to other cultures and periods is open to question?

Clearly, in epochs where the composition of the family, its spiritual and economic character, and life expectancy are very different from ours, definitions of the successive crises of life would have to vary. Erikson might say they would need modification. But a historian confronted, for example, with data on Florence 1426-1427 indicating that the average age differential of husband and wife was twenty years and that fathers died early in their children's lives, could feel that in this instance the schema would have to undergo drastic alteration.[22] A historian may hold with Plato and Aristotle, Locke and Descartes, yes, and Freud and Erikson that the earliest experiences are far and away the most potent (we remember Descartes' analysis of his predilection for cock-eyed girls based on an early fixation). And he will surely welcome Erikson's shift from exclusive emphasis on infancy and the early family romance to a more extensive view of ego development including periods of life that are better documented and hence more accessible to historical treatment. But can he accept without debate the proliferation of later "crises" in the Eriksonian design, or Erikson's assignment of weight to each of eight crises? The historian should be warned that the selection of materials to fill the boxes of the eight stages may make of the schema a self-fulfilling prophecy. I find wholly credible the crisis of adolescence and what early nineteenth-century psychiatrists like Philippe Pinel called the male climacteric, for these are vocal, articulate periods whose anguish is attested by cries and confessions. The rest of the eight stations of life appear rather arbitrary; the traditional divisions of the Church Fathers or Dante's four or Vincent de Beauvais' six may be quite enough. Before I can seriously evaluate the Eriksonian model as a historical tool, I feel that the history of the epigenetic cycle itself, diversified in time and place, needs to be written—and initial soundings in this direction have been made.[23] These reservations aside, however, Erikson's stress upon the total epigenetic cycle, whatever its form, seems to me a permanent acquisition of historical consciousness.

In the two studies of men he calls politico-religious geniuses, Luther and Gandhi, Erikson found a motive drive to heroic action in the need of the sons to outsrip their fathers and compensate for their failures. When he generalizes these conjectures about a small and special sample to all geniuses, he is speaking as a theorist of psychoanalysis, eager to find uniformities, and a historian's judgment must remain suspended. His catalogue of the common characteristics of geniuses—a secret foreboding that a curse lies upon them, a tie to the father which makes open rebellion impossible, a sense of being chosen and carrying a superior destiny, a feeling of weakness and shyness and unworthiness, a precocious conscience in childhood, an early development of ultimate concerns, a brief attempt to cast off the yoke of their fate and a final settling into the conviction that they have a responsibility for a segment of mankind—is troubling, even to a historian who has wandered far from the all-too-commonsensical positivists. As a description of Gandhi's and perhaps Luther's experience, yes; as a historical typology, no.

In his Gandhi, Erikson closely scrutinized the manner in which a group of followers resonated to their hero, identified with him in terms of their own life cycles. The skill and imagination with which he handles their recollected dreams, fantasies, and symbolic acts is unmatched in contemporary psychological history-writing. On the other hand, the general relationship between the world historical figure and his age is not advanced much beyond Hegel's lectures. There is no theory of social change in Eriksonian psychology, any more than in Freud's, except for the assumption that each new generation strives to surpass the older one, to innovate upon its works, risking oedipal ambivalence in the process. Erikson does not offer us any help in comprehending either the tempo or the direction of change beyond the categorical assertion that at certain moments mankind is prepared for epoch-making transformations—an epochal identity vacuum is created, he tells us [24]—and the hero comes along and sounds the clarion-call. Each such moment has its potentialities for new creation and redemption from historical psychic blocks that inhibit a society from embarking on a course for which it is ripe and which it desires in its innermost being. The genius leader first releases himself from psychic bondage or points the way to a release for others which he may not have personally achieved.

There is too much of the sacred drama for me in this model of the historical moment. That the hero responds sharply to forces in his world, that he has antennae in his head giving him prescience, foreknowledge, is metaphoric language that German *Zeitgeist* historians have resorted to for many decades. Though Erikson does not mention him, I keep hearing those overtones of Hegel's world-historical person, who incarnates the on-going history of absolute spirit. I am left unenlightened as to what brought about the historical crisis and unconvinced that the hero's

prescience is the force that resolves it. On occasion there is a
prophetic quality to Erikson's heralding of the next stage in world
history, with its ever broadening area of common identities, that
leaves the agnostic behind. The austere and rigorous criteria for
"psychohistorical evidence" that he set forth in a theoretical
statement are not always observed in practice.[25]

Deriving from a totally different tradition is Sartre's existen-
tialist amalgam of psychology and history. He has at least one
thing in common with Eriksonian psychohistory, and that is a
humanist emphasis upon personality in history and the freedom
of, shall we say, ego-will—though Sartre is now prepared to give
greater weight to the fetters of inherited psychological condition-
ing than he was previously.

Sartre renders existential the legacy of a psychologized Marxist framework, fills in the interstices in the history of socio-eco-
nomic development with choices of human wills as he presumes
Marx would have done, and subjects the action of these wills
to psychological analysis. A general Marxist class determinism is
postulated, but, in addition, he believes that a humanist history
can show how it is possible for individuals with a variety of class
and psychic identities to sacrifice their lives in common historic
actions. He has fleshed out a Marxist historical dialectic based
on production relations and class structure with an existential
account of how men who in an inert state have a relationship of
mere seriality to one another—like people waiting in a queue—
come, in a given historical crisis, to assume ties that entail responsibilities of life and death in action. His convoluted argument is less interesting for a historian than the kinds of questions
he addresses to his materials. Re-reading histories of the great
French Revolution, the Revolution of 1848, and the Commune,
he asks: what really happens when a crowd moves on an objective? What is the nature of the secret psychological commit-
ments and pacts they have made with one another? How in fact
does collective historical action come about? Though Sartre's
passion for phenomenological totalization will put many of us
off, historians may be able to adapt to other times and places
his method of extracting the full existential implications of iso-

lated events. In his treatment of individuals, Sartre has created prototypes for the fusion of social and psychological knowledge. The published fragments of his Flaubert, a work in progress, are a brilliant synthesis of Marxist and Freudian insights.[26]

The penetration of the outer social and ideological world into the intimacy of the family and the psychological history of the individual in this primary field of confrontation are for Sartre the first and perhaps most significant of a whole sequence of developments. In the introduction to his *Critique de la raison dialectique,* he criticized his Marxist friends for concerning themselves solely with adults: "Reading them, one would believe that we are born at the age when we earn our first wages. . . . Existentialism, on the contrary, believes that it can integrate the psychoanalytic method which discovers the point of insertion for man and his class—that is, the particular family—as a mediation between the universal class and the individual."[27] I have considerable sympathy for this viewpoint. At the present time writers who call themselves psychohistorians are forced to use, *faute de mieux,* crude and misleading affirmations about both the economy and the interpsychic relationships of the western family. A measure of our poverty is the frequency with which Philippe Ariès' history of childhood is cited as Holy Writ.[28] Whenever I have tried to interpret the family relations of historical figures I have felt on shaky ground in relying on old-hat, impressionistic utterances about this nuclear institution. But the possibilities for research are open and the materials cry for exploitation. There seems to be a consensus among social historians, prosopographers, and historians with an interest in psychological phenomena that the history of the family represents a gaping lacuna in our knowledge to which a new generation of historians should give significant priority.

History can now be individuated and particularized in a way that Leopold von Ranke never dreamed of. The economic and social existence of individuals and aggregates today can be seen reflected in the family alongside the psychic pattern set by this primal reality at a crucial period in life. The insights of Marx and of Freud can thus be brought together not in the sibylline macrohistorical rhetoric of Herbert Marcuse or Norman Brown but in concrete historical works where life situations are depicted.

IV

A certain imperialistic character attaches to a major intellectual discovery such as psychoanalysis. When a new instrument for the study of man is developed, believers in its potency tend to conceive of it as a panacea, a solution to a wide range of problems, ultimately including the historical. If it is a successful and persuasive technique that wins assent in one area of the study of man, why should it not be introduced elsewhere? Proclamations are issued raising high hopes and staking out large claims. The new technique is often applied with a heavy hand. Revolutionary results are awaited, as it pretends to answer questions for which there already exist explanations more elegant and plausible or more nuanced. It becomes totalitarian. Under attack the proponents of the new technique may withdraw from their most advanced outposts: their position was misunderstood, their theory was not meant to be all-embracing. It is only the most important interpretive device and does not quite account for everything. The original formulation has been misrepresented, misconstrued.

The initial negative reaction of official historians—and there is such a body of academic mandarins in every country—to a new method like psychoanalysis in history is equally fervid. The new technique is based on a series of false assumptions; it is not acceptable even in its own discipline; depending upon it is leaning upon a weak reed. Psychology and history are declared to be different in their essence—as if either of them had an "essence" that enjoys even a partial consensus. The human phenomena that psychological analyses are presumed to illuminate are too elusive, or if they can be grasped they are insignificant and irrelevant as far as the true vocation of the historian is concerned. The evidence brought forth by these techniques is obfuscatory, raising more problems than it resolves—as if the opening up of new problems were not in itself a virtue instead of a fault.

As studies multiply—good, bad, and indifferent—the proponents cite the best as examples and the opponents the most ill-conceived and outlandish specimens. With time, however, both extreme positions are eroded. The imperialists of the new technique pull in their horns, and the absolute deniers of its usefulness permit it an humble place in the republic of knowledge. Eventually the new perceptions insinuate themselves into the most normative orthodox history-writing, often without the author's awareness, and the controversy joins the ranks of those "appearance problems" that at intervals have shaken the intellectual world and that one later reads about with some incredulity. This has been the historical fortune of Marxist conceptions and seems a fair prognosis of what will happen to Freudian ideas in the process of their assimilation by historians.

Despite serious misgivings about some of the uses of psychology in history, I feel we have come a long way from the intellectualist psychological history of the earlier part of the century. I still cast my lot with the Freudian "psychologizers." A historian can scarcely compose a narrative line without committing himself, implicitly or explicitly, to some theory of personality and motivation. In various periods since the late seventeenth century there have been dominant psychologies, like those of Locke and Descartes, that seeped into the literary language as well as into everyday speech, and through these media constrained the historian to employ their motivational terminology. Today a historian must feel at least some uneasiness about adhering to the traditional nineteenth-century patterns of motivation. A skeptic may rightly be uncertain that the more novel systems are intrinsically superior or truer in an absolute sense than those handed down by the past; but it is eccentric in 1970 to go about in satin knee-breeches or wear a Prince Albert frockcoat, even if one likes the style. The historian is probably always obliged to accept and express himself in the psychological language of his times; and thus, as I see it, there is no escape from Freud's conceptions in some form, orthodox or heterodox.

Although there may have been a general appreciation of the long interdependency of history and psychology in a wide variety of shapes and forms, on both a theoretical and a practicing level, most members of the American historical profession, positivists

and relativists alike, were nevertheless ill-prepared for the bomb-
shell that fell into their midst on December 29, 1957, when
William Langer in his presidential address before the American
Historical Association in New York announced that the historian's next assignment was an application of the findings of
psychoanalysis to history. There were visible stirrings among members of the audience that a behavioral scientist of any school
would have identified as consternation. This was the most un-
kindest cut of all, from a scholar who had produced an impressive
array of impeccably solid works of diplomatic history. Since then,
there are indications that the stubborn resistance of a phalanx
of historians generally suspicious of what they considered random
psychological associations is being overcome. Papers dealing with
psychology and history, presented at a number of recent meetings
of the American Historical Association, have attracted large audiences. In 1963 Bruce Mazlish assembled an impressive group of
theoretical statements on psychoanalysis and history, and urged
the historian to acquaint himself with the relevant texts.[29] Stuart
Hughes reiterated the general sense of Langer's manifesto and
added a programmatic statement of his own in *History as Art
and as Science* (1964), where he called for historical research
into the "shared anxieties and aspirations [of various epochs]
which may be all the more decisive for being only partially conscious." Experiences such as these, he maintains, cut across the
conventional delimitations of class or elite groups, and he has
voiced confidence in the feasibility of arriving at valid historical
generalizations about "deep-seated fears and ideal strivings." [30]
While it is probable that the American historical profession has
produced in the last decade more articles about the desirability
of establishing a bridge between history and psychology than
works animated by the new ideas, that there has been far more
talk about the subject than actual performance, some younger
historians are beginning to incorporate the findings of the new
psychology into the body of their work. For example, the June
1970 issue of the *American Historical Review* contained an article by a young historian, John Demos, "Underlying Themes in
the Witchcraft of Seventeenth-Century New England," that was

informed by psychoanalytic concepts judiciously introduced.[31] In this respect, however, American historians have lagged behind the political scientists, who have more eagerly embraced the new ideas in their studies of dominant contemporary political figures —witness the *Daedalus* issue on "Philosophers and Kings" (Summer 1968).

The collaborators of the French *Annales,* which has lately shown itself hospitable to articles on psychoanalysis and history, are beginning to explore the psychological aspects of demography, of which they are today the outstanding school in the world. The Russians for Marxist ideological reasons and the official English historians for traditionalist ones are likely to hold out longest against the new trend.

Any contemporary use of psychology in history must postulate the existence of the unconscious, a belief that the unconscious of past epochs has left behind visible traces, and a conviction that these traces are decipherable. About the interpretation of the documentary vestiges of psychic experience there will inevitably be controversy, as there has been over the reading of dead and forgotten languages, and at present the historian is faced with rival and contradictory theories of human development from among which he must choose an initial hypothesis if he is to avail himself of the new techniques. The lack of consensus among psychologists and psychoanalysts is bound to perplex him. Once even a tentative commitment is made, however, to some psychoanalytic theory—and the historian may permit himself the luxury of being eclectic and pluralist—the results can vastly enrich our understanding of historical experience. The investigation of psychological phenomena in past epochs not only will alter historical conceptions about other ages, but could lead to an appreciation of the historical dimensions and limitations of present-day psychological doctrines.

Accusations of dilettantism are commonly made against those who are introducing modern psychology into history, and the problem of professional training in two disciplines, psychology and history, is admittedly nettlesome. Yet is it not precisely at the crossroads of two forms of knowledge that the most fertile conceptions in present-day historiography are emerging? The idea of an équipe, of the teaming of a psychologist and a historian, is a too-facile solution; an ultimate synthesis must take place within the mind of the historian if the work is to have a wholeness.

On the use of a specialized vocabulary and the borrowing of technical terminology, as contrasted with concepts, my position is rather conservative. I find the psychological jargon, with infrequent exceptions, too ugly for narrative history, and am convinced that one can adopt the concepts without the nomenclature, which derives from a parochial scientistic tradition. After all, no therapist worth his salt will resort in his consultation room to technical terms, because of the obvious danger that they may be confused with common and vulgar usage. If the historian eschews technical words, he is less likely to be seduced into dogmatism. His explanations of historical phenomena can be ambiguous, multi-faceted, possible or probable; he can write suggestively, propose solutions by indirection. Psychological labels are unnecessarily restrictive; historical figures are not patients admitted to a hospital who have to be categorized for housekeeping convenience.

Acceptance of psychoanalytic concepts in history-writing presupposes, of course, a somewhat different set of criteria for historical proof than those to which traditional historians are accustomed. For some, the evidence is not concrete enough, and the element of conjecture more obtrusive than they can countenance. While the quantitative school of history continues the Galilean tradition of mathematicizing knowledge with the instruments of a new technology congenial to our age, psychology in history still has a tendency toward the sample of one and the search for uniqueness. Any prospect of quantification seems remote, though not entirely to be excluded as an element in analyses of the behavior of groups.[32]

On the whole I feel that psychological knowledge is at this stage more useful in description than in explanatory system-making. When two disciplines are locked into the same cage, the historical keepers tell me, cannibalistic tendencies well up from their unconscious and they sometimes try to devour each other. Recent attempts to merge psychology and history in a clumsily labeled psycho-historical process do presume the sort of grand monist thesis to which history has always been refractory. Since so many historico-psychological problems have not been mapped even in a crude manner, I am reluctant to embrace elaborate theoretical structures. In the end I conceive of psychology as playing a more modest role, adding a set of vivid psychedelic colors to the historian's palette, offsetting the mournful black-and-white of structure and number that in this technological age will inevitably suffuse a large part of the historical.

The new psychologies can open up whole areas of inquiry by encouraging the historian to ask some direct, perhaps impertinent questions. The restriction of the method to biography, where it has enjoyed at least partial acceptance, should not be a lasting confinement. Historians will have to wrestle anew with symbolic representation on a broad scale. There are central problems in the history of ideas that cannot be treated adequately on an intellectualist and conscious level of expression alone and that invite the use of new psychological tools: the history of feelings about time, space, utopia, myth, love, death, God. The "unconscious mental habits" that Arthur Lovejoy hoped to analyze in his history of ideas had little or nothing to do with Freud's unconscious. Perhaps the fundamental shortcoming of his work and that of the Febvre school was their exclusive intellectualism. We all know that the experience of love and death and aggression has changed through the centuries. If a professor dared to propose a course on the history of love he would certainly take a ribbing from his colleagues. Yet this emotion has been as protean in its forms and as vital to human existence as, let us say, shipping or banking, whose respectability as subjects for historical treatment in university teaching is quite unchallenged. When a psychologist investigating contemporary attitudes toward death looks for historical comparisons, we can only provide him with impressions and isolated, sparse instances. Particularly dramatic intrusions of death, such as great plagues, have been studied by historians in their psychological as well as their economic, political, and artistic consequences; Millard Meiss's study of the Black Death is a prototype.[33] But there is need for an exploration of the long-term, changing meaning of death on the unconscious as well as on the conscious level. Death in the eighteenth century had its special character, but I think we know far less about it than we do about the diplomatic relations between Parma and Venice in that period.

The particular forms of psychic repression have a history and so do the forms of sublimation—their instrumentalities differ widely in time and place. The overt manifestations of neuroses have changed, as any sampling of case histories over the past seventy years will show. As far back as 1913 Karl Jaspers in a section of his *General Psychopathology* entitled "Social and Historical Aspects of the Psychoses and the Personality-Disorders" recognized that "the neuroses in particular have a contemporary style."[34] Few historians have yet coped with the intricacies of presenting to their readers the varying patterns of libidinal satisfaction in different epochs. You can read that grand masterpiece of provincialism, the *Cambridge Modern History*, in its newest version, without even suspecting the existence of these transformations.

The histories of fashion, clothes, sexual and marital customs, punishments, style, and a hundred other questions which have traditionally belonged to "la petite histoire" and to the antiquarians need to be explored for their symbolic content. Freud's second most important legacy to a historian may well be the dissolution of a hierarchy of values among historical materials. If all things can become vehicles of expression for feelings and thoughts, then the state document, grand philosophical affirmation, and scientific law may lose some of their prestige to other more intimate records of human experience. The day of Dilthey's elitist psychological history is over. Conversely, classical psychoanalysis, with a dubious future as a therapy, might be reborn as a historical instrumentality. The dead do not ask to be cured, only to be understood.

A great expansion in our comprehension of the past might be effected through the re-reading of old or neglected documents with a different apperception. Notebooks and scribbles that seemed destined for the ashheap of history may be rescued and made to live again—as exciting a reconquest of the past as a new archaeology. A great body of dream literature and of fantasies of past ages is unexplored. In Western Europe and in America there are voluminous materials—legal, political, medical, literary —in manuscript and print, to say nothing of representations by the plastic arts, that have not been researched for their psychological meaning. The questions have not been asked, and therefore historians have not been on the *qui vive* for the answers that lie concealed in the texts.

Economic history has become respectable, and who would now demean the history of labor, or the history of consumption patterns? I merely advocate adding to them a history of other needs and expressions of living. In defense of his idealist history of Spirit as the definition of human existence, Hegel once wrote with utter contempt of nutritive history. Now that we have, in despite of Hegel, recognized the claims of hands and stomach to a share in human history, let us make ready to welcome the other more secret and hidden parts of man into the temple.

NOTES

1. Wilhelm Dilthey, *Einleitung in die Geisteswissenschaften: Versuch einer Grundlegung für das Studium der Gesellschaft und der Geschichte* (Leipzig, 1883), I (no further vols. published). A second ed., with additions from unpublished manuscripts, forms vol. I, ed. Bernhard Groethuysen (Leipzig, 1923), of Dilthey's *Gesammelte Schriften.* With the exception of vol. II, *Weltanschauung und Analyse des Menschen seit Renaissance und Reformation* (1914), the collected works appeared from 1921 to 1936. *Der Aufbau der geschichtlichen Welt in den Geisteswissenschaften. Studien. . .* , Part I, was published in the *Abhandlungen der Königlich Preussischen Akademie der Wissenschaften: Phil.-hist. Klasse* for 1910; a new ed., with additions from unpublished manuscripts, forms vol. VII, ed. Bernhard Groethuysen (1927), of the *Gesammelte Schriften.*
2. Wilhelm Dilthey, *Die Jugendgeschichte Hegels*, which appeared in the *Abhandlungen der Königlich Preussischen Akademie der Wissen-*

schaften in 1905, now vol. IV, ed. Herman Nohl (1921), of the *Gesammelte Schriften; Leben Schleiermachers,* published with *Denkmale der inneren Entwicklung Schleiermachers, erläutert durch kritische Untersuchungen* (Berlin, 1870), I (no further vols. published).

3. Wilhelm Dilthey, *Das Erlebnis und die Dichtung,* 13th ed. (Stuttgart, 1957; original ed., 1905), p. 289.

4. Karl Jaspers, *Strindberg und Van Gogh: Versuch einer pathographischen Analyse unter vergleichender Heranziehung von Swedenborg und Hölderlin* (Bern, 1922).

5. Karl Jaspers, *Psychologie der Weltanschauungen* (Berlin, 1919; 4th ed., 1954).

6. Lucien Paul Victor Febvre, *Un destin: Martin Luther* (Paris, 1928); quotation is from *Martin Luther: A Destiny,* trans. Roberts Tapley (New York, 1929), pp. 33, 35.

7. Lucien Febvre, *Le Problème de l'incroyance au XVIᵉ siècle: La Religion de Rabelais* (Paris, 1947; original ed., 1942), p. 163.

8. Lucien Febvre, *Combats pour l'histoire* (Paris, 1953), p. 229.

9. Robert Mandrou, *Magistrats et sorciers en France au XVIIᵉ siècle: Une analyse de psychologie historique* (Paris, 1968).

10. See, for example, Joel Kovel, *White Racism: A Psychohistory* (New York, 1970).

11. Michel Foucault, *Histoire de la folie à l'âge classique* (Paris, 1961); *Les Mots et les choses* (Paris 1966).

12. Jean-Paul Sartre, *Critique de la raison dialectique, précédé de Questions de méthode* (Paris, 1960).

13. Sigmund Freud, "Brief an Maxim Leroy über einen Traum des Cartesius" (1929), in *Gesammelte Schriften,* XII (Vienna, 1934), pp. 403-405; for English trans., see the *Standard Edition of the Complete Psychological Works of Sigmund Freud,* ed. James Strachey with the collaboration of Anna Freud, XXI (London, 1961), pp. 203-204.

14. Sigmund Freud, *Eine Kindheitserinnerung des Leonardo da Vinci* (Leipzig, 1910); for English trans., see *Standard Edition,* XI (1957), pp. 63-137; *Der Wahn und die Träume in W. Jensen's "Gradiva"* (Vienna, 1907); English trans., *Standard Edition,* IX (1959), pp. 3-95; *Dostojewski und die Vatertötung* (1928), published as a preface to *Die Urgestalt der Brüder Karamasoff* (a supplementary volume in the German edition of Dostoevsky's works by René Fülöp-Miller and F. Eckstein) and republished in the *Gesammelte Schriften,* XII, pp. 7-26; English trans., *Standard Edition,* XXI, pp. 177-196.

15. Sigmund Freud, *Der Mann Moses und die monotheistische Religion. Drei Abhandlungen* (Amsterdam, 1939; Parts 1 and 2 published in German in *Imago* in 1937; English trans. by Katherine Jones, *Moses and Monotheism* [New York, 1939]); Ernst L. Freud, ed., *The Letters of Sigmund Freud and Arnold Zweig,* trans. Elaine and William

Robson-Scott (New York, 1970), p. 91, Freud to Zweig, September 30, 1934.

16. Marie Bonaparte, *Edgar Poe: Etude psychanalytique*, 2 vols. (Paris, 1933).

17. Ernst Kris, *Psychoanalytic Explorations in Art* (New York, 1962; original ed., London, 1953); Editha and Richard Sterba, *Beethoven and His Nephew: A Psychoanalytic Study of Their Relationship*, trans. Willard R. Trask (London, 1957).

18. Harold D. Lasswell, *Psychopathology and Politics* (Chicago, 1930), pp. 75-76.

19. Alexander L. and Juliette L. George, *Woodrow Wilson and Colonel House: A Personality Study* (New York, 1956); Sigmund Freud and W.C. Bullitt, *Thomas Woodrow Wilson, Twenty-Eighth President of the United States: A Psychological Study* (Boston, 1967).

20. Augustin Cabanès, *Grands névropathes, malades immortels*, 3 vols. (Paris, 1930-1935).

21. Erik H. Erikson, *Childhood and Society* (New York, 1950); *Young Man Luther* (New York, 1958); *Identity and the Life Cycle: Selected Papers* (New York, 1959); *Insight and Responsibility* (New York, 1964); *Gandhi's Truth* (New York, 1969).

22. David Herlihy, "Vieillir au Quattrocento," *Annales: économies, sociétés, civilisations*, November-December 1969, pp. 1338-1352.

23. Creighton Gilbert, "When Did a Man in the Renaissance Grow Old?" *Studies in the Renaissance*, XIV (1967), pp. 7-32, is an example of what needs to be done on a broad scale.

24. Erikson, *Insight and Responsibility*, p. 204.

25. Erik H. Erikson, "On the Nature of Psycho-Historical Evidence: In Search of Gandhi," *Daedalus*, Summer 1968, pp. 695-730.

26. Jean-Paul Sartre, "La Conscience de classe chez Flaubert," *Les Temps Modernes*, 21st year, no. 240 (May 1966), pp. 1921-1951, and no. 241 (June 1966), pp. 2113-2153; "Flaubert: Du poète à l'artiste," *Les Temps Modernes*, 22nd year, no. 243 (August 1966), pp. 197-253; no. 244 (September 1966), pp. 423-481; no. 245 (October 1966), pp. 598-674.

27. Jean-Paul Sartre, *The Problem of Method* (prefatory essay of *Critique de la raison dialectique*), trans. Hazel E. Barnes (London, 1963), p. 62.

28. Philippe Ariès, *L'Enfant et la vie familiale sous l'ancien régime* (Paris, 1960).

29. Bruce Mazlish, ed., *Psychoanalysis and History* (Englewood Cliffs, N.J., 1963).

30. H. Stuart Hughes, *History as Art and as Science* (New York, 1964), pp. 61, 62.

31. John Demos, "Underlying Themes in the Witchcraft of Seventeenth-Century New England," *American Historical Review*, LXXV (1970), pp. 1311-1326.

32. An interesting attempt to deal with the psychology of a social aggregate that raises the problem of quantification is Marc Raeff, *Origins of the Russian Intelligentsia: The Eighteenth-Century Nobility* (New York, 1966).
33. Millard Meiss, *Painting in Florence and Siena after the Black Death* (Princeton, 1951).
34. Karl Jaspers, *General Psychopathology*, trans. J. Hoenig and Marian W. Hamilton (Chicago, 1963; original German ed., *Allgemeine Psychopathologie*, 1913), p. 732.

3

IN DEFENSE OF
PHILOSOPHICAL HISTORY

In 1765 there appeared under an Amsterdam imprint a work by the Abbé Bazin entitled *Philosophie de l'histoire*. It was probably one of the first usages of this particular combination of words as the subject of a book, though as far back as 1572 Jean Bodin had already employed the adjective *"philosoph-historicus"* in describing Philo Judaeus. Implicit philosophies of history are, of course, much older. But reflections in rabbinic literature and the Church Fathers, the mystical schema in Joachim of Fiore, and the realistic insights of Ibn Khaldun are to be distinguished from the explicit, self-conscious philosophies of history of the last two centuries.

Bazin's work was a most inauspicious beginning for the presentation of a form of knowledge that has consistently irritated and sometimes outraged empirical historians who conceive their primary mission to be the indefatigable pursuit of the all-too-numerous facts. The Bazin book was really a pamphlet of about 200 pages and dealt mostly with Biblical history, raising such disturbing questions as whether Moses was not really Bacchus in disguise. It did not at all justify its pretentious title nor its grand dedication to the Empress of Russia. Moreover, to compound its

many blasphemies and inaccuracies, it was not written by the
Abbé Bazin at all, but by none other than Monsieur de Voltaire.
The title took hold, and, for better or for worse, philosophies
of history have been with us ever since.

At about the same period a slew of works began to appear
in Germany calling themselves *Philosophie der Geschichte*. By
this time Turgot had delivered his epoch-making harangues before
the Sorbonne on the "History of the Progress of the Human
Spirit," and Vico's *Scienza Nuova* had seen its definitive edition
in 1744. World chronology, which had still been the central
problem of universal history in the seventeenth century, gave
way to philosophical history in the eighteenth. Then, for about
a solid century, roughly from the middle of the eighteenth through
well past the middle of the nineteenth, there was a vast outpouring of grand systems. While philosophical history was a general
intellectual problem everywhere in Europe, the most original
writing was concentrated heavily in France and Germany. The
Italian Vico had no important successor in his native land. And
in England, except for the rather imitative works of Price and
Priestley in the eighteenth century and Spencer and Buckle in
the nineteenth, the subject was not seriously cultivated. In France
and Germany two separate catenas were established, and there
are parallel developments in both countries in which influences
from one thinker to another can be described with meticulous
detail. In the French School the main current ran from Turgot
through Condorcet, Saint-Simon, and the Saint-Simonians, culminating in the mammoth structure of Auguste Comte. In Germany
the line is traceable from Herder, Lessing, and Kant through
Fichte and Schelling, again culminating in a *summa*, Hegel's
Lectures on the Philosophy of History in the academic year 1822-
1823. Karl Marx who followed is probably more in the German
than in the French tradition, though he synthesized elements from
both sides of the Rhine.

For about half a century after Marx, the literature did not
decrease in quantity, but it was manifestly the work of *epigoni*.
Not until the decade of the first World War did the subject
experience a major revival at the hands of Oswald Spengler.

Finally, in the last great enterprise in this field, many of the pretensions of Germanic philosophical history have been decently hidden under a modest title in the traditional manner of English understatement: Toynbee's *A Study of History.*

Since World War II there has been a proliferation of briefer works, particularly from the pens of theologians. Slavophile and rather mystical Russians had already resurrected Christian world history in a Greek Orthodox form in the late nineteenth century. Contemporary Catholic philosophers like Maritain and D'Arcy and Protestant theologians from Bultmann through Tillich and Niebuhr have added their sectarian versions of the pivotal role of sin in universal history.

Now it is not difficult to define the two major and most obvious uses to which the philosophies of history have been put in the course of the last two centuries. They have served either as a civil theology, an apologetic of God's way in the world, a theodicy, a religious drama, or they have accompanied a program of political and social action. These two uses were, to be sure, never mutually exclusive, since the civil theology often involved precepts of moral human behavior in this world, and when men read secular philosophies of history they sometimes experienced emotions akin to that oceanic feeling which Romain Rolland once described to his friend Sigmund Freud as the essence of his own religious sentiment. Thomas Churchill, the late eighteenth-century English translator of the works of both Condorcet and Herder, has himself naively depicted the romantic religious emotion awakened in him by working with philosophies of history. "It has made my breast glow with the fervor of virtuous sentiment," he wrote in 1795, "I have almost felt myself the inhabitant of another world." [1] Freud, of course, would identify this vague sense of communion with the infinite which philosophical history generated in its devotees as nothing more than an infantile wish to return to the womb. Vico's civil theology is probably the most magnificent statement of a profound religious purpose in philosophical history. It is a demonstration of a Providential order accompanied by a moral admonition to mankind. The persistence of this religious idea—as distinguished from the rather shallow emotivity of a Thomas Churchill—is clearly visible even in Toynbee's work. Like Old Testament prophets, Vico and Toynbee exhort mankind to choose the path of divine reason and to live. If you follow the way of hyper-sophistication, you will again fall into the dregs of Romulus, threatened Giambattista Vico. If you build military empires and deny the moral truths of benign Deism, you will be utterly destroyed, warns Toynbee.

The second use of the philosophy of history, its relation to a specific program of social and political action, an idea first set forth by Condorcet, Saint-Simon, and Comte but not really exploited until Marx, requires no extensive documentation, since in our day a large portion of the world has officially adopted the Marxian philosophy of history, though in a form somewhat amended by Chairman Khrushchev. For the history-intoxicated revolutionary before he came to power, philosophical history had served as a heady stimulant, an assurance to the elect of ultimate triumph, a guide to action, an organizing intellectual force which created single-mindedness, a marvelously effective, self-fulfilling prophecy. The dictum pronounced by Condorcet in one of his manuscripts, *Maîtriser l'avenir*, "master the future," was perhaps the earliest realization by a philosopher that he was forging an instrument of great potency while writing a sketch of past world history. That among these secular reformers and revolutionaries the philosophy of history became an *ersatz* religion which adapted and often plainly translated religious terminology has been noted frequently before. The martyr of a revolutionary cause was sustained in his darkest moments by the consolations of history. The contemplation of the eternal chain of human destinies was for him "an asylum in which the memory of his persecutors cannot pursue him," wrote Condorcet while in hiding from Robespierre's agents, "There he lives with his peers in an Elysium which his reason has created for itself and which his love for humanity enhances with the purest pleasures." [2]

In recent years, the renascence of the philosophy of history has provoked a series of virulent assaults against the whole subject among both historians and philosophers. The general grounds for attack are virtually self-evident. The philosophy of history, having become a tool, a mere engine of class or international warfare in the hands of princes and peoples seeking advantage, cannot be taken seriously as a form of knowledge. It is ill-disguised propaganda and should be excluded from the university if it cannot be banished from the city. Similarly, if the philosophy of history is a sacred work, an instrument conducive to spiritual renovation for men with or without God, it should be cultivated in schools of divinity and in religious establishments and has no place in the academy. Of course, a third type of criticism, reflecting our contemporary preoccupation with methodology, doubts whether a philosophy of history is possible at all. This could be answered with a Johnsonian gesture by stubbing the toe on the ten volumes of Toynbee, the two quartos of Spengler, the four of Auguste Comte, and sundry less substantial works.

The problem can be posed on a quite different level, however. Admitted that philosophies of history have become handmaidens of theology and politics, the vital question still remains: of what use have they been and can they still be to the professional historian or to every man in quest of historical knowledge?

At the outset, it is necessary to deal with what might be considered the parochial interest of professionals defending their status. One type of criticism which can be disposed of rather quickly, and with an ad hominem argument, is the self-righteous attack of Mr. Dry-as-Dust. He may be honest enough in his fashion when he is writing his doctoral dissertation well-nourished with facts, but place a textbook publisher's contract in his hands and open up before his dazzled eyes a prospective market of four million copies for a one-volume history of civilization, and his purity melts as he latches on to the first philosophical generality that comes to hand. What Toynbee calls the antinomian western historian is transformed into a true believer, a believer in anything modish. It is good to remember the subtle mockery, the wry humor, with which Carl Becker dealt with the worshipers of the cold, hard facts. When you next open your favorite textbook, scan it for its philosophico-historical generalizations, count up how many mutilated borrowings there are from Herder and Condorcet, Marx and Toynbee, when the author is not parading

a crude bit of manifest destiny, *grandeur de la France,* chosen
people, tight little island, or democratic values. Indeed, it might
be maintained that everybody wears a philosophy of history; some
are draped in rich Renaissance brocades; some cover their naked-
ness with hand-me-downs, second-hand Marxisms, third-hand
Toynbees, almost unrecognizable tatters of Turgot and Spengler.
We read the philosophers of history, plagiarize them, and then
damn them in public. You cannot escape the philosophy of history by assuming the tough visage of the famous television dick
who constantly demands: "The facts, the facts, nothing but the
facts."

I shall dwell no longer on professional Tartuffism—and I
write as one not entirely without sin.

Other attacks must be taken more seriously. Philosophies of
history are accused of being systems of high abstraction—or reduction—and as such, it is charged, they make the historical world lie.
Back in 1883, Dilthey delivered a telling blow when he ridiculed
the presumption that the philosophical historians had found truth
by distilling some universal essence from the infinite variety of past
human experience. In their arrogance, they imagined that history
would reveal to them its ultimate word. History has no such secrets. History has no unitary message to convey. Moreover, the true
historian, philosophical or otherwise, Dilthey insisted, cannot be a
mere abstractor of what others have accumulated. He must have
immediate and direct contact with historical reality in some form,
dig for the original ore, get dirt under his fingernails. He cannot be
a generalizer alone. I should like to associate myself with these
strictures, though I wish to forewarn the reader that I intend to
abandon the maligners of philosophical history in mid-stream.

In their attempt to imitate Christianity or monistic scientific
systems, the philosophers of history have often ended up with a
few gnomic phrases—far from any direct historical experience. I
shall not defend the philosophers of history for their obsessive sys-
tematization, wrong footnotes and citations, a prioristic tendencies,
mystical utterances. I join their enemies in attacking their pom-
posity, sibylline speech, and dogmatism.

But the majority of the classics, Vico and Herder, Hegel and

Marx, Comte, Spengler, and Toynbee, remain among the great educators of the historical race. And, paradoxically enough, it is their empirical observations rather than their structure-building which I have found intellectually most rewarding. Their luxuriant flow of analogies contains metal far more precious than the ultimate object of their quest. They were unsuccessful in finding a succinct alchemical formula to describe all historical being, but in the process they made wonderful new combinations of historical elements. They are like the explorers who sought for gold, often enough discovered only fool's gold, but in passing opened up new continents of far more durable riches. In a recent work Ludwig von Mises, a rigid scientific thinker, dogmatically asserts: "A philosophy of history has to be accepted as a whole or rejected as a whole." [3] If that is either a moral imperative or a scientific law, I shall proceed to violate it.

In certain respects, the relationship between the philosopher of history and the workmanlike professional historian is akin to that uneasy meeting between the religious mystic and the institution-bound theologian. Such men are often enthusiasts whose vision of the historical world comes to them in a moment of sudden illumination. Having descended from the mountain, they have even recorded for us the external circumstances surrounding their revelation. That rather pedestrian, mid-eighteenth-century Basel official, Isaak Iselin, has described the fervent enthusiasm which forced him to write his *Geschichte der Menschheit*. Nicolas Boulanger was gazing at sea shells in the roadbeds he was digging for King Louis XV, when there came to him a vision of world history as the consequence of a trauma inflicted on mankind by the deluge. Auguste Comte noted on his manuscript the precise minute when the dynamics of the historical world were unfolded to him. In our day, Toynbee has left the most detailed autobiographical testimony of all: fittingly, the original burst of light occurred on the Orient Express, but there were also minor raptures like the one he describes near the duck pond in Kensington. Professional historians necessarily look askance at such mystical or poetic experiences: we are housebroken and they are not. But good empiricists that we are, shall we not have to concede that the

visions of the mystics, respectably draped, have often in the end
been accepted by church councils, holy synods, legislative assemblies, party congresses, even historical associations?

The fact that these philosophers of history have often been
motivated by a desire to alter the social, political, or intellectual
structure of their times and have composed patently partisan pam-
phlets should not blind us to their discoveries. We are, after all,
above such reduction of a man's total work to what *he* may conceive to be its underlying purpose. Voltaire wrote anti-clerical bro-
chures disguised as philosophical history, but he also broadened
the scope of history immensely by including the new dimension of
manners and morals and customs. And, may I confess it, a para-
graph in Voltaire drawing upon the conformities between the
naked Hebrew prophet walking through the streets of Jerusalem
and the Indian holy man impresses me with its simple significance
even today. I prefer it to the frock-coated, gentlemanly presentation of the prophet which is still widely prevalent. Karl Marx
plotted to change the economic structure of the world and the
character of its fundamental human relationships, and in doing so
he has left us new insights into the nature of work and human
personality, into the historic role of the struggle for subsistence,
and into the dynamics of the conflict of classes. In one sense Toynbee may have written a ten-volume sermon in which Anglicanism
and Deism are fighting for supremacy, but he has also illuminated,
by the mere act of juxtaposing similar circumstances in different
civilizations, a great number of real historical situations. His description of common elements in frontier societies, his analysis of
the Levantine personality through the ages, his depiction of the
syndromes of disintegration, themselves based on empirical studies,
can in turn fertilize others.

The emininet Dutch historian, Pieter Geyl, in his now famous
onslaught on Toynbee, begins by giving the devil his due. Toynbee
"is sensitive to the colorful world of phenomena—to life." But
Geyl cannot rest with this affirmation. He gives vent to what seems
to me to be a thinly-disguised Puritan negation of the sheer richness of Toynbee's historical imagery. When he feels himself en-
snared and enchanted for a moment, he draws back into his

professional austerity, into what, in the Terry Lectures at Yale, he refers to as his "calling." "Splendid as are the qualities of the work, fascinating as I have found it," writes Geyl, "grateful as I shall ever remain to the author for profound remarks, striking parallels, wide prospects, and other concomitant beauties—the system seems to me useless." [4] Handsome, yes, but not handsome enough to tempt me, said the hero of *Pride and Prejudice*. But it is precisely these characteristics, not only of Toynbee, but of the other great philosophers of history of the past two centuries, which bestow upon them a unique worth and lasting value. To stimulate thought and to activate the historical imagination is the highest praise. These men are to be read, not as antiquarian curiosities of literature, but because in the vigor and freshness of their analogies they have expressed empirical truths. Philosophers of history are the great vivifiers of actual history-writing. They have enlarged our understanding of man and of human behavior. They speak with tongues. They venture grand schema, they focus a strong light upon one aspect of human nature—often to the exclusion of others—the importance of man's everyday economic activities, or the all-pervasiveness of a unifying historical temper, or the growth and exhaustion of style, or the resistance of man's psychic nature to change, or the identifying elements of class and nation and epoch.

Let us take Vico as an example. A good deal of his writing was decadent humanism even in his own day. What etymological nonsense, silly Roman history, what sheer fantasy about the giants who peopled the globe, about the interpretation of specific myths, about the Merovingians. And yet, approximately a century after the first edition of Vico's major work, the young French historian Michelet discovered in him the inspiration for a romantic view of history which saw in all aspects of human existence at a given moment in time keys, traces, indices, revelations of the spirit of an age. Vico taught Michelet to use the lowliest event and the greatest as symptom. Vico gave him a sense of the wholeness of an epoch's character—the harmony of its feeling, thinking, and willing—and inspired him to create romantic masterpieces. There come to mind a few pages on the wild libertinism and scientific creativity of the Directorate—pages alive with true emotional greatness. And we can still derive nourishment from reading Vico. He shows the ideal in the sensate, never allowing us to forget the particular, never enshrouding us in pure vapor. Of all the philosophers of history, Vico perhaps now has most to teach as we seek to explore the history of the Western mind and sensibility in recent centuries.

One may argue that the tenets of romantic history are available elsewhere and that one does not care for this lush foliage anyway. But try Herder's definitions of the *Volk* spirit. Generations of Germans and later Slavophile historians lived under the spell of the idea of the folk-genius, that hard core of character and cultural personality which seems to identify a modern nation. You do not have to swallow Herder's *Schwärmerei* to be moved by his depiction of the contest of genesis and climate. Even those of us least prone to see the nation as the key unit of historical development cannot fail to sense the vitality of this conception. Herder defined the problem, asked the question. He had the idea of an ineradicable or nearly unalterable stamp of cultural personality—a conception, incidentally, which has been more fruitfully exploited by anthropologists than by professional historians. We in this generation may be less attuned to the rationalist progressists of the Condorcet-Turgot type, but they did sustain a whole nineteenth century of Whig historians, in good books and in bad. Admittedly, the philosophers of history are time-bound. It is no longer Marx's history of a struggle for subsistence that can fascinate young American students—it is "alienation." But that possible reality, that question of the quality of the relationship between a man as subject and the object into which he pours himself, is a profound one, and it must henceforth be asked of all ages where it may be remotely relevant.

The philosophers of history have posed the valid issues. They have forced us to wrestle with the morphological analogy. When dealing with a real historical situation, we must ask ourselves about decadence or new birth. But when Geyl challenges Toynbee to answer in so many words—yes or no—are we in an age of historical decadence or growth, the question so phrased may be pushed aside with an historical fifth amendment without losing one's membership in the profession. It is a legitimate inquiry— the one Spengler answered with such absolute assurance—as to whether different collectives—he calls them cultures—have significantly variant reactions to time and space. The centrality of the problem has thrust itself upon empirical historians. There is nothing metaphysical about it.

Few of the great philosophers of history were closeted visionaries. Among them were activists who themselves experienced in various forms what they described. Saint-Simon, the déclassé noble, knew in the flesh the conflict between classes and social systems. Toynbee, the classical scholar and Near Eastern political expert before and after Versailles, watched the death throes of historic Islam and the birth and proliferation of military nationalisms about which he later wrote. It is because of their particular insights and world experience raised to a high level of generality that I find the philosophers of history worthy of profound meditation. That is the word I mean. They should be our Platonic *Dialogues,* our *Discourse on Method,* our *Treatise of Human Nature.* They should be the education of the young historian. Instead he is often brought up on a bibliography of bibliographies of bibliography.

Empirical observation, broadened and generalized by a philosopher of history, in turn enriches further empirical observation. My contention is that the philosophers of history, themselves moved by direct contact with reality, have provoked and inspired the professional historian—the historian who rightfully insists upon retaining *his* direct and immediate relationships with experience. The philosophers of history should be defended as renovators of historical perception, as men who have broadened our grasp of the world, even as Cézanne has introduced novelty into our perception of a landscape, and Freud has deepened our understanding of the human psyche. Philosophies of history are rich in one-sided earthy apprehensions of experience. Herder's description in the *Ideen* of the tragic outcome both for conquerors and conquered of the fast amalgamations of what once were individuated societies; in Vico, the loneliness and barbarism of the intellect in the society of the human stage become over-refined; Comte's daring equation of societal evolutionary stages with his own regression into what he calls fetishistic perception during his madness; the tension between sociability and a desire for anarchic freedom depicted with stark simplicity in Kant's brief essay on philosophical history; the Saint-Simonian analysis of a crisis generation in the public exposition of the doctrines of the cult—all these are examples of the brilliant new ideas which the philosophers of history have poured abundantly into the cultural treasure-house of western society. May I adopt a phrase of Saint-Simon about the diffusion of such new ideas? "They are like musk. You do not have to see or touch it in order to sense the odor." [5]

When Comte's philosophy of history is reduced to the law of three states, Hegel's to the play of thesis, antithesis, and synthesis, the Saint-Simonians' to the alternativity of critical and organic epochs, Vico's to the three types of nature in the *ricorsi*, Condorcet's to all-inclusive rectilinear progress, Marx's to a dogmatic economic interpretation, Toynbee's to the five stages of the civilization cycle, Spengler's to mechanical chronological equations of the duration of "cultures" and "civilizations" in various stages—and such *is* the treatment they receive at the hands of their detractors—then we are indeed boiling these men down to their dead skeletal remains. And it is not in praise of such rattling bones that I would write.

One of the more common and widely-known recent attacks of this nature on philosophers of history has been the riotous tarring of the victims with the black pitch of the idea of inevitability. The emotional overtones of freedom are so powerful that few things arouse our antagonism more readily than the notion that we are bound, that possibilities are not infinite. However grim the reality, we balk at being deprived of the last vestige of our childhood dream of liberty. I should like to vindicate the philosophers of history as a body from the accusation that they ever meant to squeeze mankind into the straitjacket of inevitability. It can be maintained that even when they subscribed to the idea, it was at most a loose and partial swaddling which left important members free; that the inevitabilities they dwelt upon were varied; and that a discussion of abstract inevitability is less useful than an examination of the concrete propositions which each evolved. This apology for the true and authentic nature of philosophies of history should be accompanied by animadversions both against the simplistic *epigoni* whose sins they have unjustly borne and against Sir Isaiah Berlin's *Historical Inevitability*.[6]

Virtually no major philosopher of history (with the possible exception of Spengler) has claimed that everything in historical development is inevitable. On the contrary, in large measure their work has revolved around the problem of demarcating the realm of the inevitable and defining the possibilities of free human action. In the process, they have molded new concepts on the relations of culture and personality, freedom and necessity. Their structuring of the realm of the inevitable was merely a way of defining some aspect of human nature, and the sum of their definitions, contradictory as they may be, has served to extend our total understanding of human nature and of the historical process. It is doubtful whether Sir Isaiah can demonstrate from the texts that any but the most vulgar popularizers believe in absolute inevitability—and as soon as he accepts the identification of scientific norms and apparently repetitive phenomena in the historical process, he is arguing merely about degrees of determinism. All things are inevitable, but some are more inevitable than others, might be the responsive chorus of most philosophical historians if they could answer his slashing attack in, of all places, an Auguste Comte Memorial Trust Lecture. In the establishment of a hierarchy of the inevitabilities, reasonable men will differ; they will no doubt reveal diverse types of inevitability as they are swayed by religious, political, or psychological considerations. They will, above all, reveal themselves and their generation. And in this historical confession they will make more complex and more varied our knowledge of man.

In summary, I submit that the philosophers of history have increased our appreciation of concrete, real experience. In this respect I have received illumination from the religious philosopher of history, from the historical sociologist, from the Marxist. My attitude may be called eclectic, but I would prefer to relate it to an idea of plenitude. You can, of course, adopt toward philosophical history all of the traditional attitudes that have been adopted toward God. You may believe in the one true system, you may deny the existence of any. You may be agnostic, militantly skeptic, or even acataleptic. But *all* philosophies of history are revelations of true history, and as such I would exclude none of them. I embrace all philosophies of history outside the asylum—and I do not really draw the line there. The institution, after all, harbored Auguste Comte.

Many professional historians would prefer to forget these historical enthusiasts, in the same way that certain schools of philosophy today exult in their break with the philosophers of the past. Some are afraid that the philosophers of history might seduce us into bad habits. Granted. They are as dangerous to the development of the historian as poets and novelists, and they are as vital to his existence.

NOTES

1. Thomas Churchill, Preface to his translation of Marie Jean Antoine Nicolas de Caritat, Marquis de Condorcet, *Outlines of an Historical View of the Progress of the Human Mind* (London, 1795).
2. Condorcet, *Esquisse d'un tableau historique des progrès de l'esprit humain*, 4th ed. (Geneva, 1798), p. 359.
3. Ludwig von Mises, *Theory and History* (New Haven, 1957), p. 323.
4. Pieter Geyl, *Gebruik en Misbruik der Geschiedenis*, The Terry Lectures, October 1954 (Groningen, Jakarta, 1956), p. 55 ff.
5. Henri de Saint-Simon, *Introduction aux travaux scientifiques du XIXᵉ siècle*, in *Oeuvres choisies* (Brussels, 1859), I, p. 68n.
6. Isaiah Berlin, *Historical Inevitability* (London, New York, 1955).

UTOPIAS ANCIENT
AND MODERN

4

THE GOLDEN AGE:
A MYTHIC PREHISTORY
FOR WESTERN UTOPIA

Sometime in the latter part of the ninth century before Christ, a Greek merchant-sailor from Kyme, a commercial center on the mainland of Asia Minor, returned to the countryside of southern Boeotia from which his ancestors had fled in the wake of the Dorian invasion. There he bought land on the slopes of Mount Helikon, cleared the fields of rocks, and built a farm. After he died, his two sons fell to wrangling over their inheritance. One, who was the poet Hesiod, took the occasion to write an expostulation to an unsatisfactory brother as an introduction to his great moralizing epic of Greek rural life, *Works and Days*. Sadness over the loss of fraternal love was intermingled with a more universal feeling of man's bleak isolation in an age of social disarray.

Twilight had descended upon the age of the heroes and the tone of life was melancholy. Agglomerations of wealth had been dispersed and there was a pervasive atmosphere of decline. Hunger had become a familiar in the house of the Boeotian farmer. The barons who ruled his destiny were venal and rapacious—they

had taken bribes from brother Perses. Hesiod saw little hope for
the future, for he was of the men of the iron age. Bickering and
strife, suffering and travail were their daily lot, and the gloom
of life was relieved only by rare intervals of good fortune. When
in the course of their steady degeneration the present race of
men were born greyheads, the poet-seer prophesied, Zeus would
put an end to them, a fate they deserved, for they were incapable
of justice and righteousness and controlled, lawful behavior. Hesiod
cried out in despair:

> And I wish that I were not any part
> of the fifth generation
> of men, but had died before it came,
> or been born afterward.
> For here now is the age of iron. Never by daytime
> will there be an end to hard work and pain,
> nor in the night
> to weariness, when the gods will send anxieties
> to trouble us.
> Yet here also there shall be some good things
> mixed with the evils.
> But Zeus will destroy this generation of mortals
> also,
> in the time when children, as they are born,
> grow gray on the temples,
> when the father no longer agrees with the children,
> nor children with their father,
> when guest is no longer at one with host,
> nor companion to companion,
> when your brother is no longer your friend,
> as he was in the old days.[1]

The bitter lament concluded a long, mythic sequence on the
five races of men, in which is embedded the most famous passage
in western culture on the golden age. Hesiod's disheartened strophes
on the age of iron were preceded by a nostalgic evocation of a
primeval epoch of ease and innocence, when a fortunate golden
race peopled the earth. By a strange though not uncommon historical alchemy, the dark world of Hesiod gave birth to its opposite, the canonical Greek version of the golden age of Kronos,

a myth that in time was amalgamated with the companion myth of the Blessed Isles and with a rich inheritance of Near Eastern visions of paradise. Eventually the three myths, syncretized in a thousand different shapes, became powerful subterranean currents flowing through the body of utopian thought. From this early mythopoeic experience there is neither escape nor recovery; it remains an inexhaustible source of great strength and tragic weakness for European man.

In the opening verses of Hesiod's description of the golden race, many elements of the utopia of calm felicity, a dream of happiness that will endure until the end of the eighteenth century, are already present. The abode of the golden race has no name, but it is a serene and tranquil place where food grows without cultivation and the curse of hard labor has not yet fallen upon mankind. The earth gives forth fruit of itself, *automate* (αὐτόματη), a fantasy that will often be renewed in the utopian imagination and contrasts dramatically with the unremitting toil of the iron men. The golden ones, in a state of eupsychia, spend their days merry-making and feasting. The life they lead is free from violence, sorrow, grief, and hard work—a pastoral idyll. Evils of old age are outside their ken, and so are the terrors of dying: in their golden well-being they glide into death as if they were falling asleep. Great utopias will always provide for good dying as well as for good living.

> In the beginning, the immortals
> who have their homes on Olympos
> created the golden generation of mortal people.
> These lived in Kronos' time, when he
> was the king in heaven.
> They lived as if they were gods,
> their hearts free from all sorrow,
> by themselves, and without hard work or pain;
> no miserable
> old age came their way; their hands, their feet,
> did not alter.
> They took their pleasure in festivals,
> and lived without troubles.

When they died, it was as if they fell asleep.
   All goods
were theirs. The fruitful grainland
   yielded its harvest to them
of its own accord; this was great and abundant,
   while they at their pleasure
quietly looked after their works,
   in the midst of good things
[prosperous in flocks, on friendly terms
   with the blessed immortals].[2]

   Perhaps only one adornment of later utopias is conspicuously absent: while the golden race is beloved of the gods, they know no women. Their generation antedated the events narrated in the myth of Pandora, even though in the present arrangement of Hesiod's poem the misogynist tale of the gods' vengeful creation of women as the origin of evil is placed before the myth of the races. The men of the golden race were sons of Mother Earth and were conceived without the intervention of the male, neither god nor human—a sharp contrast to the creation of Adam, which is accomplished by the Lord, a paternal figure, acting alone.

   After the golden ones there was an abrupt decline, and the race of silver men who succeeded were born abject and vicious. Maturing late, they remained children hanging on to their mothers' skirts until a hundred, and in the brief span of adult life allotted to them were incapable of refraining from savage insolence toward one another. The bronze race, even more bestial, were possessed by psychic evils. They were bloodthirsty creatures who reveled in war, and aggression became endemic among them. The race of heroes, which Hesiod interpolated at this point, has no metallic equivalent. Toward this generation immediately preceding his own iron men he betrayed a measure of ambivalence. The heroes of Thebes and Troy could not be ignored, though their inclusion interrupts the general pattern; but there is no unreserved admiration for the Greek intruders who launched a thousand ships against the land of his father's birth. The Homeric warriors were not practiced in the virtues of diligence and industriousness that Hesiod extolled. Nonetheless, their life-span over, they were allowed to dwell in the Islands of the Blessed in circumstances approximating those of the golden age, while the bronze race were despatched to Hades.

This literal-minded recapitulation of Hesiod's myth of the five races assumes that Hesiod existed as a historical personage and was not a mere name for a collectivity of Boeotian bards, and it passes over a multitude of scholarly interpretations to which the seemingly innocent lines have given birth over the past century. Some recent readings are so subtle and sophisticated that the farmer-poet of Askra might have had difficulty in comprehending their argument. But the rationalist commentators who have raised a host of queries in the spirit of the higher criticism should not be dismissed without at least a hearing.[3] If Hesiod intended to present the decline of the races as inevitable, they ask, how could the myth serve to encourage either his brother or the rest of mankind to return to the ways of work and justice? Does the interjection of the race of heroes between the bronze and the iron races, on the face of it rather clumsy, have a more recondite meaning? Is he telling of a one-way, linear descent from golden excellence to iron degeneracy, or does he hold forth the promise, or at least the remote possibility, of a renewal of the metallic cycle from the beginning? Does he allow for a counter-movement as the genealogy of the races is reversed and they swing pendulum-like from iron race to heroes to bronze to silver to gold in a variant of the theme of eternal recurrence? If the underlying four-metal division of the races was transmitted from the Orient, from Indian or Zoroastrian mythology or both—as many scholars believe—was Hesiod's originality limited to the invention of the race of heroes? Do the metals have hidden symbolic significance—the identification of gold with royalty or divine brilliance—or was the myth a poetic real history of the progressive introduction of new forms of metallurgy, a model for our archaeological nomenclature?

The conclusions of present-day interpreters are nothing if not ingenious. The opening myths of *Works and Days* are looked upon as two related accounts of the origin of evil in the world that recall in passing a time before the existence of sickness, suffering, and death. There is a moral behind the myth of Prometheus and Pandora: men must accept the harsh decree of Zeus that henceforward the sustenance of life will be hidden from them and they must work to survive. The myth of the five races was a lesson to Hesiod's hapless brother Perses as well as to the mighty princes of the earth that they must pursue Dikè and shun Hybris or suffer the dismal fate of the evil races. Alternatively, for critics who stress the final destiny of the races, the myth serves as an explanatory system of the world natural and supernatural, since the first two races become *daimones,* the bronze men are the people of the dead in Hades, and the heroes have been wafted away to the Blessed Isles. Alongside the immortal gods, the superseded races continue to exist in another form, and the myth establishes the extramundane structure of the universe, a total hierarchy of being. Skeptical of the traditional acceptance of the chronology of the races, some mythographers deny any vital links among these self-contained entities. The sequence is not temporal but is an order of merit, and the serialization of the myth is disregarded as a latter-day innovation. This is an attractive hypothesis, though the heroes, who are in fourth place, are manifestly superior to the bronze race who are in third, thus upsetting the descending ladder of excellence. One commentator interprets the myth as a constant dialectic between Dikè and Hybris, rather than a simple decline from race to race. He posits a major break after the first two races, who represent higher types of reality, embodiments of justice—gold the positive image and silver the negative. The third and fourth races can only be defined in terms of violence, the opposite of justice. While the first two become *daimones* and are worshiped by the pious, the third and fourth, inferior beings, are not comprehended in the ranks of the divine. The iron race is the most complex of all, for it has two stages of existence: in one, justice still rules, moral laws are obeyed, men go through a natural life cycle, and good is mixed with evil; in the other, Hybris alone will triumph, a state of absolute evil symbolized by the birth of greyheads and neglect of the laws of filial piety, hospitality, and respect for oaths. Hesiod thus conceived of himself as living in a transitional moment of the iron age, when both Dikè and Hybris still coexisted and men had a choice between good and evil. The moral admonition to brother Perses is now understandable. A world ruled by Hybris alone inspires terror, though there is a prospect that after the reign of Hybris is over, Justice may return. It is the poet's anguished complaint that he was not born either in an earlier generation or later under a new reign of Justice.

Provocative as these interpretations are, the encrustations of recent scholiasts have rendered the myth virtually unrecognizable, like barnacle-covered statues raised from the bottom of the sea. Prior to the projections of modern scholarship, most of western culture was content to read Hesiod at the surface level, without probing for secret complexities. Whatever Hesiod's design may have been—and he was not rigorously rationalistic and philosophical, but probably using older mythic materials in a free and poetic way—in the three thousand years following his death, his golden race, or the golden age into which it was soon transformed, was cherished as a shining ideal of human existence, and the remaining races or ages were lumped together as times of sorrow. Of the entire myth, often only the golden-age utopia was remembered and the anti-utopia of the other periods forgotten. A didactic epistle in verse addressed to a wayward brother, exhorting him to lead a continent, blameless life by tilling the soil and forswearing contentiousness, seems an unlikely place to find the Greek counterpart of the Garden of Eden. But *Works and Days* remained the *locus classicus* of the idea, and every phrase reappeared countless times in utopias well into the eighteenth century. Lifted from its context, Hesiod's myth of the golden race lived on, adapted, altered, telescoped, amplified, and historicized.

In antiquity, the metamorphoses of Hesiod's myth of the golden race vied in number with those of the gods. As the myth was passed along through the Greek and Roman literary worlds, the conditions of life for the golden race were constantly modified to accord with current philosophical and religious preconceptions. Eventually the myth of the golden race, with all the ambiguities of a myth in Greek culture, was reduced to a matter-of-fact description of an actual historical epoch. In the intermediate stages along the way, the mythic and historical components were inextricably intermingled. At some point difficult to establish, but surely by Hellenistic times, Hesiod's idea of five races was completely supplanted by four ages (the races of heroes was dropped) and the golden race became a golden age. When this occurred, the temporal and historical character of the myth was firmly established.

In the second century before Christ the original Oriental myth of four metallic ages which had inspired Hesiod sprung another offshoot, the redaction of the myth in a mixed Hebrew and Aramaic form in the Book of Daniel. When adopted into the Biblical canon, Nebuchadnezzar's vision of the colossus composed of four metals and feet of clay gave rise among interpreters to the doctrine of the Four Kingdoms, the most tenacious frame for a universal history until the eighteenth century.

Greek lyric poets of the sixth and fifth centuries before Christ evoked a bygone age of innocence and virtue without calling it golden, but Hesiod's imprint on their writing is unmistakable. Theognis of Megara bewailed the passing of the pious men among whom had once dwelt Hope and Good Faith and Moderation and Justice in a vein reminiscent of Hesiod, though his vision may have been much narrower. He may only have deplored the usurpation of power once exercised by his own social class, the good nobles, on the part of the evil, vulgar upstarts greedy for money without any sense of fidelity to the old ways. The Agrigentine poet Empedocles, in a fragment appropriately preserved in a treatise on vegetarianism written by the Neoplatonist Porphyry eight hundred years later, added abstinence from blood among men and animals to the attributes of an age anterior to and even more perfect than the reign of Kronos. In Empedocles' mystic cycle of Love and Strife, the primal age corresponds to a time when Strife is yet unborn. Kupris, who in this fragment is Aphrodite and the cosmic force of Love, reigns a solitary goddess at the beginning of things. She is honored with animal offerings, not in the flesh, not in life-destroying ritual sacrifice, but merely with images. "They had no god Ares nor

Kudoimos nor king Zeus nor Kronos nor Poseidon, but Kupris was queen. Her did they propitiate with holy images, with paintings of living creatures, with perfumes of varied fragrance and with sacrifice of pure myrrh and sweet-scented frankincense, casting to the ground libations of golden honey. Their altar was not steeped in the pure blood of bulls, but rather was this the greatest abomination among men, to tear out the life from the goodly limbs and eat them." [4] Empedocles' text on the alternativity of the ages of Love and Strife has recently given rise to as many variant interpretations as Hesiod's apparently synchronic order of the races, though for most of western culture Empedocles was simply the poet of the contrariety of Love and Strife in a temporal sequence.

In the *Dialogues*, Plato used the myth of the races in a wide variety of ways. The third book of the *Republic* incorporated a transformed version of Hesiod's myth into the noble lie, a technique for imposing hierarchic order upon his ideal city. "While all of you in the city are brothers, we will say in our tale, yet God in fashioning those of you who are fitted to rule mingled gold in their generation, for which reason they are the most precious—but in the helpers silver, and iron and brass in the farmers and other craftsmen." [5] In the third book of the *Laws*, his last work, he used the first part of the same myth to an entirely different purpose. He told of periodic geological catastrophes after which civilization had to start its cycle of existence over again with only a remnant of mankind, and in a limited sense each new beginning became a golden age. By this time the myth of Hesiod had been wedded to an origins-of-civilization myth. Through the mouth of the "Athenian," Plato reconstructed the life of the few survivors of the human race preserved somewhere on the mountain-tops on the morrow of one of the great periodic deluges. The first generations after the flood, bereft of all arts and sciences, lived in a primitive state of innocence. Though simple-minded, they had exalted natures; and Plato appreciated their unspoiled way of life. Civilized mankind could not recapture their guilelessness, but Plato linked the ideal state of the past with the future good society when he tried to inculcate their

moral virtues into his urbanized citizenry, whom he would deprive of useless and corrupting luxury. Men of the first age
were kindly disposed and friendly toward one another because
they had the necessaries but not the superfluities of life. "Now
a community which has no communion with either poverty or
wealth," he argued, "is generally the one in which the noblest
characters will be formed; for in it there is no place for the growth
of insolence and injustice, of rivalries and jealousies." [6]

Many later utopias would seek to reproduce the continence
and benevolent spirit of Plato's early ages of mankind. More
than two thousand years after Plato, a young French engineer,
Nicolas Boulanger, member of the philosophical circle of the
Baron d'Holbach, revived much of the Platonic phraseology in
his L'Antiquité dévoilée, an impassioned re-creation of the human
condition after upheavals in the physical structure of the earth.
His purpose was not unlike Plato's—to relate the naturally moral
post-diluvians with the rational good men who were being fashioned in European society by the Enlightenment. The Platonic
lawgiver aimed to institute at one fell swoop what the most sanguine of the eighteenth-century philosophes hoped to achieve
only gradually. What for Plato was still a myth became scientific
truth for the engineer-philosophe, who could prove that the deluge
had in fact occurred by pointing to sea-shells on the mountains
and who derived the image of a tender and gentle post-diluvian
man from mythology and Plato's text. Nothing in Plato ever
died; in a thousand new guises his images were born and reborn
in the utopian fantasies of later generations.

The vision of man in a primitive state of nature in Rousseau's
Discourse on Inequality, its most noteworthy modern envelopment, makes only peripheral reference to Plato's fable of early
mankind, though Rousseau knew the Dialogues. From his notes
we gather that he was inspired rather by the work of a later
writer, Dicaearchus of Messana, a pupil of Aristotle who spent
most of his life at Sparta. His Βίος Ἑλλάδος, the first universal
history of culture ever written, is preserved in a summary by
Porphyry in that same treatise to which we owe the fragment
from Empedocles on the primitive reign of love, and came to

Rousseau circuitously through excerpts in Saint Jerome.[7] Dicaearchus completely demythicized the golden age and reduced it to
plain historical reality. Virtually all the physical or moral qualities
that grace Rousseau's state-of-nature man have an antecedent in
this Hellenistic portrait of the first generations, an age extolled
as the best life ever enjoyed by men, when they were truly like
unto the gods. They ate little—no heavy foods—and therefore did
not sicken from being loaded down with foul matter. The arts
had not yet been invented, and men thrived, without care or
toil, on the spontaneous fruits of nature. Similarly, Rousseau's
natural man was superior to societal man in "physique" and in
"morale," he never suffered from disease, and he needed no
doctors, the bane of civilized existence. Both in Dicaearchus and
in Rousseau the acorn sufficed the peaceful primitives. There
was no rivalry or emulation among them because there was
nothing of value about which to contest. To the later multiplication of desires Dicaearchus, a true forerunner of Rousseau, im-
putes all the evils that have beset mankind.

By the time Aratus of Soli wrote his astronomical poem the
Phaenomena for the Macedonian court in the third century
before Christ, the temper of the golden age had been subtly
changed. No longer depicted as primitive, it was a philosophical
epoch in which the first men practiced the rationalist moral virtues esteemed by the author. When Aratus reached the Maiden
in his versified description of the constellations, he was minded
to celebrate her ancient beneficent reign: "But another tale is
current among men, how of old she dwelt on earth and met men
face to face, nor ever disdained in olden time the tribes of men nor
women, but mingling with them took her seat, immortal though
she was. Her men called Justice; but she assembling the elders, it
might be in the market-place or in the wide-wayed streets, uttered
her voice, ever urging on them judgements kinder to the people.
Not yet in that age had men knowledge of hateful strife, or carping
contention, or din of battle, but a simple life they lived. Far from
them was the cruel sea and not yet from afar did ships bring their
livelihood, but the oxen and the plough and Justice herself, queen
of the peoples, giver of things just, abundantly supplied their every

need." [8] Life had lost something of its easygoing character as men ploughed the fields with oxen, but the air of the pastoral idyll was preserved: existence remained simple, nature was generous, and the pernicious influences of foreign trade had not yet corrupted men by stimulating a taste for luxury. The poem of Aratus was popular in the Roman world—it was translated by Cicero and adapted by Hyginus (who added nothing to the original).

The Romans, who have virtually no utopias of their own, dreamed of the happiness of the reign of Saturn, whom they identified with Kronos, and in the Saturnalia enjoyed, if only for a brief moment and in a debauched form, a revival of the golden age. In Roman literature the epithet "golden" was usually applied to a historical period rather than to a mythic race. Far better known than the Greek poets, Ovid is the pivotal figure in the transmission of the myth to the Middle Ages. Beginning with the Renaissance, his *Metamorphoses* was one of the most popular schoolbooks in western Europe; and his portrayal of the golden age in Book I, which filled out Hesiod's spare text, was the definitive form in which the myth was infused into utopian thought. Ovid, who was a friend of Hyginus, did not disguise his close kinship with Hesiod, for all his rich embellishments of the *aurea aetas*; but the atmosphere has become heavily scented with the primitivist nostalgia of an over-sophisticated society. "Golden was that first age, which, with no one to compel, without a law, of its own will, kept faith and did the right. There was no fear of punishment, no threatening words were to be read on brazen tablets; no suppliant throng gazed fearfully upon its judge's face; but without judges lived secure. Not yet had the pine-tree, felled on its native mountains, descended thence into the watery plain to visit other lands; men knew no shores except their own. Not yet were cities begirt with steep moats; there were no trumpets of straight, no horns of curving brass, no swords or helmets. There was no need at all of armed men, for nations, secure from war's alarms, passed the years in gentle ease. The earth herself, without compulsion, untouched by hoe or plowshare, of herself gave all things needful. And men, content with food which came with no one's seeking, gathered the arbute fruit, strawberries from the mountain-sides, cornel-cherries, berries hanging thick upon the prickly bramble, and acorns fallen from the spreading tree of Jove. Then spring was everlasting, and gentle zephyrs with warm breath played with the flowers that sprang unplanted. Anon the earth, untilled, brought forth her stores of grain, and the fields, though unfallowed, grew white with the heavy, bearded wheat. Streams of milk and streams of sweet nectar flowed, and yellow honey was distilled from the verdant oak." [9] The reign of natural righteousness without legal sanctions, with which Ovid began, was in itself utopia for the law-ridden society of Rome and its heirs. The elimination of any need for the external compulsions and restraints of law remained a dominant theme in utopian thought down through Marx's *Critique of the Gotha Program*, albeit his concept was animated by a romantic idea of *Gemeinschaft* which no Roman would have countenanced.

The stage-scenery of the human imagination can readily be shoved about and the same props put together in many different patterns. Though there are those who would sharpen the distinction between the vision of a glorified past in Hesiod and a complete utopia that looks forward to the future, many Western thinkers have joined the notion of a primitive golden age with a promise that the happy epoch now vanished will be reborn. Secular versions of this union of ideas were widespread in the eighteenth and nineteenth centuries: a typical history of mankind began with an age of blissful innocence, followed by an interim of misery, and concluded with a progressive attainment of a state of terrestrial happiness. While Hesiod's epic reflected an age of social disintegration and looked backward, the fortunate human condition of the age of Kronos could be made part of a utopian vision if translated into the future. Utopian fantasy, like the dream-world of our nightly existence, is not very insistent on precise chronology. Early in the nineteenth century Henri Saint-Simon stood Hesiod's mythic conception on its head and proclaimed: "The imagination of the poets placed the Golden Age in the cradle of mankind, in the ignorance and brutality of early times. It is rather the Iron Age that should be relegated there. The Golden Age of the human species is not behind us, it is before us." [10]

A second mythic element in utopia, Elysium, which first appears in Homer's *Odyssey*, is said to be a survival from Minoan religion. It is a death-free, comfortable haven for selected heroes in a place that is neither Olympus nor Hades. "And now, King Menelaus," the royal hero was assured by Proteus, "hear your own destiny. You will not meet your fate and die in Argos where the horses graze. Instead, the immortals will send you to the Elysian plain at the world's end, to join red-haired Rhadamanthus in the land where living is made easiest for mankind, where no snow falls, no strong winds blow and there is never any rain, but day after day the West Wind's tuneful breeze comes in from Ocean to refresh its folk. That is how the gods will deal with Helen's husband and recognize in you the son-in-law of Zeus." [11]

In Hesiod's version of the same myth, when Kronos, king in heaven during the golden age, was overthrown by his son Zeus, he was banished to the Islands of the Blessed to rule over the heroes. Conditions in the Blessed Isles were about the same as those that prevailed for the golden race:

> And there they have their dwelling place,
>   and hearts free of sorrow
> in the islands of the blessed
>   by the deep-swirling stream of the ocean,
> prospering heroes, on whom in every year
>   three times over
> the fruitful grainland bestows its sweet yield.
>   These live
> far from the immortals, and Kronos
>   is king among them. [12]

The stream of the ocean is common to both versions of the Elysian myth, though only in Hesiod is the island nature of the site explicit. The human foetus too is an island, and in their island utopias men have often expressed a longing for the security of the fluid that once protected them. The maternal symbols of most paradisaical utopias are compelling and need not be labored: the gardens, islands, valleys have reappeared with simple constancy through the ages. The vagueness of Homer's language gave the exegetes an opportunity for free play, as they shifted Elysium about until they landed it on the moon, another female symbol. And though Hesiod stressed the distance of the Blessed Isles from the immortal gods, inevitably there was a blurring of the line between the blissful existence of the heroes under King Kronos and the carefree ways of the gods on Mount Olympus, the grandest creation of Greek utopian fantasy.

In Greek and Roman mythology there were many permutations of Elysium and the Blessed Isles. They assumed kindred shapes as the garden of the Hesperides, the Isle of Ogygia where Calypso offered Odysseus immortality, and Leuke, the white island, to which Thetis carried the body of Achilles. Servius, the commentator on the *Aeneid*, identified Elysium with the Fortunate Isles. The related idea of Elysium-like places that were the abodes of mortals was born early. Homer himself left a description of good King Alcinous' orchard, where "fruit never fails nor runs short, winter and summer alike. It comes at all seasons of the year, and there is never a time when the West Wind's breath is not assisting, here the bud, and here the ripening fruit. . . ." [13] Belief in an earthly garden paradise for mortal men thus had Hellenic as well as Judeo-Christian origins.

By the time of Pindar, the Theban poet of the fifth century before Christ, the character of the population in Elysium had radically changed. In Homer, the next world had been located in two distinct regions, the dark underground Hades across the River Styx to which most men repaired as shades and the exclusive Elysium reserved for the immortal heroes in a rather unidentifiable faraway place "at the end of the earth." Under Orphic influence this aristocratic division was modified by a doctrine of punishments meted out for breaches of the laws of the gods, and by a belief in the transmigration of souls through successive existences and purifications until their final release to the Blessed Isles. Pindar's second Olympian ode and a few threnodic fragments that are ascribed to him expressed the Orphic faith

of Theron, tyrant of Acragas. The Orphic cult had taken root in
Sicily, and in this ode, at least, Pindar accepted its mystic eschatology. The ode has a consolatory opening on the vicissitudes
of life addressed to Theron, and it closes with a baffling attack
on Pindar's literary rivals; but its magnificent central passages
are devoted to a prophecy of the fortunes of the soul in afterlife
that elevated the poem to a great religious revelation. Immediately
after death on earth, good and evil spirits would be judged in
a nether Hades, Pindar foretold, and their fates determined: the
righteous would lead a life of ease and the wicked suffer pains
that no one dared look upon. After purgation some good souls
would be sent back to earth to experience again the cycle of life
and death. Only a small group who had survived this process of
reincarnation three times and remained innocent of wrongdoing
both on earth and in Hades might then proceed along the high-
way of Zeus to the Blessed Isles. The cooling ocean breezes of
this abode of the pure recall Homer and Hesiod, but new elements are added. Radiant trees and flowers of gold blaze all
about and the blessed ones entwine their arms and crown their
heads with chaplets. According to a threnody that has been related to the ode, the immortal souls are more sportive than in
the passive Homeric Elysium: "Some there delight themselves
with feats of horsemanship and the athlete's practisings. Some
with draught-play, others with the music of lyres." [14] In the ode
itself the governance of the place has been entrusted by Kronos
to Rhadamanthus, its ruler in the Homeric version as well, and
Pindar gives a partial list of the goodly company assembled there
—Peleus and Cadmus and Achilles.

Though secular portions of the ode celebrated Theron's victory in 476 B.C. and praised wealth and hard-won achievement,
frequent Pindaric themes, salvation in Elysium depended neither
upon earthly good fortune nor success in contests, but upon freedom from wrongdoing demonstrated in repeated trials in this
world and in Hades. Whereas in Homer Elysium had been the
predestined lot of a few humans who were transported there as
relatives of the gods, in Pindar the Blessed Isles became the
reward for a life of struggle and of overcoming sin. It coexisted

with a Hades where the wicked were tormented. Achievement of felicity had become a more active masculine goal; translation to the Blessed Isles was not a birthright, but required a life of strenuous effort, a moral equivalent of the athlete's training. The Church Fathers will have to go only one step further than Pindar, when they allow the saints in Christian heaven, who have endured in virtue, to gaze out of the celestial windows and rejoice in the spectacle of the torture of the damned. In their emphasis on orthodoxy and chastisement, there are modern "utopian" societies that have closer affinities to Christian heaven than to the calm Elysium of Homer.

While Plato in the *Phaedrus* accepted into his own myth of the soul an Orphic doctrine, not unlike Pindar's, of three incarnations and a final release of the soul for the philosopher without guile or the philosophical lover, he was bitterly scornful of other Orphic renderings of the afterlife in Elysium. In the second book of the *Republic*, speaking through the mouth of Adeimantus, he denounced as contemptible the materialist rewards that some Orphic poets in the name of the gods promised those who lived in justice and piety, and he mocked Musaeus and his son Eumolpus, who had left a song of alcoholic gratification in the next world for the righteous initiated into the mysteries: "They conduct them to the house of Hades in their tale and they arrange a symposium of the saints; where, reclined on couches and crowned with wreaths, they entertain the time henceforth with wine, as if the fairest meed of virtue were an everlasting drunk." [15] This utopia of vulgar pleasure was repugnant to Plato the censor, who would expel the poets from the city—even Homer and Hesiod— for prating about worldly prosperity as a recompense for upright conduct.

In later Greek writings the Elysian Fields were often transposed to other planets or to the celestial sphere.[16] Doubt over its whereabouts beset the Neoplatonists, in part because Plato had shifted the final haven of the soul from one to another of his eschatological myths. Plutarch and the third-century disciple of Plotinus, Porphyry, showed through a skillful exegesis of the Homeric text on Elysium that the poet meant to situate the fields of the blessed on the moon. In his *Face one sees on the moon,* Plutarch supported his conclusion with evidence from an ancient parchment found at Carthage, which maintained that Persephone, who receives the souls of the dead, is not the queen of the under-world but of the moon. Contrary to the myth, she spends all her time with her husband, who is the atmosphere of the moon, though periodically she approaches Demeter the earth-mother and their shadows are intermingled in space. Homer's end of the earth is therefore the moon, because it is the place to which the earth's shadow extends, and the space between the earth and the moon is an atmospheric purgatory through which souls still sullied must pass. Once having found peace on the moon, the spirit is separated from the psyche and returns to its origin, the sun, while the psyche retains its exterior corporeal form and continues for some time to live an attenuated dreamlike existence —much like what Homer recounted of the shades in Hades. In his Ἐκλογαί the fifth-century compiler Stobaeus quoted a fragment of Porphyry to prove incontrovertibly that Homer's Elysium flour-ished on the moon. Porphyry starts with an etymological argument, that Elysium derives from *heliosis*, meaning that side of the moon exposed to the sun and enjoying brilliant illumination. The defini-tion is then reinforced by an astronomic explication of the enig-matic Homeric words "end of the earth": "Night say the mathe-maticians [he meant the Pythagoreans] is nothing but the shadow of the earth which often falls on the moon. The moon is thus really the extreme limit of the earth, since its shadow cannot hit anything beyond the moon." [17]

Perhaps because it was the newly-established site of Homer's Elysium, the moon became a favorite destination of extra-mundane voyagers in search of a perfect society. From Lucian through Cyrano de Bergerac and Godwin, more or less serious lunar utopias proliferated for centuries—though the marked preference voiced by American astronauts for the plains of Texas over the face of the moon may presage the definitive extirpation of this fantasy from our consciousness. The physical presence of man in a place where he had once situated his utopia will invariably desacralize it and make him look elsewhere. The moon has suffered the fate of Tahiti.

NOTES

1. *Hesiod*, trans. Richmond Lattimore (Ann Arbor, 1968, c.1959), p. 39.
2. *Ibid.*, pp. 31-33.
3. See J.P. Vernant, "Le Mythe hésiodique des races. Essai d'analyse structurale," *Revue d'histoire des religions*, CLVII (1960), pp. 21-54; Paul Mazon, "Hésiode: la composition des Travaux et des Jours," *Revue des études anciennes*, XIV (1912), pp. 328-357; René Schaerer, *L'Homme antique et la structure du monde intérieur d'Homère à Socrate* (Paris, 1958), pp. 77-80; Victor Goldschmidt, "Théologia," *Revue des études grecques*, LXIII (1950), pp. 33-39; Friedrich Solmsen, *Hesiod and Aeschylus* (Ithaca, 1949); Rudolf von Roth, *Abhandlung über den Mythus von den fünf Menschenge-schlechtern bei Hesiod und die indische Lehre von den vier Weltal-tern* (Tübingen, 1860); W. Hartman, *De Quinque Aetatibus Hesio-deis* (Freiburg, 1915); Ernestius Graf, *Ad Aureae Aetatis Fabulam Symbola*, Leipziger Studien zur classischen Philologie, VIII (Leipzig, 1885); Woldemar Graf von Uxkull-Gyllenband, *Griechische Kultur-entstehungslehren*, Bibliothek für Philosophie, XXVI (Berlin, 1924).
4. H. Diels, *Die Fragmente der Vorsokratiker*, 6th ed. (Berlin, 1951), I, pp. 362-363, Empedocles, Fragment 128.
5. Plato, *Republic*, with English trans. by Paul Shorey, Loeb Classical Library (Cambridge, Mass., 1958), I, p. 305.
6. Plato, *Laws*, with English trans. by R.G. Bury, Loeb Classical Library (Cambridge, Mass., 1961), I, p. 175.
7. K. Müller, ed., *Fragmenta historicorum graecorum* (Paris, 1841-1868), II, pp. 233ff; Jean-Jacques Rousseau, *Discours sur l'origine . . . de l'inégalité*, in *Oeuvres complètes*, Pléiade ed. (Paris, 1964), III, p. 199.
8. Aratus of Soli, *Phaenomena*, with English trans. by G.R. Mair, Loeb Classical Library (Cambridge, Mass., 1960), p. 215.
9. Ovid, *Metamorphoses*, trans. Frank Justus Miller, Loeb Classical Library (Cambridge, Mass., 1960), I, pp. 9, 11.
10. Henri de Saint-Simon, *De la réorganisation de la société européenne*, in *Oeuvres choisies* (Brussels, 1859), II, p. 328.
11. Homer, *Odyssey*, trans. E.V. Rieu, The Penguin Classics (Harmonds-worth, 1946), Book IV, pp. 77-78.
12. *Hesiod*, trans. Richmond Lattimore, pp. 37-39.
13. Homer, *Odyssey*, Book VII, p. 115.

14. Pindar, *Works*, trans. Lewis Richard Farnell, I (London, 1930), p. 333, Fragment 129.
15. Plato, *Republic*, with English trans. by Paul Shorey, Loeb Classical Library, I, p. 131.
16. Félix Buffière, *Les Mythes d'Homère et la pensée grecque* (Paris, 1956), pp. 482-499.
17. Joannes Stobaeus, Ἐκλογαί, in *Anthologium* (Berlin, 1958), I, pp. 421 ff., 448.

5

PANSOPHIA,
A SEVENTEENTH-CENTURY
DREAM OF SCIENCE

This is the history of a fantasy that never bore fruit, a lost cause, the seventeenth-century hope of a reconstituted Christian commonwealth in Europe that would serve as a prelude to a universal millennium on earth, a millennium unpolluted by the wild enthusiasm of the Anabaptists, a millennium based on calm and orderly science as a way to God. While the utopia of a perfected Christian society assumed widely diversified shapes, in this lecture I shall search for shared ideals in a broad spectrum of writers—and of course I shall find them, since the discovery is predetermined—in the works of two Dominican friars, the Italians Giordano Bruno and Tommaso Campanella, the Englishmen Francis Bacon and John Wilkins, the professors of the Rhineland area Johann Heinrich Alstedt, Christoph Besold, and Johann Valentin Andreae, the Moravian bishop John Amos Comenius, the expatriate Prussian businessmen in London Samuel Hartlib and John Dury, and above all that supreme embodiment of European

The Lovejoy Lecture, The Johns Hopkins University, Baltimore, November 8, 1968.

culture, Gottfried Wilhelm Leibniz. Though these thinkers were dispersed throughout Europe, they learned from one another and sparked one another's imaginations; the core of their grand illusion was the same. As individuals they have been studied often enough before. My perception of the total configuration of their enterprise may add something new.

In part these men were extending a mode that had been revived by Thomas More in the previous century, and his name was called to witness by Protestants and Catholics alike. But both in form and in spirit, their new Respublica Christiana was radically different from his Christian humanist "Optimum Republic"; for by 1600 the idea of utopia had broken through the ramparts of his tight little island and fused with the new intellectual and scientific atmosphere of the age. Though simultaneously there developed a literary genre that continued to follow the bare outline of More's fable—a colloquy in which a returned traveler or shipwrecked sailor drew a "speaking picture" of a distant society for an amazed European—the word "utopia" began to be used adjectivally and loosely in the early seventeenth century, without restriction to the Morean tale, and came to connote visions of an ideal state of man in this world. It might also characterize the general feeling of hopeful youth, as in John Donne's wistful reflection in a letter to Sir Henry Wotton: "If men . . . Durst looke for themselves . . . They would like strangers greet themselves, seeing than Utopian youth, growne old Italian."[1] Or it could be applied to any reformist project of colossal dimensions— designs or "ideas," as Samuel Hartlib's group called them. The overtones of the term fluctuated from mockery to admiration. If there were occasional parodies of utopia like John Hall's *The Discovery of a New World* (ca.1609), Milton could write of utopia with glowing warmth as "that grave and noble invention which the greatest and sublimest wits in sundry ages, Plato in Critias, and our two famous countrymen, the one in his Utopia, the other in his new Atlantis chose, I may not say as a feild, but as a mighty Continent wherein to display the largenesse of their spirits by teaching this our world better and exacter things, then were yet known. . . ."[2] My usage takes for granted a broad meaning and then, with a measure of scholarly license, deliberately stretches it further to cover a number of esoteric philosophical and scientific visions that might not ordinarily be subsumed under the rubric utopian. After all, the only one whose right to the title cannot be challenged is King Utopus himself.

It is easy to isolate the enduring influence of Plato's *Republic* and More's *Utopia* in the Respublica Christiana. More amorphous and elusive are the traces of Joachimite prophecy that keep cropping up in seventeenth-century social and political movements. The writings of Joachim of Fiore were first printed in Venice early in the sixteenth century, and his sibylline phrases reverberated in the sermons of Thomas Münzer, who openly avowed his indebtedness to the *profeta*. Seventeenth-century Christian millenarianism derived from many sources, but much of the foretelling of a reign of light on earth under an order of brotherly love and community has a Joachimite resonance, though few may have read his work in the original. In his abortive rebellion in Calabria in 1599 Campanella consciously adopted Joachim's style and said so to his Inquisitors. Paradisaical fantasies would, of course, never be lacking in Protestant societies possessed by bibliolatry. Nor was the Renaissance hermetic tradition, with its promise of plainly magical benefits to mankind, by any means dead. The influence on the seventeenth-century utopian imagination of the enchanted City of Adocentyn, described in a widely-known Latin translation of an Arabic hermetic text entitled *Picatrix*, has recently been commented upon with virtuosity by Frances Yates.[3] Almost all of the utopians, especially the Lutherans like Alstedt and Besold, were steeped in the Christian mystical tradition of the previous two centuries. One of the greatest of them, Comenius, ended his life the dupe of a charlatan prophet of doomsday. But who among the giants of the seventeenth century, including Descartes and Newton, did not have his moments of religious illumination?

A final element worth recalling is the growing realization that novelty was feasible in the physical world, both in geography and in experimental science. The frontispiece of Bacon's *Great Instauration* is a sailing ship symbolizing the dual aspect of discovery, accompanied by a citation from the prophecy of Daniel.

If there were new lands and new inventions, there could be new societies molded by man's accumulated knowledge. The building of a new Atlantis, a Christianopolis, a new Jerusalem, a City of the Sun, was now eminently practicable. Thomas More had concluded his second book with the rather doleful reflection: "But I readily admit that there are very many features in the Utopian commonwealth which it is easier for me to wish for in our countries than to have any hope of seeing realized." [4] By contrast, the seventeenth-century figures, imbued with a completely different spirit, were virtually all men of action who believed passionately that their plans, however fantastic they may be to us, could and would be crowned with success here and now, or at least within a foreseeable future. As a young man in the first flush of adolescent universalism Bacon had hoped to put his great reform into execution all at once by government fiat; and the *Parasceve* of his middle age still expects the whole scientific system to be completed within a brief period of time. Utopia, having left the realm of fiction, became a manifesto. The religious schisms and their divisive political concomitants, the fanaticism of the Reformation and the obscurantism of the counter-Reformation, were threatening Europe with fratricidal wars of annihilation. Great designs for the survival of Christendom were of the utmost urgency, and their inventors dedicated themselves to this sacred purpose, prepared to sacrifice their lives in its pursuit.

It would not be useful to follow the fortunes of utopian thought in seventeenth-century Europe in all its peculiar manifestations, for that would reduce us to mere cataloguers, and the antiquarian bibliography of utopia is already overnourished. Instead, I mean to single out one of its noblest embodiments, the prospect of a Christian commonwealth comprising the whole of mankind, supported not only by the revelations of the two Testaments, but by two young and buxom handmaidens, a vast encyclopedia of knowledge of the concrete world and a growing body of experimental science. Often it was no more than a dream of science expressed in non-mathematical terms; its mathesis clung to an older meaning of the word.

The novel seventeenth-century attempt to recapture an authentic Christian vision represents the last major effort to establish a unity of European culture upon a common Christian foundation, free from sectarian malice. It is profoundly Christian in two respects: the identification of scientific research into all the possible powers of nature as a way of knowing and loving God, and the use of the new discoveries for the benefit of mankind as an act of Christian charity, of obedience to the commandment to love one's neighbor. In the preface to the *Great Instauration*, Bacon addressed a "general admonition to all" that the true end of knowledge should be charity, not power. The Christological aspects of this prospect are perhaps open to question, though all the utopians, with the possible exception of Bruno, incorporated Christ as a vital mediator in their systems. Even though Bruno's Christ was another Magus, the informer who turned him over to the Venetian Inquisition testified that the heretic planned to work for the general transformation of the moral world within the Catholic religion.

The practice of science as a virtuous activity in Christian, aristocratic, seventeenth-century Europe should not be taken for granted. It had to overcome the inveterate prejudices of various segments of the population. One group of the religious looked upon the absorption with secondary causes as a deflection from contemplation of the divine Primary Cause and hence suspect, if not heretical—especially when scientific propositions like the Copernican hypothesis seemed to contradict the literal sense of the Bible. Aristocrats who had an Aristotelian contempt for manual labor and a certain fastidiousness in personal habit were offended by the very idea of a man of quality dirtying his bare hands with offal and black coals and animal carcasses. The mass of the people, not free from the image of the scientist as a sorcerer or one possessed by the devil, were frightened by clandestine experiments said to bestow dark powers upon the natural philosopher. And some literary wits, beginning to be jealous of the honors heaped upon men who toyed with rulers and triangles and circles rather than lofty poesy, soon found an easy mark for ridicule in the portrait of the obsessed scientist.

At the outset, to establish the credibility of my subject, I should like to set forth schematically the personal links in the historical chain of the seventeenth-century Christian utopians. An examination of the intricate web of their relationships is a necessary prolegomenon, because these men have usually been considered in isolation, within the restricted context of their national societies.

The list of philosophers whom we shall consider is headed chronologically by the Dominican friar Giordano Bruno of Nola, though he lived no more than forty-eight days into the seventeenth century before he was burned at the stake by the Inquisition. Whether there was a coherent moral or scientific system in the poetical writings and dialogues of this extravagant half-genius, half-charlatan, remains moot. The Inquisitors who interrogated him about the fantasy of his conversations of the gods, *The Expulsion of the Triumphant Beast,* believed that it contained the seeds of a Christian heresy rather than a reformed Christian morality cleansed of vice and hypocrisy and false conceptions of the cosmos.[5] Under the mask of a rehabilitated Jovian pantheon, expressed in imagery that will always resist interpretation in detail, one can recognize an allegory of the transformation of mankind through the reign of pure love free from concupiscence, the exercise of a benign authority tolerant of human difference, and devotion to true knowledge devoid of Aristotelian pedantry. Though grave doubts have been raised about the Christian quality of the Egyptian hermeticism in which Bruno's utopia was enveloped, it seems difficult to question either his reckless zeal to reform the whole world, or the tragic simplicity of his belief that his doctrines were reconcilable with Thomas Aquinas and that the Pope could serve as an agent in the great work. Tommaso Campanella, another South Italian Dominican, twenty years Bruno's junior, was implicated in a conspiracy to overthrow the Spanish hegemony and to establish an ideal city in Calabria. Incarcerated after the fiasco, in 1602 he finished the Italian version of the *City of the Sun,* and then continued to labor for the realization of his utopia on a world scale through the most outlandish political mechanisms for thirty-seven years longer, most of them spent in prison, where he was subjected to tortures that would have destroyed a less fanatical believer. Though Bruno was mentioned only once by Campanella in his writings—and then pejoratively—Campanella was a strange replica of his predecessor. And while there is compelling evidence that Campanella drew from the same hermetic sources as Bruno had, the Christian nature of his utopia is less debatable.

Though Bacon's *The Great Instauration* did not appear until 1620, the first decade of the century was for him a period of prodigious creativity during which he composed nine different works, only two of which he printed: *The Advancement of Learning* and the *Wisdom of the Ancients*. The *New Atlantis* was published posthumously in 1627. The private life of this corrupt and self-revealed man was in some respects a constant denial of his spiritual mission; but the literary heritage he left obtrudes everywhere, and his ambitious program for the new science in a Christian commonwealth initiated a separate intellectual stream that quickly flowed through Europe and merged with Campanella's. Within a decade Bacon's whole scientific scheme was incorporated into the first continental encyclopedias, and Campanella's theological manuscripts even quote the epigraph of the *New Instauration* with a Baconian interpretation.

The utopian fantasts and the programmatic scientists—as distinguished from the sober experimenters and *investiganti*— were in the early years of the seventeenth century intimately joined. Intellectual relationships between the English and the Italians were always close. Bruno's dreams of science in a spiritually reformed society were published as dialogues in Italian in England when he was there in the 1580's, a member of the most sophisticated Elizabethan literary circles and a lecturer at Oxford whose teachings raised tumults. Though Bacon looms as a giant in his own right, mutual influence during this period is not precluded—Bacon at least knew Bruno's name and the general drift of his writing, even if he was critical of the wildness of his imagination. Bruno remains an underground source that erupts in unexpected places—in the writings of that polymath, millenarian, and encyclopedist Johann Heinrich Alstedt, for example, who published some of Bruno's manuscripts and was the teacher of

Johann Valentin Andreae at the University of Herborn in Nassau. Bacon maintained ties with the Continent through the intermediary of his "littel" favorite, Sir Toby Matthew, who wrote a preface to the Italian translation of his moral essays in 1618 and kept him informed about the work of Galileo.

Andreae, a Lutheran pastor and son of a pastor, author of about a hundred works, published his *Christianopolis* in 1619,[6] after he had dramatically repudiated the Rosicrucian pamphleteers of Tübingen (of which he and Besold had been the leaders) and the plans for a secret Christian brotherhood—sometimes called the Invisibles—that was to serve as a nucleus for the "reform of the whole of mankind," a phrase that was the actual title of one proselytizing leaflet. The enigma of the Rosicrucians in the early seventeenth century has baffled historians: Andreae probably invented the whole mythology of the vision of Christian Rosenkreutz, the purported fifteenth-century founder of the knightly order, and the *Chemical Wedding*, "discovered" in 1604, was written by him. Report of the actual existence of a farflung Order of Rosicrucians, with their promise of a universal reordering of the world through a theosophy, was doubtless a hoax perpetrated by Andreae and his friends. But word of the brotherhood spread across Europe from Poland to England—Descartes was once accused of membership—and a motley group of mystics, alchemists, and Christian reformers like Michael Maier and Robert Fludd considered themselves to be of the secret fraternity and defended the principles set forth in the *Fama Fraternitatis* (now known to be Andreae's work), published in Cassel in 1614. In the seventeenth century more scholarly young men throughout Europe were touched by the Rosicrucian faith than were willing to confess when they had grown staid and old.

Andreae's connections with Campanella from whom he derived and Comenius who was his disciple are amply documented. Wenceslaus Wense of the Tübingen circle had visited Campanella in his Naples dungeon and at one time proposed calling the Rosicrucian brotherhood a City of the Sun. And the Christian utopia of all of these thinkers can easily be related to a host of esoteric movements that had lived on from past ages. Even when the new science tried desperately to differentiate itself from philosophical alchemy, judicial astrology, cabalist numerology, millenarianism, hermeticism, Rosicrucian theosophy, or Neoplatonic mysticism, elements of the occult were intermingled with the most commonsensical scientific and political insights. The two worlds often lived together in the same persons—this was clearly so in the case of Bruno, Bacon, Andreae, Besold, Alstedt, Campanella, and Comenius. Only in later ages were the rationalist and mathematically ordered elements in their writings isolated in compendia of thought, which pared away the living flesh and spirit to expose mere dry bones.

Present-day scholarly debates over questions of priority in utopian discovery among partisans of Bacon, Campanella, and Andreae are anachronistic. Theirs was an intellectual community. Oral and manuscript converse was still important, and ideas were freely exchanged and borrowed. The sequence of printed books is not a good determinant of precedence. Andreae's *Christianopolis* was doubtless influenced in some degree by Campanella's work—not yet published—through the agency of Besold and Tobias Adami, German scholars in Andreae's circle who, like Wense, had visited Campanella in prison. In fact, a number of Campanella's philosophical works and the *City of the Sun* itself were printed for the first time in a Frankfurt 1623 edition in Latin, prefaced with a moving introduction about the sufferings of the author written by Adami, who had carried the manuscripts north and had earlier published a précis of Campanella's doctrines.[7] It would be easy to establish further relationships among the major figures. Christoph Besold translated into German Campanella's vision of a universal Spanish monarchy,[8] and his own millenarian quest ultimately led this prodigious scholar and polymath to the bosom of the Catholic Church, to the outrage of his Lutheran colleagues at Tübingen. Both Thomas More and Campanella appear in episodes of Comenius' *The Labyrinth of the World and the Paradise of the Heart*. But even when the utopians copied from one another verbatim, as Comenius certainly did from Andreae, plagiarism is not the word for their incorporation of one another's ideas. The bitter quarrels among productive physical scientists that streak the seventeenth century with cries of "thief" are not often repeated here. The brotherhood of Christian utopians were contributors to a common treasury and there were no sharp disputes about priority in their dreams of Christian science.

Comenius, a bishop of the Moravian brethren, who after the Battle of the White Mountain wandered an exile through Poland, Germany, Sweden, and Holland, corresponded with Andreae and considered himself his follower. His own collected works published in Amsterdam in 1657 began with a long excerpt from his mentor, and he makes reference to his divine appointment to carry on Andreae's mission. Comenius is thus the midway figure in the catena of seventeenth-century Christian utopians. From him the educational ideas of a Christian *pansophia*—he popularized the term, which was borrowed from the title of a now forgotten book of 1633 by Peter Laurenberg [9]—spread throughout the world. What appeared in print during his lifetime was only a small portion of his vast storehouse comprising 450 items, according to a recent Czech bibliography.[10] Five manuscript volumes of a seven-part system were discovered in the library of an orphanage in Halle as recently as 1935: Panegersia (Universal Awakening), Panaugia (Universal Dawning), Pansophia (Universal Wisdom), Pampaedia (Universal Education), Panglottia (Universal Language), Panorthosia (Universal Reform), Pannuthesia (Universal Admonition). But contemporaries knew of this wanderer's grand design to inculcate universal wisdom in all men capable of receiving it, using universal education as a means and a universal language as a mechanism, with the ultimate goal of a universal reformation of mankind. Translations of Comenius' works into Arabic were made in Aleppo; and there are even stories of a rendering into "Mongolian." He became the educator of the American Indian when his textbooks were introduced into Harvard, where an Indian college had been established. Comenius served as a bridge to the utopians of the English Commonwealth, who at first glance appear to be more concerned with ambitious economic plans for the improvement of agriculture, relief of the poor, and organization of public employment offices and clearinghouses for scientific information than with the ultimate hopes for Comenius' pansophia. Samuel Hartlib, a German merchant's son living in England, and John Dury—both of whom came from Elbing in Prussia—hastened to publish Comenius' manuscripts, even without his consent. Though the men of the Commonwealth who had invited Comenius to England in 1641 never fulfilled their promise to found a pansophist college, his impress remains deep on the great Puritan "projectors" and on John Wilkins and Joseph Glanvill, apologists for the Royal Society.[11] But even when the Englishmen, or expatriate Prussians, turned their attention to specific reforms limited in scope, these were always conceived as parts of the *great* reform of mankind through pansophia, partial fulfillments of the final goal. Samuel Hartlib's Bureaus of Accommodations and Communications—a plan for the mobilization of England's scientific and economic resources—were explicitly committed to the implementation of the grand designs of Bacon and Comenius. As the Commonwealth's "Agent for the advancement of universal learning and the public good," Hartlib published the aim of the spiritual director of his projected bureaus: "To put in Practise the Lord Verulams Designations, De Augmentis Scientiarum, amongst the Learned" and "To help to perfit Mr. Comenius Undertakings Chiefly in the Method of Teaching, Languages, Sciences, and of Ordering Schools for all Ages and Qualities of Scholars." [12]

Comenius' pansophia was the culmination of a movement that had its origins in the writings of the thirteenth-century illuminated doctor from Majorca, Ramón Lull, whose *Ars magna generalis* foreshadowed many later attempts to fix the elements of universal knowledge and to use this new science as an instrument for the propagation of the Christian faith among infidel Mohammedans and Jews. With the publication of his numerous writings in the sixteenth century, Lull was posthumously recognized as an eminent forerunner in the quest for a logic that would unify the sciences, for a methodical science of sciences, and above all for an encyclopedia that would illustrate the unity of basic ideas in the diverse branches of knowledge. The pansophist program also involved the fabrication of a universal language composed of artificial characters that represented the true nature of things ordered along rational principles. By the mid-seventeenth century all these scholarly and philosophical projects, in which the art of memory played a crucial role, were considered not mere exercises of virtuosi but instrumentalities serving a Christian religious ideal of universal brotherhood. The real language, when finally devised and adopted by all Christian men, would put an end to religious disputations, since the words for all things and concepts would then have precise, undebatable meanings free from the cloudiness and confusion of vulgar spoken languages that inevitably led to misunderstanding and theological dissension. Pansophia would end quarrels and wars among nations. Knowledge would have a solid sensory base—the true image of things, not their inflated, scholastic, verbal definitions. The universal language and knowledge logically integrated would make the learning process easy, and a rational pedagogic system based on visual aids, as in Comenius' *Orbis Sensualium Pictus*—perhaps the most famous textbook of modern times—would make literacy general and thus facilitate man's ascent to godliness. The true Christian commonwealth delineated in miniature models by Comenius' predecessors, Campanella in the *City of the Sun* and Andreae in the *Christianopolis*, would then become a universal reality.

The pansophists were committed to Christian progress in the scientific understanding of things as a way of drawing together the peoples of the world. There were recognized grades of perfection in pansophia as there were in cabalism and in the various gnostic sects to which it was related; but with the new philosophical and scientific tools at their disposal they firmly believed that the general spiritual level of the whole of Christendom would be raised. When words were related to real things, the idols and superstitions of mankind would crumble. Bacon's attack against false intellectual idols in *The Advancement of Learning* was refurbished as pansophist weaponry. Men would live more harmoniously with one another as in their inner beings they recognized and submitted to the influence of the truly divine harmony in the world of things, revealed in that mirror of the world, the orderly encyclopedia of knowledge. Comenius' encyclopedia, a *Theatrum universitatis rerum*, was planned to comprise a mere twenty-eight volumes, another of his ideas that remained a will-o'-the-wisp.

Eventually, all the strands of the Christian utopia merged and culminated in the heroic labors of Leibniz, who in his youth had written a poem in praise of Comenius, and devoted his life to the elaboration of a philosophical system demonstrating the pre-established harmony of God's creation. But this restless man was never restricted to the philosopher's cabinet. He called upon the great princes of Europe to serve as God's agents for realizing the grand design of a Respublica Christiana and propagation of the faith through the sciences. At one time he provided a verbal apology for the ascendancy of Louis XIV, exhorting him to move against the Mohammedan flank in Egypt. When his proposal was ignored, he turned to supporting the traditional power of the Holy Roman Emperor as the ideal Christian knight; or, alternatively, to the election of the House of Hannover, that new Sparta among the nations, whose history he was commissioned to write. European culture was endangered by the Turks at the gates of Vienna. Leibniz offered one of his few finished manuscripts, *The Monadology*, to Prince Eugene, conqueror of the Turks, in an act symbolic of their common purpose. Inconsistencies in his attitude toward one or another potentate—and he switched his protectors often, as Campanella had before him—are of no consequence; the princes were only emissaries of the Lord, first in the reconstitution of a Christian Europe, and ultimately in the Christianization of the whole world. The great utopian missionaries have at times been called Machiavellian; they were merely adept at changing instrumentalities. Leibniz' diplomatic memoranda should not be appraised primarily in the context of German nationalism, as they sometimes have been east of the Rhine. The hundreds of independent German princelets spending themselves in internecine wars were creating confusion and anarchy. They had to be welded together if Europe were to survive. But this "Teutscher" monad was only one element in the great hierarchy of Christian European society. Leibniz never believed that it could stand by itself.

For Leibniz, the most dramatic proof that science was des-

tined to be the conquering arm of the new Christian polity was
the triumph of the Jesuit missionaries in converting so many of
the mandarins of China, a success that he attributed solely to the
wonderment aroused by their introduction of European inventions
and discoveries. He saw a movement parallel to the Christian expansion in China on the other side of the globe—in the harboring
of the Indian colleges by centers of learning like Harvard and
William and Mary. A proposed network of scientific academies in
Berlin, Dresden, Petersburg was envisaged as a chain of outposts
against barbarism and a defense of Christian civilization. When
he wrote a memorandum to the Duke of Württemberg on the
founding of a new university (1668-69), he stressed the need for
locating it in an urban area, lest scholars become isolated in
monkish cells and defeat the aim of free exchange between men
of learning and ordinary citizens for their mutual edification and
enlightenment. Science had to penetrate the very life-blood of
the Christian polity. His science, of course, was far closer to what
the members of the Royal Society called science than to the fantasies of the first half of the century—but it was not divorced
from the more extravagant pansophic projects of his youth, to
which he remained loyal.

You may have remarked that the French have not been conspicuous in our genealogy of pansophists. There were to be sure
French men of science who touched at the periphery of the movement. Father Marin Mersenne, active in the first half of the
seventeenth century, appreciated the pansophic ideals of Comenius, and received Campanella in Paris after his liberation,
though with a measure of skepticism. Absurd as it may sound,
the dying Campanella, disillusioned with the Spaniards, hailed
the government of Richelieu as an incarnation of the City of the
Sun in the new edition of his book in 1637. The eclogue he wrote
on the birth of the Dauphin, the future Sun King Louis XIV, is
an example of Campanella's remarkable flexibility:

> The Cock will sing; Peter will spontaneously reform himself;
> Peter will sing; the Cock will fly over the whole world, but will

submit it to Peter and be guided by his reins. Work will become a pleasure amicably divided among many for all will recognize one Father and God. . . . All Kings and peoples will unite in a city which they will call "Heliaca," which will be built by this noble hero. A temple will be built in the midst of it, modelled on the heavens; it will be ruled by the high priest and the senates of the monarchs, and the sceptres of Kings will be placed at the feet of Christ.[13]

Cyrano de Bergerac's utopian *Voyages to the Sun and the Moon*, slight things in themselves, drew inspiration from Campanella. And even Descartes had had a mild flirtation in his youth with the literature of the Rosicrucians and with ideas of a universal science, though he rejected the feasibility of a universal language as mere romance, and he had contempt for the aged Campanella, who tried in vain to track him down in Holland. The French seem to have contributed primarily political schemes to the idea of Europe, and the excessive concentration upon political mechanics in memoranda like the Duke de Sully's Grand Design and in Emeric Crucé's *Le Nouveau Cynée* shows that their conceptions tended to be essentially plans for achieving a European peace through a balance of power, not an integrated Christian world-order.

The relative insignificance of France in this enterprise may be explained in part by the simple reality that the consolidated French monarchy was providing a new framework for the reestablishment of hierarchy, whereas in revolutionary England, pulverized Italy and Germany, and chaotic central Europe, which had no such centripetal force, the visionaries looked outward to a revival of the concept of universal monarchy. In the deliberations of the private "academy" of that strange French entrepreneur Théophraste Renaudot which served as brain-trust and propaganda mechanism for Richelieu, there might be occasional mention of Bacon and Campanella, even of the Rosicrucians; but amid scores of practical projects of a scientific and philanthropic nature, many of which were copied verbatim by Hartlib, there is not a single grand conception. Even the Christian agrarian utopia of Fénelon was addressed primarily to the French monarchy; it was perhaps universalist and mystical in spirit, but its chief concerns were the realm of France and it turned its back on the new science.

Having roughly fixed the historical sequence of the utopians and established their interconnections, in the remainder of this paper I shall attempt to distill an essence that is the same in the visions of the men from Moravia, Tübingen, London, Paris, Elbing, Nola, and Calabria, whom I have identified as bearers of the seventeenth-century utopia. The discernment of similarities among these highly individualistic men of genius, whose voracious appetite for knowledge and philosophical stature appear larger than life-size, does not for a moment imply that as thinkers they are being leveled to some common denominator. The reduction of a Campanella, an Andreae, or a Leibniz to a system escapes me; but common elements persist.

Let us begin with a negation. The Christian-scientific utopians were unanimous in their rejection of a dogmatic acceptance of scholastic Aristotelian philosophy. In the ideal Christian polity —whether the City of the Sun, Christianopolis, a new Atlantis, or the Christian Brotherhood of Comenius—men would be joined in knowledge *in rebus*, knowledge that was concrete, sensate, based on objects in the real world. All men would perceive things and their relationships with a new clarity. This would be true illumination. War was declared on purely verbal definitions that confused and obfuscated. Few diatribes have reached the peak of vituperation with which Bruno and Bacon denounced the empty definitions in the accepted scholastic Aristotelian tradition that still dominated the universities of Europe despite the attack of Peter Ramus. In an early manuscript Bacon was mild-mannered but deadly on the whole of Greek philosophy.

> Your learning we have said, is derived from the Greeks. But what sort of people were they? I mean to go in for no abuse. I shall neither repeat nor imitate what others have said. I am content simply to remark that that nation was always precipitate mentally, and professorial by habit—two characteristics inimical to wisdom and truth. What could be more childlike

than a philosophy prompt to chatter and argue and incapable of begetting works, a philosophy inept in dispute and empty of results.[14]

Among the Christian utopians great emphasis was placed upon the senses, above all sight, as a primary source of true understanding. Campanella, follower of Telesio, prescribed that everything that was known about nature and the cosmos should be depicted in images on the circular walls of the City of the Sun for all men to see. Symbolic representation and mathematical signs were good and sound means for teaching and memorizing and for universal communication, and there was a certain derogation of words, surely of wit and literary conceits and flourishes. A predilection for plain speaking associated with this outlook was later reflected in the style laid down for its *Transactions* by the Royal Society, whose very motto is telling—*Nullius in verba.* John Wilkins' *Universal Character*, a language of rational signs akin to ideograms, had numerous predecessors in the seventeenth century and many later admirers, not the least of them Wilhelm Gottfried Leibniz.

For most of the century the utopian program-makers, beginning with Francis Bacon, thought of the central problem of scientific knowledge as an ordering of disparate materials in accordance with a uniform, rational schema; hence the pivotal role of encyclopedism and the crucial position of Alstedt's seven-tomed Herborn *Encyclopedia* of 1630 [15] in the history of pansophia. The arrangement of the materials for any prospective encyclopedia was the key to its character. The great eighteenth-century encyclopedias avoided the whole issue of the unity of knowledge, as we still do today, by resorting to the alphabet— even though they dutifully reprinted Bacon's formulas for the rational division of the sciences. The seventeenth-century Christian utopians had not yet surrendered to this mechanical device. They looked for an order that was rooted in a real logic and that led to God, an *Allweisheit die zu Gott hinführt.* Fragmented knowledge of things for its own sake was meaningless. Andreae and Comenius repeatedly warned that unless universal knowledge were deliberately classified to demonstrate a divine purpose, it might end up serving the devil.

If sensate knowledge and the science of things were the beginning of wisdom, they were not its end. The regulating of man's physical, animal needs, even his allowable pleasures, with which most earlier and later utopians were preoccupied, was not the final goal of the Commonwealth. All this was simply preparatory for the contemplation of higher things. Virtually without exception, these are transcendental utopians, despite the circumstantial detail with which economic and sexual matters are sometimes handled. The itching of the flesh had to be quieted so that superior men might be able to function freely as spiritual beings. Honest pleasures were permitted, as in More's *Utopia*, but sensate enjoyment was not valued in and of itself. The leaders of Bacon's Bensalem did not linger at the table, despite their discovery of new tastes and combinations of liquids in the laboratory. The senses were to be satisfied, with the expectation that once appeased in a modest way, they would no longer distract men and impede the communal quest for knowledge leading to God. Most of the utopians, including the two great friars Bruno and Campanella, were antipathetic to extremes of ascetic behavior, considered inimical to sound and healthy inquiry. The meticulous ordering of material things in the regulation of the city, of production and consumption among the masses of the population, was a way of assuring peace, of minimizing breaches in the calm felicity of life so that those who were capable of climbing the ladder of wisdom to higher levels of communion with the divine could fulfill their innate capacities, undisturbed by the kind of social and military turbulence that tore Europe apart in the Thirty Years' War. Only thus would the Christian destiny of man on earth be realized.

In the face of the growing power of the unified political, territorial state, typified by the aggressive policy of Louis XIV's long reign, pansophia turned to the whole world, not to a single dynastic state, as the proper unit of Christian life. If subsidiary state forms were recognized as desirable, as they were by Leibniz, these political monads were mere elements in a hierarchy of being; they were not ends in themselves. Hartlib's ideal plans for a functional government of England were meant to be adopted by other Christian states, too; they were not unique prescriptions. When he was appointed official utopian of the Puritan Commonwealth, he formally stressed the universality of his duties, their application to the whole Christian brotherhood.

In these Christian utopias the spiritual power in society was acknowledged as manifestly superior over its ancient temporal rival, and both were usually vested in the same bodies. The rulers were to be philosopher-kings, or an aristocracy of scientist-priests governing a virtual theocracy. It was taken for granted that all spiritual power was to be imbued with scientific knowledge. Even so homely a utopia as Samuel Hartlib's *Macaria*, one of the most insipid of an unbearably dull literary genre, ordained that ministers of religion had to be medical doctors, too. The king of Campanella's Solarians was the very personification of power and knowledge and love—a new trinity. Even Bacon, who in the fragmentary *New Atlantis* said little about the political institutions of its capital, Bensalem, entrusts the real power in the land to the fathers of Salomon's House. Robert Hooke, probable author of an anonymous continuation of the *New Atlantis*, was explicit in concentrating religious, political, and scientific headship in Salomona, a hereditary king-bishop, whose rule on earth corresponded to God's governance of the universe. In Leibniz' utopia set forth in his *Treatise on Sovereignty* (1676) a dualism was preserved: two unified powers, a spiritual papacy and a temporal Holy Roman Emperor, would together rule the world of the Christian Republic.

The Christian utopians differed in their estimate of the ability of the mass of mankind to participate actively in furthering the ideals of their commonwealth. Comenius and the Moravian Brothers and some of their Puritan followers had far greater respect for the innate potentialities, the seed for development, in every man, than did Bacon and Campanella, who were bound to the ancient Platonic tradition, with its contempt for the man of brass, and who were in the temper of the aristocratic Italian utopias of the Renaissance, when they did not shroud themselves completely in hermeticism. It was Comenius and his English followers who stressed the feeling of Christian brotherhood, the idea of fostering knowledge of nature and God in all men, *omnes omnia omnino*, though the consequences would not be equal because men varied in their capacities. This brotherhood tended to lose some, though not all, of its mystical quality in the matter-of-fact and business-like projects of popular utility advanced by Samuel Hartlib under the Commonwealth. But the Christian goal was still there in Hartlib and his fellows, even if it seems to recede into the background in his plans for a public employment office. Bacon, on the other hand, a precious aristocrat, had no direct interest in the common people; if anything, their present benighted state made him distrust them as a repository of dangerous superstitions. Since the benefits that would accrue to all mankind from scientific investigation would inevitably multiply the conveniences of their lives and alleviate their pains, they were merely passive benefactors of a Christian charity, which remained the goal of science. Campanella also was chary of the people, and his poetry often dramatized the pathos of his distance from them, the *bestia*. The mob had to be kept in check through an awesome authority of knowledge and power. No elaborate system of police guardians was necessary, however. Separated from the run of mortals by a spiritual chasm, the head of Salomon's House rarely had to exercise his authority punitively, for his great superiority was spontaneously recognized and respected. He walked about as if he pitied men. The king of the City of the Sun was a veritable God. But the dominion of these leaders rested on knowledge, never power without knowledge, which would have been as odious as *voluntas* without *ratio*. And the whole problem of the sanction of force played no great role since eventually a reformed educational system would take care of most incipient deviations from the true order.

Education made attractive was the chosen instrumentality for inculcating a spirit of voluntary obedience in all members of the commonwealth. The course was open to talent, to those who had a natural vocation for spiritual lordship. The others, according to the gospel laid down in Comenius' *Great Didactic*, were not taught beyond their needs and capacities. And even though the higher forms of education were accessible to some women, it was understood that as a rule they would be excluded from exalted studies. If there was a careful regulation of pleasure in utopia, hardship and pain in training were not extolled as goods. The learning process was to be gradual and easy, chastisement rare and never brutal—Comenius recalled his boyhood schools as "slaughterhouses." Under the new system, teachers would strive to penetrate into the characters of their charges, in order to be able to guide them effectively. The careful gradation of learning from concrete, immediate things to the complex and the abstract was the imitation of a kind of divine chain of being. Wherever Comenius' system was instituted, there was a revolutionary departure from learning by mere rote. In the end, a measure of educational reform was perhaps the most enduring achievement of the seventeenth-century utopians.

The Christian Commonwealth was rigidly unified. Many institutions like the "community of women" in Campanella's *City of the Sun* have been grossly misconstrued because of a failure to recognize its overriding spiritual purpose, the creation of oneness. Women were to be awarded to men selected on eugenic grounds only, at times carefully designated as astrologically propitious, but not for the sake of sensual pleasure. Children were to be held in common, not for communism's sake but to promote the unity of the city, making all men brothers who were equally loved by the fathers. The Platonic fixation on unity, which Aristotle considered so exaggerated, was an all-pervasive force in the Christian utopia; it was a polar reaction to the chaotic break-up of existing society into unco-ordinated units moving in different directions.

Except for a few virtually godless political utopias attached to "extraordinary voyages," most of the seventeenth-century ideal societies had a strong religious frame. Some, like Campanella's *City of the Sun* and Andreae's *Christianopolis*, were suffused with mystical and other esoteric ideals to which we do not always have access unless we are attuned to these ways. One of the faults of many attempts to appreciate utopias like those of Bacon and

Campanella lies in the tendency of later secularists to excise them from their religious matrix. They forget that it was the miraculous appearance of the Cross of light in the sky which led to the conversion of the men of Bensalem to Christianity. Campanella's name is inscribed on an obelisk that stands in Red Square in Moscow recording the fathers of the Soviet Revolution; Campanella the religious mystic, follower of Hermes Trismegistus and judicial astrologer, numerologist, and propagator of the faith, would hardly approve of the company into which the stone-cutter has cast him. In the Christian utopias of the seventeenth century the political and social mechanisms were always overshadowed by religious and metaphysical visions of the universe.

The utopia was irenic. It was a vision of a Christian Europe in which sectarian theological differences among Protestants and Catholics had either been reconciled or were tolerated as of no consequence. This entailed either a Protestant consolidation as in Comenius, Dury, and Hartlib, or a great union of the churches as in Leibniz, or even so bizarre a solution as the imposition of a universal theocracy through the Machiavellian manipulations of the Spanish monarchy, which in an act of self-abnegation would turn over its world power to the spiritual authority of a pope. This solution was the second version of Campanella's utopia, which only his dialectical powers could reconcile with the earlier conception of the City of the Sun. Each of the utopian thinkers in his own way struggled to combat the doctrinal fragmentation of Europe: if they could not achieve the total unity of Christendom all at once, they would accept a partial amalgamation of the churches. Bruno, Campanella, and Leibniz, in their more sanguine moments, expected an imminent union of Catholicism and Protestantism. Campanella's published plan for encouraging the practice of science in England as a scheme to wean England away from her plans of conquest—a prologue to world union—only made science suspect in certain English quarters and inspired some critics of the Royal Society, with a logic that is truly twentieth-century, to cite such utterances by Campanella as proof positive that the Society itself was in effect nothing but a secret tool of the papist Spanish monarchy.[16] Leibniz' correspondence with Bossuet in a futile attempt to bridge the theological gap is the most famous of a long series of proposals of reconciliation whose authors included Grotius and Calixtus and Spinoza.[17]

Samuel Hartlib may be looked upon as a transition figure from the more metaphysical utopias to the pragmatic schemes of the later seventeenth century. Though rooted in Comenius' watery metaphysics, he opened the door to a proliferation of concrete ideas of improvement that soon removed themselves from the philosophical ideal and sought justification primarily on grounds of immediate utility. In James Harrington's *Oceana* and in Locke's political thought and constitution-making, the metaphysical envelopment of utopia has been virtually shed in favor of mechanistic solutions to social problems. Harrington has a Council of Religion in *Oceana*, but its role is strictly circumscribed. Powers and forces are manipulated to achieve an equilibrium that is valued in and of itself, not because it corresponds to an imagined vision of the cosmos or the divine. Most of the utopians of the earlier part of the seventeenth century had operated in a very different spiritual atmosphere: suddenly faced with the infinity of the universe, they found man's role in this newly-expanded space acutely problematic. It seemed to supersede the minor issues of social arrangements, which by contrast appeared petty on the enlarged horizons. The world had to be ordered, but with the aim of giving man access to the divine wisdom as it was being revealed by the new science in all its glory, complexity, and harmonious grandeur. In the second half of the seventeenth century there began to appear social thinkers who pulled in their reins, as did many scientists, and returned to wrestling with particular problems of science and traditional questions of political power, to the neglect of the grand world vision.

Leibniz, coming at the end of the seventeenth century, towered above the multitude of seventeenth-century utopians, a Janus-like figure looking both ways. For he alone was capable at one and the same time of sustaining the pansophic ideal of Comenius and his predecessors and working out the laborious details for its achievement through philosophy, theology, a new logic, an *ars combinatoria*, diplomacy, and specific scientific investigations. His lonely end in Hannover in 1716 signaled the death of the idea of a Christian world order, despite its political survival in an attenuated form in the schemes of the Abbé de Saint-Pierre.

When in the seventeenth century old hierarchical structures had been simultaneously disintegrating in the vision of the cosmos, in religious and state institutions, and in economic relationships, the utopia of pansophia tried to re-establish a harmony by integrating the new science with traditional Christian culture. The attempt failed, though not without leaving some residue. The utopian quest was resumed in the next age, but under very different auspices. In the eighteenth century cosmopolitanism, the universal vision, became militantly anti-clerical and even anti-Christian. It was naturist and it was scientific. Its conception of nature, however, was sensual and pleasure-seeking; and its science, popularized by the French *philosophes*, was used to fight the religious establishment and, for good and for evil, to secularize European culture beyond redemption.

NOTES

1. Quoted in the *Oxford English Dictionary* (Oxford, 1961), XI, p. 486.
2. John Milton, *An apology against a pamphlet call'd* A *modest confutation of the Animadversions upon the remonstrant against Smectymnuus* (London, 1642), p. 10.
3. Frances Amelia Yates, *Giordano Bruno and the Hermetic Tradition* (Chicago, 1964), p. 370.
4. St. Thomas More, *Utopia*, in *The Complete Works*, IV, ed. Edward Surtz, S.J., and J.H. Hexter (New Haven, 1965), pp. 245, 247.
5. Giordano Bruno, *Spaccio de la Bestia Trionfante* (London, 1584).
6. Johann Valentin Andreae, *Republicae Christianopolitanae descriptio* (Strasbourg, 1619).
7. Tommaso Campanella, *Realis philosophiae epilogisticae partes quatuor, hoc est de rerum natura, hominum moribus, politica. . .& oeconomica, cum adnotationibus physiologicis. . .A Thobia Adami nunc primum editae (Appendix politicae Civitas solis)* (Frankfurt, 1623); Tobias Adami, *Prodromus philosophiae instaurandae, id est, Dissertationis*

de natura rerum compendium secundum vera principia, ex scriptis Thomae Campanellae praemissum. Cum praefatione ad philosophos Germaniae (Frankfurt, 1617). Adami also published Campanella's *De sensu rerum et magia libri quatuor* (Frankfurt, 1620).

8. Tommaso Campanella, *Von der Spanischen Monarchy oder Aussführliches Bedencken welchermassen, von dem König in Hispanien, zu nunmehr lang gesuchter Weltbeherrschung, so wol ins gemein als auff jedes Königreich und Land besonders, allerhand Anstalt zu machen sein möchte. . .auss dem Italianischen. . .in unser Teutsche Sprache versetzt* (Strasbourg, 1620). This was probably the first edition in any language. A Latin edition was published in Amsterdam in 1640.

9. Petrus Laurenberg, *Pansophia, sive paedia philosophica: instructio generalis. . .ad cognoscendum ambitum omnium disciplinarum, quas humanae mentis industria excogitavit. . .ad methodum Aristotelicam* (Rostock, 1633).

10. Josef Brambora, *Kniznî dilo Jana Amose Komenského* (Prague, 1954).

11. Robert Fitzgibbon Young, ed., *Comenius in England; the visit of Jan Amos Komensky (Comenius), the Czech philosopher and educationist, to London in 1641-1642; its bearing on the origins of the Royal Society, on the development of the encyclopedia, and on plans for the higher education of the Indians of New England and Virginia, as described in contemporary documents* (London, 1932); George Henry Turnbull, *Hartlib, Dury and Comenius; gleanings from Hartlib's papers* (Liverpool, 1947).

12. Samuel Hartlib, *Considerations tending to the Happy Accomplishment of Englands Reformation in Church and State* (London, 1647), p. 47.

13. Quoted from Yates, *Giordano Bruno and the Hermetic Tradition*, p. 391.

14. Benjamin Farrington, *The Philosophy of Francis Bacon. An Essay on its development from 1603 to 1609, with new translations of fundamental texts* (Liverpool, 1964), p. 109.

15. Johann Heinrich Alstedt, *Encyclopaedia, septem tomis distincta*, 7 tomes in 2 vols., 2404 pp. (Herborn, 1630). In 1610 Alstedt had already published at Herborn a *Panacea philosophica, id est Methodus docendi et discendi universam encyclopediam.*

16. See *Thomas Campanella, an Italian friar and second Machiavel, his advice to the King of Spain for attaining the universal Monarchy of the World: particularly concerning England Scotland and Ireland, how to raise division between king and parliament, to alter the government from a Kingdome to a commonwealth. . . . Translated into English by Ed. Chilmead. . . .With an admonitorie preface by William Prynne* (London, 1659).

17. François Gaquère, *Le Dialogue irénique, Bossuet-Leibniz* (Paris, 1966), I, *La Réunion des églises en échec* (1691-1702).

6

TOWARD A PSYCHOLOGICAL HISTORY OF UTOPIAS

The waking fantasies of utopia are subject to diverse interpretations on as many different levels as ordinary dreams. In one sense they are private worlds whose geography and laws of movement are explicable in terms of their creator's life experience. There are utopias which become so exclusively personal that they border on schizophrenia—*The Description of a New World, called the Blazing World,* by Margaret Cavendish, Duchess of Newcastle, published in 1666, has much in common with the delusions of Dr. Schreber which Sigmund Freud analyzed in a famous paper.[1] Uncounted utopian worlds of this character are being conjured up every day, though few of them are ever set in print. But if one avoids solipsistic manifestations and restricts oneself primarily to those utopias which have won a measure of public acceptance (and become at least *folie à deux*), the maincurrents of utopian feeling, the dreams shared widely enough to be social utopias with a general history, can be identified. Some dreams express so forcefully a poignant longing of masses of men that their words reverberate for centuries.

Thomas More's book is *ex definitione* a utopia, but what else to include under this rubric may be subject to debate. My attitude is latitudinarian and ecumenical. The conception encompasses "extraordinary voyages," moon-travelers' reports, fanciful descriptions of lost islands, ideal constitutions, advice to princes on the most perfect government, novels built around life in a utopian society; the works of men like Owen, Saint-Simon, and Fourier, who surely would have spurned the epithet utopian which Karl Marx, in the wake of Louis Reybaud, thrust upon them, and also of Marx himself, who tried so hard to differentiate his vision from theirs; and finally a group of modern philosophical psychologists and biologists who would be ambivalent about the term, as well as a number of contemporary philosophers of history who have ventured to speculate about the future nature of man. The boundaries need not be demarcated with nice precision. It is moreover not the literary form that establishes the universe of discourse—in the nineteenth and twentieth centuries utopian thought hardly belongs to belles-lettres and is often unbearably prosy and jejune—but the intent to evoke a vision of the life of man in an earthly paradise that would be radically different from the existing order and would presume to render its inhabitants happier in some significant sense of that ambiguous yet unavoidable word.

The utopia should perhaps be distinguished from the religious millennium because it comes to pass not by an act of grace, but through human will and effort. But neither specific reforms of a limited nature nor mere prognostications of the invention of new technological gadgetry need be admitted. Calendar reform as such would not qualify as utopian; but calendar reform that pretended to effect a basic transformation in the human condition might be. Bacon and Campanella, Andreae and Morelly, Fénelon and Condorcet, Restif de la Bretonne and Edward Bellamy, Wells and Hertzka, Wilhelm Reich and Norman Brown, Fromm and Marcuse, Maslow and Julian Huxley, J. B. S. Haldane and Teilhard de Chardin all find a place on the roster of utopia—some, to be sure, against their will.

Surveying the body of writings since the publication of Thomas More's *libellus*, one may ask a few simple questions: what secret wishes of mankind do these works seek to express?

how have they described the "happiness" they hope to see
realized? what is the temper and character of the life they idealize?
what conflicts of psychic desire were they aware of and how did
they resolve them? While the responses of the hundreds of utopias written in a Christian western world since the sixteenth
century have something in common, they may also be regarded
as psychological documents that significantly reveal the sensibility
of the particular historical societies in which they appeared. There
may be a perennial utopian theme, but there are also important
historical variations of a psychological order in the 450 years under
review, and these shall preoccupy us. If the ordinary dream often
derives its content from a need denied or a wish repressed and
transformed, the utopia may well be a sensitive indicator of where
the sharpest anguish of an age lies. In modern utopian thought,
there have been a number of marked shifts of direction, reflecting
the total changing realities of the world—not alone revolutions in
its political and social spheres—and these fluctuations of expression are matters for historical analysis.

The concept *utopia* has from the beginning been used in
both a positive and a pejorative sense; it has connoted at the same
time an ideal longed-for and a crackpot scheme. The negation of
the great dream has always constituted a parallel stream, from
the very inception of utopian thought. The anti-utopia was not
the invention of Aldous Huxley and Zamiatin: after all, the
Parliament of Women by Aristophanes was contemporaneous
with Plato's *Republic*; More's *Utopia* produced a galaxy of mock-
ing parodies; and even in the body of many a dead-pan utopia, a
mischievous little imp occasionally raises its head to debunk. But
such intrusions from the real world, the satirical utopia or what
has been variously called the dystopia, anti-utopia, or contra-
utopia, are excluded from our inquiry. The same applies to the
weird, biologically transformed supermen invented for Edward
Bulwer-Lytton's *The Coming Race* (1871), and Olaf Stapledon's
Last and First Men (1930), another subject passed over in order
to preserve Thomas More's humanist frame. High seriousness and
earnest affirmation of the possibility of human happiness are demanded of all those who approach the blessed isle, as More's poet

laureate said in the eulogy appended to the main body of the work:

> Wherefore not Utopie, but rather rightely
> My name is Eutopie.

The true dreamer, I am told, rarely if ever utters a negative.

In the present sketch the utopias since More have been divided into three ages of unequal duration. The periodization is of course somewhat arbitrary—it is certainly meant to be illustrative rather than definitive—and in a more detailed study subsidiary trends would have to be enlarged upon. The first group might be called utopias of calm felicity, running roughly from More to the age of the French Revolution; the second comprises the dynamic socialist and other historically determinist utopias, which span the greater part of the nineteenth century; and the last are the psychological and philosophical utopias of the twentieth century, for which I borrow from Professor Abraham H. Maslow the term "eupsychia." Throughout this essay the new themes in the utopian dreaming of each period—the most recent fashions in utopia—will be pushed to the fore and highlighted, in full awareness that hackneyed motifs from earlier times are constantly being reiterated in the background. If a broad definition of utopia is accepted, a headcount would show a vast increase in the number of utopias produced in the last fifty years, but most of them are mere mastication.

Of necessity this *esquisse* will neglect many aspects of life in utopia, such as science, art, and religion, the epigenetic cycle, and death, to concentrate largely on love, work, and aggression—which perhaps immediately defines my orientation.

UTOPIAS OF CALM FELICITY

The utopian idea, already richly explored in antiquity, was in modern times first embodied in a specific form and baptized by Thomas More, whose Latin work (Louvain, 1516) was translated during the sixteenth century into all the major European languages and has since been republished somewhere on the continent at least once every few decades—there is now even a Chinese version. No other work of this character has enjoyed anything like its popularity, well over a hundred editions. It set the pattern for western utopia (after Plato, of course). The main-springs of the good life lay in the wise order, and the solution to the problem of happiness was vested almost exclusively in the "beste state of a Publyque Weale." Through the end of the eighteenth century this stereotype predominated in hundreds of derivative works, for the most part ephemeral, in which typical literary elements were the isolated island, the shipwrecked or adventurous sailor, and the systematic description upon his re-turn home of a government-controlled economy, benign social customs and manners, and a peaceful, tolerant religion. More's way of perceiving things stamped European consciousness so in-delibly that his schema was adopted in scores of authentic travel reports as well as imaginary narratives, and it became the frame-work for many circumstantial accounts of newly-discovered lands. Writers like Garcilaso de la Vega seem to have viewed the reality of the Incan empire, for example, through More's utopian eyes.[2]

In European utopias prior to the nineteenth century, it was assumed that discord in relationships among persons, dissension, conflict, hostility, strife, or sharp competitiveness generated a social climate which brought forth the greatest unhappiness for all men. The panacea lay in the discovery and establishment of social arrangements under which expressions of psychological and physi-cal aggressiveness were virtually eliminated. A supremely good society was feasible because, though by nature man might be capable indiscriminately of both good and evil, appropriate laws and institutions could be devised to cooperate with the loving tendencies in his nature, as well as with his fear of pain and punishment, to create utopia, continuous pleasurable enjoyment subject only to the natural ills of sickness and old age—and even these might be sharply reduced. With proper educational con-ditioning, mostly through the good example of seniors, it was believed possible to achieve this end so perfectly that transgres-sions of the established order would be rare.

In most pre-Revolutionary utopias in the Morean tradition,

unbridled acquisition of property is identified as the chief, if not the sole, source of all dissension. There is a presumption that with the abolition of monopolies of property and with the establishment of some sort of communism or commonalty the antagonistic spirit, the cause of evil, no longer would find significant expression in society. It would simply vanish. "In this they establish three good qualities of man: equality, the desire for peace, and the contempt for riches, as the world is tortured primarily with the opposites of these," wrote Johann Valentin Andreae in the *Christianopolis* (1619).[3]

A carefully regulated marriage system also contributes to orderliness by reducing to a minimum the possibilities of competition in the gratification of sexual desire. In More's *Utopia* a viewing in the nude of prospective mates in the presence of elderly witnesses avoids the subsequent discovery of secret faults and keeps the marriage secure. Though divorce is possible, it is not encouraged. The social organization thus assures not only a stable order but an absolute one, so that change is confined to the natural seasonal environment, whose capacity for inflicting pain is fairly well controlled by human invention. These Christian utopias have succeeded in imitating among men on earth the constancy and invariance of God's creation. The terrible anxieties of the quest for food and for traditional work on the land or in the guild during a period of social upheaval have been allayed in an established, fixed order. The fear of violent death in war or at the hands of outlaws dispossessed of their inheritance has been assuaged. And the arrogant band of bedecked and bejeweled courtiers, the contumacious new officials of a society witnessing the breakdown of feudal relationships without yet having achieved the relative consensus of the policed nation-state, have been banished from Utopia.

The feelings suffused by this state of commonalty—whether communistic as in Thomas More, or based on small holdings, or even somewhat hierarchized by status in later works—are those of equality and Christian brotherhood. The orgiastic chiliasm of the Anabaptists was merely an exaggerated form of the same temper. "Equality cuts all our vices at their root," say Restif's

Megapatagonians.[4] In those spheres of life where emulation was still tolerated, it was carefully contained within bounds in order to avoid envy and hostility—for example, in the choice of magistrates in More's *Utopia*, or of marital partners in Restif de la Bretonne's *Andrographe* (1782), where the whole procedure is regulated with the punctilio of a minuet. In the works written after More there is no consensus on absolute equality, and in late eighteenth-century utopias published in the wake of Rousseau's *Discourse on Inequality* there is a tendency to distinguish between "natural" inequalities, which are allowed some measure of extra reward, and those alien inequalities introduced by "civilization"; but gross inequality is not countenanced. French eighteenth-century utopias might be communistic, as in Morelly's *Code de la nature* (1755), or might idealize a system of private agricultural holdings whose size was strictly controlled or of independent artisan enterprises whose expansion was regulated. In any case, at least the spirit of communal equality prevails, without engrossing or monopoly. The enlightened despot or philosopher-king who emerges "naturally" at the apex of society does not contaminate the general egalitarian atmosphere. Louis XXXVI, the reigning monarch in Sébastien Mercier's *L'An Deux Mille Quatre Cent Quarante* (1770), accompanied by a few companions, walks the streets of the city without pomp or ceremony. When property is allowed, the lands are frequently redistributed and the inheritance laws manipulated to preserve more or less equal holdings. Pierre de Lesconvel's Naudelians are allowed to own no more than twice the land necessary for sustenance.[5] The mode of life is that of an idealized agricultural society, a fantasized early Roman Republic. This small independent farmer's utopia lives on well into the Chartist movement of the nineteenth century—in the writings of James Bronterre O'Brien for example—and it has its partisans even in our own day. (It cropped up again during the Great Depression of the thirties.)

In many pre-Revolutionary utopias an exception from the rule of equality is made for those with an inclination toward studies. Philosophers and scientists are preferred as leaders, but their natural superiority is not envied, neither does it always yield them substantially greater material benefits than the work of a farmer or an artisan. Perhaps there is inequality of esteem—occasionally special memorials for scientific benefactors are erected in the marketplace—but in many utopias there is no essential difference of economic condition. There are, to be sure, a few apparent exceptions. The Master of Salomon's House in Bacon's *New Atlantis* is an awesome figure who lives in a grand public building. But if Harrington's *Rota: or a Model of a Free State* (1660) is against "Community," it nevertheless holds to its own version of the idea of equality and is still called an "equal Commonwealth." [6] The leaders of the Sevarambians invented by Vairasse do enjoy more women than ordinary citizens, but these extra wives are leftovers or widow ladies. Extraordinary emoluments for outstanding excellence do not undermine the rule of order, more or less equality, and sufficiency for all.

In More a conquering King Utopus had to inaugurate the new system, and the abandonment of his utopian laws and institutions would immediately result in an abrupt weather-change to an atmosphere of depravity, conflict, and misery. The order of happiness is within human capacity but it is not innate. Thus Utopian man is not natural—he has been fashioned by institutions—but the result is not unnatural since the founders of Utopia utilized benign instincts and repressed harmful ones through education and the dictates of the law. In contrast to our contemporary absorption with the problem as a major source of dolorous psychic disturbance, the Utopian conception of repression envisages a process that is neither very painful nor very complicated. As a consequence, the social environment in which every new-born Utopian first sees the day is uniformly pleasurable and his whole existence will be passed in the same mild emotional climate.

Tranquillity is the highest good. Since only moderate pleasures are deemed to be pleasures at all,[7] there is nothing to disrupt the order of calm felicity, once it has been instituted, as long as the world endures. More's Utopia is not even subject to the natural decay that Plato considered inevitable for his Republic.

Labor in moderation is judged to be a good in most utopias,

not only to satisfy man's economic needs, but to maintain sound mental hygiene, and both the Biblical curse and the Aristotelian have been lifted. "The Islanders love work and they regard it as a special gift of God's grace," wrote Philipp Balthazar Sinold in *The Happiest Island in the Whole World or the Land of Contentment.*[8]

Though not regarded as a source of great pain, work is nonetheless kept at a minimum in order to allow ample social time for the awakening of other salutary human interests such as learning. While Christian asceticism and the mortification of the flesh are rejected, the spiritual and intellectual life is nevertheless valued above any other. The early utopias are still deeply rooted in the rationalist tradition. More's Utopus made a deliberate and crucial decision when he limited the consumption of commodities to the necessary and the comfortable in order that any surplus labor might be devoted to study. Recognized needs are generally held to the small number necessary for commodious but not luxurious living. The six-hour day was promulgated as adequate under ordinary circumstances; but if it proved excessive for the satisfaction of basic requirements and for building up a reasonable stockpile, Utopians would not go on ceaselessly producing additional commodities—as we do in a society where expansion, not knowledge, is the goal—but would immediately curtail the hours of labor. "What time may possibly be spared from the necessary occupations and affairs of the Commonwealth, all that the Citizens should withdraw from the bodily service to the free liberty of the mind and garnishing of the same." [9]

The psychological assumptions of the pre-nineteenth-century utopias were that man normally sought sensate happiness, that this state of pleasurableness was easily definable, that the condition was derivative from the establishment of an appropriate institutional order, and that this order was not difficult to achieve once its virtues were made known. Man required food, clothing, sexual gratification, some means of protection against foreign enemies, and an educational system to guarantee the transmission of utopia from one generation to another. There were general needs for religious adoration, a bit of good clean fun in the

evening, amiable conversation, the respect due to one's age and
sexual status, but there were no powerful drives and no stormy
passions to upset the equilibrium.

The mood of the system is sameness, the tonus one of Stoic
calm, without excitation. Utopia is unchanging; one day is like
the next except that natural holidays related to the seasons and
nuptial rites punctuate the year with occasional festivities. It is
only a rare dystopian—Abbé Gilles Bernard Raguet in the *Nouvelle Atlantide de François Bacon* (1702)—who complains of the
boredom of existence. No one would ordinarily want more than
a fair share and if normal desires were adequately satisfied there
would be no monstrous outbursts of irregularity. Should an infrequent disturbance ruffle the calm of life, it would be handled
by a minor police system (which is somehow never described).
The natural passions are depicted as mild and gentle, and punishment is merely a bridling of excess. The voracious one, the man
of uncontrolled lusts, the hardened criminal, is eliminated, but
without wrath or vindictiveness, after he has been persuaded
to choose his own doom, as in Mercier's description of the
execution of a criminal in *L'An Deux Mille Quatre Cent Quarante*.
Indeed, the wretch might have continued to live in obloquy
had he been so depraved as to desire it. Shame and public dis-
approval are the ordinary means of insuring an obedience to the
law that soon becomes spontaneous.

There is no need for privacy, no "lurking corners," to use
More's phrase, no capricious travel without a social purpose, for
in all these might reside new possibilities for inequality in pleasure. The problem of liberty is rarely posed in this phase of
utopian literature because the goals are set in a different direction:
a quest for serenity, quiet happiness, peace, perhaps virtue, above
all order, what Abbate Pietro Chiari called "stabile felicità" and
Thomas Floyd, the perfect "caulme of permanent felicitie." [10]

An Epicurean-Stoic could be totally self-fulfilled in this
environment; nobody else would be—neither the romantic, nor
the voluptuary, nor the hero, nor the entrepreneur, nor the saint,
nor the ascetic who inflicted pain upon himself. In this period,

the inhabitants of utopia are all practicing ancient philosophers of varying degrees of moral attainment.

In Bacon's *New Atlantis,* the dominant tone set by the inventive scientists, who mix concoctions for physic and man's delectation, offhand seems to be one of movement rather than stability. But I think it could be shown that recent interpreters have gone far beyond the author's original intent when they identify him as the father of modern industrial chemistry eternally in search of novelty. Inquiry into everything that is possible might serve for the prolongation of life and Bacon is not averse to adopting convenient mechanical instruments; but he still thought of science as a body of knowledge that could be acquired in a finite period of time through assiduous cultivation of his method. He surely would not have been in favor of widespread escalating luxury, which could only lead to softness. The rule of the scientists in *New Atlantis* is an example of precedence for the learned, but in this unfinished piece there is no suggestion of a wildly dynamic republic of science, innovating endlessly, such as Condorcet depicted in his *Fragment sur l'Atlantide,* a commentary on Bacon, some two hundred years later.

Perhaps the greatest distinction between the sixteenth- and the eighteenth-century utopias lies in the redreaming of ideal sexual and marital happiness. As the Christian character of utopia began to wear off, the utopian fantasy allowed itself more and more to envision a wider gamut of sexual relationships. Particularly after the discovery of the Blessed Isles of the Southern Seas and the publication of travelers' reports—many, of course, written in Paris garrets—a flood of utopias depicting various exotic forms of marriage inundated Europe. If the utopia was situated in a climatic zone where the bounty of nature was overflowing and little or no labor was required, work regulations, no longer meaningful, gave way to the problems of sexual gratification. Here one can discern two contrary tendencies—sometimes in the same writer. From Restif de la Bretonne, whose vivid portrayals of eighteenth-century sexual life are the best known of his two hundred-odd volumes and who wrote a sexually unrepressed utopia in *Le Dédale français,* come plans that feature maniacally detailed, elaborate, and often terribly repressive, sexual ordinances. In his *Andrographe,* for example, even after marriage free sexual intercourse between couples is prohibited until the age of thirty, at the same time that successful evasion of the girl's vigilant parents is encouraged. Restif reflects the tales he read of esoteric sexual practices among savage peoples, as well as the fears generated by his own extravagant desires. But throughout this rather dull sexual utopia, the ideal of stability and inflexible order is unassailed— if anything, the chains are tightened.

A trend in a different direction, also inspired by Tahiti and the simultaneous de-Christianization of Europe, looks toward complete sexual freedom as an ideal, insists on new, more intricate marriage forms, or at least pleads by implication for the mitigation of existing legal restrictions with their cruel punishments for adultery and homosexuality. In these utopias, Christian monogamy, not rooted in nature, is exposed as both hypocritical and provocative of strife. A freer sexuality, as the utopia purports to demonstrate, does not lead to the disruption of the social order and the exacerbation of hostile emotions among men, but on the contrary contributes to peaceful, amicable relationships among the fortunate islanders. Thus, despite important sexual emendations, the Morean ideal of stability remains intact. The sexual relations described by Diderot in the *Supplément au Voyage de Bougainville* are pleasurable yet innocent, not debauched, without deleterious consequences for moral character or order—essentially More's requirements for honest permissible pleasure. True, in the writing of subtle moralists like Diderot the new sexual pattern is never described without ambivalence, but in many cruder works all manner of sexual combinations are attempted, as for example, the *poli-antropie* described in the *Histoire d'un peuple nouveau dans l'isle de la raison* (1757), where eight men and four women living together without jealousy comprise the rational marital unit, because "woman has received from nature a greater aptitude for and a stronger tendency toward plurality." [11] In some respects the utopia of the Marquis de Sade is still part of this rather naive, eighteenth-century naturalistic vision of free-

dom from sexual repression; in others it points to the more complex twentieth-century resuscitation of the problem.

THE OPEN-ENDED UTOPIA OF THE NINETEENTH CENTURY

About the time of the French Revolution, or shortly thereafter, depending upon how accurately one presumes to pinpoint
the origins of something as intangible as a change in the waking-
dream habits of a society, trouble came to the utopia of calm
felicity. The disturbing elements were so numerous and varied
that the transformation seems overdetermined: a reorganization
of industry, though picayune by our standards, in the eyes of
contemporaries a revolutionary upheaval that posed unprecedented
problems for urban life; a growing awareness among some of the
misery of the new industrial working classes, generating a pathos
as intense as More's reaction to the first impact of the enclosure
movement; a new historical consciousness epitomized in a theory
of inevitable, endless progressions; a conception of past—and
hence at least the probability of future—biological metamorphoses
of the species; a new definition (or a revival of an old one) of
human nature that cast doubt upon the hitherto unchallenged
Greco-Christian belief in the superiority of man's rational over
his passionate and manual-administrative capacities; a further re-
consideration of monogamy as the absolute sexual institution;
a reappraisal of the need for equality; and, last but not least,
the birth of a romantic cult of personality, self-expression, and
individuation.

Whereas before the nineteenth century utopias are invariably
stable and ahistorical, ideals out of time, they now become dynamic and bound to a long prior historical series. They should
henceforth be called euchronias—good place becomes good time.
In some respects they hark back to the mystical temporal doctrines of medieval dissidents like the followers of Joachim of
Fiore and the chiliasts of the Reformation. In *time* we shall have
utopia. The early utopia was usually restricted to an island or a
similarly isolated environment, and there was a steady counter-
point between the tiny haven of happiness and the greater world

outside. By the end of the eighteenth century, historical utopias, typified by Condorcet's canonical depiction of the future of mankind in the Tenth Epoch of his *Esquisse,* can be confined to no narrower limits than the whole globe. The old-fashioned model —or at least some of its elements—may reappear in the nineteenth century: witness Cabet's *Voyage en Icarie* and a host of other dreary utopian novels. But the mainstream of creative utopian thought has moved in another direction, and the fable is often discarded. An introductory philosophy of history now replaces the traditional prefatory literary contrivance.

The goal of the historical progression depicted in nineteenth-century utopias has sometimes been interpreted as static because Christian millenarian images, along with pastoral motifs from the classics, have crept into the writings. In a relatively continuous culture such as the western one, older utopian fantasies, Greek, Judaic, Christian, Renaissance, and eighteenth-century, are never entirely obliterated, and verbal elements from the past survive with altered meanings. Nietzsche and others less well informed have made sport of the eternal Sabbath of nineteenth-century utopians, calling their blue heaven on earth dull, insipid, and as uneventful as the heavenly Jerusalem of the City of God. And vulgar expositions of Saint-Simon, Fourier, Marx, and Comte make it appear that their ultimate worldly *telos* is fixed and codified. Comparison with the earlier examples of utopia, however, immediately points up their unique quality: virtually all the great nineteenth-century utopias have continued metamorphoses built into their very frame; they are open-ended.

H. G. Wells was in error when he advertised his own dynamic utopia of 1905 as setting a new style in the genre; his was rather among the last of the nineteenth-century utopias—the Saint-Simonians would have found nothing novel in it but peripheral details. Condorcet's Tenth Epoch, the utopian one, is indefinite, by which he meant that ideal transformations in the distant future could not even be imagined until a further higher level of progress had been reached. There is no finish to his dynamic scientific utopia; happiness itself becomes boundlessly progressive with new discoveries. Saint-Simon often talked of a golden age in the future, an image from Hesiod's lexicon, but his disciples understood their Master well when they prognosticated an expansive movement without a cutoff.[12] Auguste Comte's portrayal of humanity-to-be in the second volume of the *Système de Politique Positive*—usually forgotten—predicted a complete turning-away from preoccupation with rationalistic science and technology once nourishment for the maintenance of life could be provided without work and inhaled as odors. But this dawn of a world of pure love and play does not inaugurate a static utopia, since Comte foresees a ceaseless extension of the dimensions of human emotiveness and its expression. Marx has few passages that describe the future with customary utopian detail, but the realm of freedom initiated by the passage from prehistory to true history, once man is emancipated from necessity, is dynamic, forever spawning new possibilities for individual self-actualization. In Fourier's phalanstery, a day of life and love is very unlike the yesterday, especially for those whose psychological nature, the butterfly type for instance, drives them to welcome frequent change.

Pre-Revolutionary utopians are physically immobile. The Saint-Simonians in utopia, on the other hand, are continually building roads, railways, and canals, the great arteries for the unification of mankind, and they are constantly moving over them, making occasional overnight stops at well-furnished motels. The Fourierist may have a home base in a small phalanstery; but there are armies of bayadera and their male counterparts who are always touring, vast programs of cultural interchange, and great itinerant battalions of young workers for public projects. A little-known German fantasy of 1828, *Die Unterwelt*, conceived of a tremendous subterranean expansion of world-wide communications. Wells' utopians are inveterate world travelers—though a meticulous record is kept of their whereabouts. There is an air of excitment and feverish stimulation in this nineteenth-century utopian world. Perhaps the ne plus ultra of this utopian vision was reached in the concluding sections of William Winwood Reade's bizarre universal history entitled *The Martyrdom of Man* (1872). After him, science fiction could only fill in the boring details. Disease will be extirpated; the causes of decay will be removed; immortality will be invented. "And then, the earth being small, mankind will migrate into space, and will cross the airless Saharas which separate planet from planet and sun from sun. The earth will become a Holy Land which will be visited by pilgrims from all quarters of the universe. Finally, men will master the forces of Nature; they will become themselves architects of systems, manufacturers of worlds." [13]

As a consequence of the new commitment to perpetual motion, the problem of ordering a fast-changing world became as intricate in utopia as it is in actuality. The utopia now called itself a "system" by preference. The new mobility altered the whole psychological atmosphere and eternal self-transcendence became a necessity of romantic personality. The utopian problem was how to allow individual dynamism free play and yet prevent it from degenerating into violent anarchy.

The characteristic nineteenth-century solution was epitomized in Auguste Comte's motto, which Brazil adopted as its national slogan: *Order and Progress.* From this viewpoint, a controlled Marxist revolution is still part of a utopia of order; it is merely another way of arranging the dynamic historical process. Up to the nineteenth century, the utopian ideal involved the ordering of life once and for all time. By contrast, the new vision entailed a constant management of run-away historical forces: to tame the future, to know in order to predict and control, to change the world—but always in accordance with its historical destiny.

Many nineteenth-century utopias are organismic and hierarchical, rooted in "scientific" theories of biology and physiology. As the new physiology of popular writers like Bichat, whose ideas both Saint-Simon and Comte took over, dwelt on the fundamental ineradicable differences among men, the egalitarianism of the old utopias was abandoned. Equality, no longer a psychic need, was decried as *égalité turque* by Saint-Simon and condemned as a source of discord because its presumption that human beings were interchangeable counters forced men into the wrong slots, creating social chaos. French nineteenth-century utopians were in quest of an order that emphasized individualism, self-expression, and self-fulfillment. It is perhaps symbolic of the contrast between the two utopian styles that while in More's *Utopia* the identification of people is not an issue, the Saint-Simonian orators had to assure their prospective adepts that under the new system personality would be preserved and their individual names emblazoned upon their costumed breasts. (If the utopia provides what men most keenly miss, the utopian of the earlier period did not fear a loss of personality because he had it, while the nineteenth-century romantic felt endangered by anonymity because his identity had already been threatened by the new industrial society.)

Order now required a complex organization in which the satisfaction of individual uniqueness, not equality, was the paramount key to happiness. Among the Saint-Simonians, utopia was based on three biological types whose Platonic origins are obvious: the rationalist, the emotive, and the motor. To the extent that the egalitarian principle survives, it signifies equality in self-actualization. Saint-Simonian happiness was founded on the fulfillment of natural creative professional capacities and the appeasement of sexual desires in a system that permitted easy divorce under the guidance of priestly love-counselors. More's utopia had also allowed people to choose their crafts freely in accordance with their predilections, but the distinctive occupations were few in number and most young men followed in their fathers' footsteps; the whole problem was unimportant. For the Saint-Simonians, who lived in a more complex world, appropriate choice of occupation as the realization of a "biological" personality was fundamental to the system. An order that was more highly differentiated was denominated the superior order from the time of the Saint-Simonians through the Spencerians.

While the Saint-Simonians constructed hierarchies within professional or sociological categories, Fourier's "passionate series" centered around psychological differences. The bringing together of eight-hundred-odd recognizable psychological types under one roof was a precondition for happiness in a phalanstery; otherwise the variety of relationships necessary for total self-fulfillment in the State of Harmony would be lacking. Since work without love was a psychological burden, a pain to be eradicated from utopia, Fourier developed the mechanism for making labor "attractive," a free expression of the whole self, never divorced from erotic inclinations. You only work with those you love; and you may have as many different work patterns as are congruent with the intricate network of your love relationships. Appropriate provision is made for the specialized psychic needs and desires of each stage of the life-cycle. Since all desires are natural and all have rights to satisfaction, Fourier's utopia operates without any concept of repression. This pathetic little bourgeois salesman may have preserved the idea of unequal returns on investment in the shares of phalanstery, but the poorest man there led a highly stimulated oral and genital existence.

The Christian humanist More had still explicitly distinguished between the lower grosser and the higher spiritual pleasures and he would restrict the former for the sake of the latter. When nineteenth-century utopians appreciated man's passionate nature as at least equal, if not superior, to his reason, the old psychological scale of values was subverted. Where More insisted on continent adequacy, Fourier dreamed of progressively greater pleasurable excitements. The gentle, restrained converse among persons in the older utopias will not suffice the romantics. Fourier widened the dimensions of utopia beyond anything that had been dreamed of before, and in retrospect he emerges as the greatest utopian after More.

How do the French prophets curb the aggressive and hostile tendencies that threaten to endanger the peace of all utopias? The Saint-Simonian system is based on the assumption that once man's natural desire for love and creative self-expression is fulfilled, none but monsters (and they can be disposed of) would have any lust for dominion over others. All energies would be turned toward the endless exploitation of nature on a global scale. Fourier was perhaps more subtle than the Saint-Simonians. He made allowance for certain forms of the aggressive instinct: he fostered emulation among rival work and love groups, which are continually being reshuffled in such a way that competitiveness is at once expressed and tamed, as in the best sporting tradition. To mitigate the pains of an amorous rejection in an order of free love, he employed wise counselors of the opposite sex who had intensely pleasurable techniques at their disposal to console the defeated. The simple Fourierist psychological principle is that harmful aggressiveness is the consequence of frustrated instinct— what he called *égorgement*—and if there are enough salutary outlets there is no eruption in destructive hostility. Fourier devised elaborate mechanisms for the diversion of murderous passions into innocent channels; in phalanstery the potential killer becomes a slaughterer of animals.

Marx's utopia is subject to dispute, since he did not leave a finished blueprint like Owen's *Book of the New Moral World* or Cabet's Fourierist *Voyage en Icarie*. In the *Critique of the Gotha Program* (1875), the slogan "Jeder nach seinen Fähigkeiten, jedem nach seinen Bedürfnissen!" seems to recall the Saint-Simonian belief that there were unique and diverse talents around which society should be organized. (Marx's slogan is, of course, an emendation of the pronouncement in the *Doctrine de Saint-Simon*: "A chacun suivant sa capacité, à chaque capacité suivant ses oeuvres.") Marx's conclusion, "to each according to his needs," is reminiscent of Fourier's language, but its full meaning is rather ambiguous. For Fourier, need surely involved sexual and psychological needs, not merely taking from the public granary as much as one wanted to eat. If Marx was also concerned with this broader definition of need, when he wrote the *Critique of the Gotha Program* he probably referred primarily to means of subsistence.

In general, in Marx's manuscripts of the 1840's the utopian elements had been more fulsomely articulated, and he foresaw a rich and varied sensate life that has distinct Fourierist overtones. He voiced antagonism to the occupational specialization resulting from the division of labor because it entailed a deformation of personality and an impairment of human faculties.[14] In the fifties he explicitly used the term "self-actualization of the individual." [15] Though the concept of alienation is primarily an economic one in Marx, on occasion it does have the psychological sense that some contemporary commentators have made central to his thought. The elimination of alienated labor, whatever its meaning, was part of his utopia. Communism would represent a regaining of personality, the reintegration and the return of man to himself, the transcendence of human self-alienation or self-estrangement. In the ultimate sense, idleness—not work—was the goal of the Marxist utopia, as it was of the Comtean.[16]

In the older utopias—the Germans named the genre "Staatsroman"—the prince or the legislator had been the promulgator of the good economic order and its preserver, In the early nineteenth-century utopias, the state became a sort of superfluous superstructure which ought, and was destined, to wither away. Solve the problem of the organization of labor—or invoke Paul Lafargue's *droit à la paresse*—and you solve the problem of human happiness. If wise Utopus was once the mainspring of the system, the inflated state mechanism of the nineteenth century came to be regarded as an oppressive foreign growth that was probably inimical to the ideal economy. Psychic happiness or misery, the joys of employment and prosperity or the horrors of starvation, flowed directly from the choice of an economy. Society could be "administered" by the central banking system of the Saint-Simonian planners, or it might be a free-functioning grocery-store, an economic anarchy in the Proudhonian manner. In either event, the state was no longer the focal utopian institution—a sharp transfer of the gravitational center from the earlier mode. Society did not have to be ruled and policed, it merely had to be organized and administered. Not until the late nineteenth century, in such state-capitalist utopias as Theodor Hertzka's *Freiland* (1889), was the state again restored to a directing role in the ideal society.

CONTEMPORARY EUPSYCHIAS

Mr. Frazier, the founder of Walden Two, exclaimed to his visitors with a gesture of impatience, "No one can seriously doubt that a well-managed community will get along successfully as an economic unit. A child could prove it. The real problems are psychological." [17] One can agree with Professor Skinner's formulation of the contemporary utopian question and yet find his solutions rather derivative, a reasonable amalgam of Morean and Fourierist elements refurbished with some of the newer experimental techniques. The real novelty in twentieth-century utopian fervor is concentrated elsewhere.

While eighteenth- and early nineteenth-century utopian thinking still fitted in neatly with physical science in the shape of the smooth-flowing Newtonian world-machine—it had served as a model for both Saint-Simon and Fourier, who fancied themselves Newtons of the social universe—in the latter part of the nineteenth century two scientific hypotheses about the nature of man appeared to raise almost insurmountable barriers to the prolongation of the utopian dream: the discoveries of Darwin and of Freud. Both were shattering to those men of the nineteenth century who had had visions of a peaceful, orderly, progressive world from which antagonism and aggression were virtually banished and where man's creativity would flower forever.

That Social Darwinism in many of its forms was a gross distortion of Darwin's thought is irrelevant. Phrases such as the "struggle for existence" came to imply that raw tooth-and-nail conflict was imbedded in man's biological nature. Bloody images intruded into the dreams of the utopians. The initial impact of Darwinism called forth a spate of imaginative new worlds representing the activities of a creature who once was man in successive future stages of his biological evolution—Stapledon has eighteen of these periods. Such writings—often in novel form—are for the most part negative, or at best ambivalent, utopias. The loathsome species whose cold aspect and newly acquired physical-scientific powers terrify such residual humans as they encounter hardly belong in a humanist utopia. The supermen of Renan's *Rêves*, for example, maintain their dominion of reason through fear. These biologically transformed beings have generally moved in one evolutionary direction: toward omnipotence and a diminution of human affect. Beast-machines, emotionally impoverished, existing only to exercise power, became a stereotype whose origins in social reality are all too apparent.

Freud's death instinct may have been a relatively late introduction into his system, but the whole of his life work had already established a deep-rooted contradiction between civilization and happiness. The desire for aggression against fathers and brothers was represented as virtually innate and only partially transmutable. In many ways Freud's was the most trenchant and devastating attack on utopian illusions—what he called the lullabies of heaven—that had ever been delivered.

If the two powerful scientific influences of Darwin and of Freud, which found parallel embodiment in great writers like Friedrich Nietzsche, tended to inhibit fresh utopian dreaming—they did not of course stop the flow of incredibly dull novelistic utopias in all European languages that merely re-hashed old social utopian themes, such as Edward Bellamy's *Looking Backward* or Anatole France's *Sur la pierre blanche*—the experience of two world wars, a mass slaughter of innocents, and the murderous aberrations of new social systems in the making even further dampened utopian ardor. The dystopia had its brilliant moment in the works of Zamiatin, Aldous Huxley, and Orwell.

But despite their flood of bitter mockery the utopian energy of man was not irretrievably dissipated. The creature, it seems, could not stop dreaming even as he stood beneath the gallows of the atomic launching pads. Certain of the hopes of old-fashioned Morean and Saint-Simonian utopias had in the meantime become partial political realities, through social legislation, in restricted areas of the world; or they had at least been incorporated as programmatic statements of intent by major institutions. The social encyclicals of Pope John XXIII, the speeches of Khrushchev at Soviet Party Congresses, and the preambles to Democratic Party platforms are a fairly wide-ranging sample of the penetration of early nineteenth-century utopian motifs into the contemporary political arena. Henceforth mankind only had to face the nettlesome problems incident to the implementation of these lofty purposes; a vague consensus about their merit had already been achieved.

Simultaneously with the realization of some reforms that once would have been deemed wildly utopian, in the realm of pure thought western writers undertook to do battle with both the Darwinian and the Freudian pessimistic denial of the utopian hope, and in the course of their counterattack they developed the two new utopian styles that are peculiar to our age.

Firstly, a group of imaginative life-scientists have transformed the emotional temper of Darwinism. They now assert that a benign spirituality is about to possess the whole of mankind and become a permanent acquisition of the species, that we are on the point of ascending to a higher stage in the autonomous and irreversible evolutionary process. Physical-biological evolution has vitually reached the utmost limits, they say—the size of the brain has hit a plateau since Neanderthal—and the development of man, who now has the power to control his own destiny, must henceforward take place in the realm of mind or spirit. Instead of being associated with tooth-and-nail capitalism, rampant nationalism, and aggressive imperialism, the theory of evolution, in a Kropotkin-like mood, has moved away from dramatization of the individual struggle for survival to envisage a future world peopled by humane, cooperative, totally conscious beings. The German romantic idea of a leap into a higher state of consciousness, a rather metaphysical concept, is replaced by an assertion of psychosocial evolution that purports to have roots in the sciences of anthropology, paleontology, and biology, broadly interpreted of course. Teilhard de Chardin has written of a noösphere, a universal belt of psychosocial forces; Julian Huxley, somewhat less Platonic, preferes the term noösytem. Both of them conceive this new world of consciousness to be stage three in the evolution of matter, which has already passed through a historical transformation from the inorganic into the organic. But for all the scientific learning that buttresses their predictions, within the context of this paper their views can only be looked upon as a dream of reason.

The future expanding order of psychosocial inheritance, they foretell, will result in earlier internalization in the child and in ever more complex psychic awareness in the adult. Through the progressive intimacy and density of the network of human communications throughout the world, a peaceful and universal morality will be achieved. In the course of time the process of natural selection will fortify the new ethical order by showing biological preference for those with superior fitness in adapting to it. The old warfare between nature and culture will be abolished since both will be dominated by rational man.

The Jesuit paleontologist Teilhard de Chardin is emerging

as the central prophetic figure of this twentieth-century cosmic historical utopia, with his arms outstretched to embrace humanist English biologists as well as French Marxists, among whom he has recently been assimilated. "Mankind," he wrote in the *Phenomenon of Man*, "the spirit of the earth, the synthesis of individuals and peoples, the paradoxical conciliation of the element with the whole, and of unity with multitude—all these are called Utopian and yet they are biologically necessary. And for them to be incarnated in the world all we may well need is to imagine our power of loving developing until it embraces the total of men and of the earth." [18] J. B. S. Haldane's man of the future will be "more rational and less instinctive than we are, less subject to sexual and parental emotions, to rage on the one hand and the so-called herd instinct on the other." [19] Julian Huxley has a vision of "psycho-social selection" that is unique to man and "decides between alternative courses of cultural evolution." This mechanism, he says, "must be primarily psychological and mental, involving human awareness instead of human genes." [20] Herman J. Muller is perhaps more hortatory than prophetic, but the biological utopia of universal love eugenically controlled is at least a prospect. "The rapid upgrading of our intelligence must be accompanied as closely as possible with a corresponding effort to infuse into the genetic basis of our moral natures the springs of stronger, more genuine fellow-feeling." [21]

These scientists belittle the prophets of doom and those so engrossed in the pettiness of living that they fail to appreciate the grand design of the future happiness of mankind, which, to be sure, is more cerebral than sensate, more spiritual and artistic than physical—in the desexualized Comtean, rather than Fourierist, tradition. Undaunted by the horrors of the twentieth century, Teilhard de Chardin was confident that we were actually witnessing the initial breakthrough into the new age. In a letter written shortly before his death, when the nations of the world, east and west, agreed to cooperate in the scientific investigations of the geophysical year, he playfully yet enthusiastically proclaimed it the first year of the noösphere.

The life-scientists have been joined by a number of eminent

philosophers of history, who seem agreed that the next stage of human life either must or is likely to entail a spiritualization of mankind and a movement away from the present absorption with aggressive power and instinctual existence. Arnold Toynbee uses the term "etherialisation" for what Teilhard de Chardin in his private language called "hominisation," and Karl Jaspers, a second "axial period" of spirituality similar to the age of the prophets. For what is the fable of the sleeper on the ledge of a mountain-side, which Toynbee has preserved from the first volume to the last, but a historian's utopian dream? One ledge separates the primitive world from the age of civilizations. But this age is drawing to a close, and the rule of circularity that governed the twenty-one known specimens of civilized society in the past is not applicable to the future. Civilization with its inner cyclical dialectic of growth and destruction is about to be transcended. When mankind reaches the next ledge above us new rules will prevail in what Toynbee, a somewhat reluctant utopian, tentatively defined as a spiritual world of brotherhood and communion.

Parallel with this readaptation of Darwinism to serve a utopian ideal of a peaceful, rational, cooperative man, are the efforts of a group of psychologists, anthropologists, and philosophers to grapple with Freud and free him from the rather somber portrait of the future of mankind which he left behind, particularly in his last works. Against the purported elimination of aggressiveness as a consequence of establishing a new order of property relationships (or the abolition of property), which Marx had assumed, Freud consistently aimed his sharpest barbs.[22]

The paltry measure of happiness an individual might attain was dependent upon far more than an ideal social order: it was rather the result of a complex interplay between a man's psycho-physiological nature and the particular forms of repression adopted at a given historical time in a specific culture. Some natures were doomed from the outset to suffer under certain cultural regimens, others to flourish; some sought refuge in insanity, while others could be restored through therapy to endure or tolerate what was essentially inimical to them. There are many ways to unhappiness in the Freudian philosophy. Civilization might create higher mental systems which contained the beast, but aggressiveness would inevitably erupt in a thousand guises. If primitive aggressiveness merely assumed different shapes throughout history, if the most that could be done in the name of civilization was to repress and sublimate, then the eudaemonist utopia was sheer nonsense. To the extent that Freud has a utopian ideal it is a Kantian one: the development of all human capacities beyond the instinctual. The preferred historical state of man is the reign of de-emotionalized reason; but this is hardly in prospect.

The first important disciple of Freud's to attempt an adaptation of his discoveries to a more optimistic view of the future of man that would be consonant with the Marxist utopia was Wilhelm Reich. The Marxist and the psychoanalytic movements had once appeared on the European intellectual horizon as profoundly antagonistic orientations. In the twenties, on the eve of the Nazi seizure of power, Reich broke ranks and summoned the German proletariat to abandon their exclusive fixation upon the Marxist sociological interpretation of man's historical destiny and to incorporate much of Freud's psychological theory of genitality into their worldview—"Dialectical Materialism and Psychoanalysis" appeared in *Unter dem Banner des Marxismus* in 1929. But Reich drew revolutionary consequences from the doctrine: instead of a future civilization resting on heightened instinctual repression, he preached an apotheosis of the body in all its parts and a worship of the orgasm. Immediate radical sexual emancipation was for him a prerequisite to the achievement of a victorious social revolution; otherwise the potentially militant masses, enthralled by the repressive psychological forces of the Oedipal family structure, would be inhibited from active political rebellion. The two most important nineteenth-century, pre-Marxist utopian schools, the Saint-Simonian and the Fourierist, had intimately coupled free sexuality with work needs, but this bond had been neglected by the Victorian, Kaiser Wilhelm Marxists. Reich's original *Sexualpolitik*, which of course did more violence to Freud than to Marx, was an authentic return to the older tradition.

Those who have followed Reich's path in the 1940's and 50's, Fromm, Marcuse, and Norman Brown, represent a characteristic resurgence of the Adamite utopia in a mechanized society where relationships are endangered by an atrophy of love. They negate the Freudian negation of the eudaemonist utopia. They reject the underlying dualism of his system and admit no intrinsic reason that the libido cannot enjoy free expression, once mankind is emancipated from the economic and sexual repressions that may have been necessary in lower states of civilization so that culture might be built.

The posthumously published manuscripts of the young Marx are the proof-text for Fromm's great conciliation. Like Hercules at the crossroads, modern man might have embarked upon a new order of free labor in companionship and love—Fromm's restatement of the Fourierist utopia—or he could again allow himself to submit to a pathological sado-masochistic order of society. Man seems to have chosen the second alternative, a competitive power-dominated society in which "alienation as a sickness of the self" is well-nigh universal.[23] He will never be happy until he finds love and security in true democratic socialism. "Man today is confronted with the most fundamental choice; not that between Capitalism and Communism, but that between *robotism* (of both the capitalist and the communist variety), or Humanistic Communitarian Socialism." [24]

Marcuse tackles Freud more directly on the concept of repression. For the purpose of the argument, at least, he accepts the Freudian system in its pure form unadulterated by the neo-Freudians, but to Marcuse's Hegelian-Marxist concept of stadially developing consciousness the idea that civilization must forever be nurtured and sustained by repressed libidinal energies is abhorrent. An era of general non-repressive sublimation will be inaugurated by reactivating early stages of the libido. "The sexual impulses, without losing their erotic energy, transcend their immediate object and eroticize normally non- and anti-erotic relationships between individuals, and between them and their environment. . . . The pleasure principle extends to consciousness. Eros redefines reason in his own terms. Reasonable is what sustains the order of gratification." [25] Fourier never said more. As in Fromm, the abolition of what Marcuse calls "surplus repression"

(Marx is not named in *Eros and Civilization*, but he is the absent hero) requires political action as a necessary prolegomenon to the establishment of his new world. As for the general tenor of this utopia without repression, it has none of the wild abandon of spontaneous philosophical anarchism, and Marcuse chides Wilhelm Reich for his failure to distinguish between repressive and non-repressive sublimation. The higher freedom will have its hierarchy à la Saint-Simon, even its general will à la Rousseau. "Repressive reason gives way to a new *rationality of gratification* in which reason and happiness converge. It creates its own division of labor, its own priorities, its own hierarchy. The historical heritage of the performance principle is administration, not of men, but of things: mature civilization depends for its functioning on a multitude of coordinated arrangements. These arrangements in turn must carry recognized and recognizable authority. Hierarchical relationships are not unfree *per se*. . . ." [26]

Norman Brown's utopia also derives from Freud. But he sees no reason for suffering through the later repressive stages of genitality when it would be more human, natural, and indeed pleasurable to stop at the period of greatest self-fulfillment, childhood sexuality. Wilhelm Reich's assumption that the sexuality which culture represses is normal adult genital sexuality is rejected as "simplified and distorted." With a wealth of literary evidence from poets and mystics, Brown demonstrates that Freud's stage of childhood is what mankind has longed for through the ages, that the redemption of the body, the abolition of dualism, the dawn of Schiller's age of play or Fourier's "attractive work" is the final solution to the problem of happiness. Brown contends that Freud himself had sensed this in one of his moods but censored it in another. Brown, too, calls upon the young Marx to bear witness, though his utopia is in general less politically oriented than either Fromm's or Marcuse's. While his argument is not as skillful a dialectical exercise as Marcuse's, he pursues much the same course: Freud is quoted against himself. "The abolition of repression would abolish the unnatural concentrations of libido in certain particular bodily organs—concentrations engineered by the negativity of the morbid death instinct, and constituting the bodily base of the neurotic character disorders in the human ego. . . . The human body would become polymorphously perverse, delighting in that full life of all the body which it now fears." [27]

Maslow's psychological utopia has its roots in a rather different way of wrestling with Freud's concept of aggression; he does not really belong with the group whom Professor Philip Rieff has recently called the Freudo-Marxists. Marx has played less of a role in his thinking than have the anthropological studies of Ruth Benedict and Margaret Mead, which seemed to show that in primitive communities polarities of aggression and mildness were culturally determined and that generally aggressive behavior was by no means universal. From Benedict's manuscripts he drew the concept of "synergy," which allows him to conceive of a society where truly spontaneous, unfrustrated, egotistic behavior would have to express itself in altruistic action—echoes of the eighteenth-century moralists. From a study of what he considers mature self-actualized people, he has come to dream of a totally self-actualized society in which the expression of hostile aggressiveness and the need for its external repression would hardly exist.

Along with the neo-Freudians, Maslow rejects such absolute concepts as the death instinct. He believes that through the discovery of the pure sources of one's own nature there can be a free outpouring of creativity, even the birth of a new way of cognition uncorrupted by the inherited categories of Aristotelian thinking. His seems to be a utopia of the will, emancipated and untrammeled, that somehow achieves direct realization of the traditional love of the great universal religious illuminations of the sixth century before Christ. Often his ideal approaches the yea-saying morality of Nietzsche, freed from its confines of aristocratic exclusivity—its fangs cut—and made available to everyman. Maslow is a psychological utopian not in the sense that he is blind to the economic and social miseries that inspired most past utopias, but that with a utopian's license he moves on to another plane, where, beyond basic needs, he posits requirements for a psychic utopia that are more or less autonomous of any existing political order: the fulfillment of "idiosyncratic potentials, of expression of the self, and of the tendency of the person to grow in his own style and at his own pace." [28]

Of late, one can detect in Maslow's writings a movement away from the definition of self-actualization in romantic terms as the expansive realization of *all* potentialities, and the acceptance of a hierarchy of values in which a kind of religious experience again becomes the highest good to which others must be made subordinate.[29] In this he seems to join those philosophers of history who foresee a new spiritualization of mankind and an end to the sensate culture of our times.

Thus the two alternative utopian visions that have come to the fore in contemporary western society (in defiance of a numerous population of dystopians) appear to be moving in opposite directions. In one, based upon the hypothesis of a growing spiritualization of mankind, the dross of the body seems to be left behind. In the other, a fantasy of greater rather than diminished sensate gratification is pivotal, and all human activity is libidinized. But the polarization of these two major present-day utopian solutions must give us pause. It has been our contention that in the past the dominant utopian types have been at least relatively uniform, each in its own age. Now we find the persistence of flagrantly divergent tendencies. We could take refuge in a conception of the psychological identity of opposites. Or perhaps these counter-currents are simply two different fantasies for dealing with the gnawing reality of aggression once the problems of work have been resolved in a world of material abundance. In the state of pure, virtually disembodied spirituality there can by definition be no room for aggression; and in the state of totally unrepressed gratification or non-repressive sublimation—however differently they are defined—the two-headed Cerberus of frustration-aggression is silenced forever.

As there is throughout the planet uneven development in the level of economic growth and in the degree of acceptance of the ways of western civilization, so there are today different utopias coexisting. For a vast proportion of the human beings on earth, the simple static utopias of the period before 1800, with their promise of an orderly society and the assured satisfaction of elementary needs of subsistence, are still pie in the sky. And the wish for eternal peace remains utopian even among those who appear to have abolished at least two of the scourges of mankind, hunger and the plague. For millions of others, the simple nineteenth-century ideal of self-fulfillment epitomized as occupational choice is still a far-off goal, even though they, too, may be free from traditional slavery, starvation, and epidemic disease. Only the most advanced and wealthy segments of western civilization, where the division of labor is highly perfected, have become so absorbed with their intense and perhaps growing psychic malaise that they deputize special writers to dream for them either of a higher mental system totally possessing mankind, or of a child-like society without instinctual repression, one of complete psychic self-actualization, overflowing with love, and occupied with play. Our affluence even supports commentators on these utopians.

In recent years utopias have in some quarters fallen into ill-repute because of their presumed deleterious political effects when masses of men have been captivated by extravagant visions. But to attack utopias is about as meaningful as to denounce dreaming. No great civilization has lived without them, whether they were reserved for future life-after-death or brought down to earth. For myself, I am not convinced that they have exerted the catastrophic influence imputed to them. Their release of imaginative energies is innocent, their reflection of the emotional reality of their times authentic. Even if they are judged by an abstract criterion of truth-telling, it may be doubted whether utopians have, in fact, distorted the future any more than historians have the past.

Perhaps our danger lies elsewhere, in the possibility that the utopian quest may become all too matter-of-fact. Moon-flight, for example, is a rather old utopian device—Cyrano de Bergerac's is one of the best known of the sixteenth-century type. Now it is an imminent reality. And this much should be said in preference for the ancient form over the moon-flights of our own time: Cyrano's voyage consumed a far smaller proportion of the national product and the national genius.

NOTES

1. "Yes, answered the Spirits; for every humane Creature can create an Immaterial World fully inhabited by immaterial creatures, and populous of immaterial subjects, such as we are, and all this within the compass of the head or scull; nay, not onely so, but he may create a World of what fashion and Government he will, and give the Creatures thereof such motions, figures, forms, colours, perceptions, &c as he pleases, and make Whirl-pools, Lights, Pressures and Reactions, &c as he thinks best; nay, he may make a World full of Veins, Muscles, and Nerves, and all these to move by one jolt or stroke: also he may alter that world as often as he pleases, or change it from a natural world to an artificial; he may make a world of Ideas, a world of Atomes, and world of Lights, or whatever his fancy leads him to. . . .You have converted me said the Duchess to the Spirits. I'le take your advice, reject and despise all the worlds without me, and create a world of my own." *The Description of a New World, called the Blazing World, Written by the Thrice Noble, Illustrious, and Excellent Princesse, the Duchess of Newcastle* (London, 1666), pp. 96-98.

   See also Sigmound Freud, "Psycho-Analytic Notes on an Autobiographical Account of a Case of Paranoia" (1911), in *Complete Psychological Works*, ed. James Strachey (London, 1958), XII, pp. 1-82.

2. Garcilaso de la Vega (pseudonym, el Inca), *Historia general del Peru* (Cordoba, 1617).

3. Johann Valentin Andreae, *Christianopolis*, trans. F. E. Held (New York, 1916), p. 236.

4. Nicolas Edme Restif de la Bretonne, *La Découverte australe par un Homme-volant, ou Le Dédale français* (Paris, 1781), III, p. 509.

5. Pierre de Lesconvel, *Nouvelle relation du voyage du prince de Montberaud dans l'isle de Naudely, où sont rapportées toutes les maximes qui forment l'harmonie d'un parfait gouvernement* (Rouen, 1706?; original ed., 1703), p. 83.

6. See also James Harrington's *Oceana* (1656), ed. S. B. Liljegren (Heidelberg, 1924), p. 186: "[If a Commonwealth] be unequal, it tends to strife, and strife to ruine."

7. "They thinke not felicity to rest in all pleasure, but onely in that pleasure that is good and honest." Thomas More, *Utopia* (London, 1639 ed.), p. 184.

8. Philipp Balthazar Sinold, *Die glükseligste Insel auf der ganzen Welt, oder das Land der Zufriedenheit, dessen Regierungs-Art, Beschaffenheit, Fruchtbarkeit, Sitten der Einwohner, Religion, Kirchen-Verfas-*

sung, und dergleichen, samt der Gelegenheit wie solches Land entdecket worden, ausführlich erzehlert wird von Ludwig Ernst von Faramond (pseudonym) (Nuremberg, 1749), p. 222. *Relation du voyage de l'isle d'Eutopie* (Delft, 1711) is an example of a Catholic religious utopia of the same type.

9. More, *Utopia*, p. 144.
10. Pietro Chiari, *L'Uomo d'un altro mondo o sia Memorie d'un Solitario senza nome. Scritte da lui medesimo in due linguaggi, chinese e russiano, e pubblicate nella nostra lingua* (Venice, 1768); Thomas Floyd, *The Picture of a perfit Commonwealth* (London, 1600).
11. *Histoire d'un peuple nouveau dans l'isle de la raison, ou Découverte d'une Isle à 43. Degrés 14. Minutes de Latitude Méridionale, par David Tompson, Capitaine du Vaisseau le Boston, à son retour de la Chine en 1756. Ouvrage traduit de l'Anglois* (London, 1757), p. 134.
12. Paris, Bibliothèque Nationale, MS. n.a.fr. 24609, fol. 457v, a canticle by Charles Duveyrier.
13. William Winwood Reade, *The Martyrdom of Man*, 18th ed. (London, 1910), p. 515.
14. Engels later expressed the same idea in *Herr Eugen Dühring's Revolution in Science* (Moscow, 1947), pp. 435-436: "In the division of labour, man also is divided. All other physical and mental faculties are sacrified to the development of one single activity."
15. Karl Marx, *Grundrisse der Kritik der politischen Ökonomie. Rohentwurf, 1857-1858* (Berlin, 1953), p. 505.
16. See Marx's notes on a work on idleness known to Pierre Naville. Naville, *De l'aliénation à la jouissance* (Paris, 1957), p. 495.
17. B. F. Skinner, *Walden Two* (1948) (New York, 1962), p. 80.
18. Pierre Teilhard de Chardin, *The Phenomenon of Man* (New York, 1959), p. 265.
19. J. B. S. Haldane, *Everything has a History* (London, 1951), p. 288.
20. Julian Huxley, "The Emergence of Darwinism," in Sol Tax, ed., *The Evolution of Life. Its Origins, History and Future* (Chicago, 1960), I, p. 20.
21. Herman J. Muller, "The Guidance of Human Evolution," in Sol Tax, ed., *The Evolution of Man. Mind, Culture, and Society* (Chicago, 1960), II, p. 456.
22. "In abolishing private property," he wrote in *Civilization and Its Discontents*, "we deprive the human love of aggression of one of its instruments, certainly a strong one, though certainly not the strongest; but we have in no way altered the differences in power and influence which are misused by aggressiveness, nor have we altered anything in its nature. Aggressiveness was not created by property. It reigned almost without limit in primitive times, when property was still very scanty, and it already shows itself in the nursery almost before property has given up its primal, anal form; it forms the basis of every relation of affection and love among people (with the single

exception, perhaps, of the mother's relation to her male child). If we do away with personal rights over material wealth, there still remains prerogative in the field of sexual relationships, which is bound to become the source of the strongest dislike and the most violent hostility among men who in other respects are on an equal footing. If we were to remove this factor, too, by allowing complete freedom of sexual life and thus abolishing the family, the germ-cell of civilization, we cannot, it is true, easily foresee what new paths the development of civilization could take; but one thing we can expect, and that is that this indestructible feature of human nature will follow it there." Sigmund Freud, *Civilization and Its Discontents*, trans. James Strachey (New York, 1962), pp. 60-61.

23. Erich Fromm, *Beyond the Chains of Illusion* (New York, 1962), p. 53.
24. Erich Fromm, *Man for himself; an inquiry into the psychology of ethics* (New York, 1947), p. 363.
25. Herbert Marcuse, *Eros and Civilization* (Boston, 1961), pp. ix, 204.
26. *Ibid.*, p. 205.
27. Norman O. Brown, *Life Against Death. The Psychoanalytical Meaning of History* (New York, 1959), p. 308.
28. Abraham H. Maslow, *Toward a Psychology of Being* (New York, 1962), p. 181.
29. Abraham H. Maslow, *Religions, Values, and Peak-Experiences* (Columbus, Ohio, 1964).

THE SCIENTIST
IN SOCIETY

7

NEWTON AS AUTOCRAT
OF SCIENCE

Among the many stories that sprang up after Isaac Newton's psychic crisis of September 1693 and set tongues wagging in England and abroad was a rumor that he was dead. Had his life actually been cut off when he was in his early-fifties, the consequences for the long-range development of western science would not have been overwhelming. The *Principia* had been published in 1687; the calculus, at least in its Leibnizian form, had been known since 1684; and his theory of light, though not in the final version of the *Opticks* (1704), had been communicated to the Royal Society in the seventies. His alchemical papers, interpretations of prophecy, and radical revision of world chronology, though they are respectable, rational texts in the spirit of the age, would not, in the long run, have been missed. And other men would have made the corrections for the later editions of the *Principia* without his supervision. Nor would the loss of Newton's "philosophy" recorded in the sibylline "Queries" to the *Opticks* and the "General Scholium" to the second edition of the *Principia* have left a major gap in the annals of thought.

Newton lived on for about thirty-four years after the encapsulated episode and the mild depression that followed. There was an opinion among some eighteenth- and nineteenth-century scientists, echoed in Lord Keynes's impish address on the tercentenary of Newton's birth, that he was never the same after that black year, that he was sort of gaga. In fact, a transformation in his person did take place, though not in this simple, pejorative sense. His genius for solving mathematical problems with incredible speed as if by sudden illumination was by no means impaired, as the continental scientists learned when they dared to test him. What occurred after his crisis was a dramatic rechanneling of his capacities. To say that an aggressiveness which had once turned inward was allowed to manifest itself outwardly during the last thirty years of his life is an oversimplification of his psychological history; but since it is not my intention to present a full-length portrait in this paper, the crude formula will perhaps suffice.

A royal appointment in 1696 made it possible for Newton to leave the university cell in which he had immured himself for decades, alter his whole mode of life and conduct, and give overt expression to a deep need for the exercise of power and to manipulatory skills which had previously been dormant. The tremendous energy with which he was endowed found new materials to mold in the world of men. A juxtaposition of the first portrait of him by Kneller in 1689 with the late ones by Vanderbank tells at a glance the story of the transformation from a sensitive, melancholy, and rather dreamy scholar clad in black to the bloated, pompous, irascible administrator in rich brocade and velvet. Through the influence of Charles Montague (later Lord Halifax), who had been his student at Trinity, Newton was made Warden (and subsequently Master) of the Mint, and to occupy the post he moved to London. For him the office was no sinecure, though it had been the original intention of his patron to provide one, and Newton spent years on the recoinage and on the organization of a campaign against clippers and counterfeiters, venting his rage in the interrogation of prisoners, wielding powers of life and death over them. Though this magistracy continued to the eve of his death and teaches us much about his character, it is less significant for our present purpose than a second office which he assumed in 1703 and held simultaneously—the presidency of the Royal Society.

The political, social, and religious worlds through which Newton moved over the years were subject to mercurial change, and
no shift in his mature life was more abrupt than the passage from
Cambridge to London. A fixated man and a Puritan in spirit,
from the early Restoration on he had led a monastic life under a
rule established by his own harsh censor. When he emerged to
participate actively in a war against Papism and the Stuarts, he
was from the outset an ardent supporter of the House of Orange,
and he remained consistently Whig until his death. But the
Whiggery of the turn of the century and the reign of Queen
Anne, though it might raise popular tumults and burn pope, cardinals, and Dr. Sacheverell in effigy, was hardly consonant with
a mid-seventeenth-century Puritan morality, not with Somers and
Halifax at the helm. The looseness of society in the reign of
Queen Anne and the first George perceptibly modified the manner of Isaac Newton, if not the demands of his austere censor.
Carried about London in a sedan chair, he grew quite corpulent.
As a public figure, he met regularly for business with the corrupt
and uninhibited Whig politicians and received foreign noble-
men, virtually all of whom were accursed Papists. Newton did not
participate in Halifax' orgies, nor was he invited to membership
in the Kit-Kat Club. He was more likely to be drawn to the millenarian Prophets of London who swallowed up his young friend
Fatio de Duillier than to the witty literary society of Pope, Swift,
and Gay. Yet he was no longer ignorant of the ways of the world.
In the privacy of his chamber he remained a devout believer, a man
of learning, concentrating more and more on history sacred and
profane as the final revelation of the divine intent. His absolute,
though secret, unitarianism was known only to a few intimates
—to William Whiston, to Hopton Haynes, an assistant at the
Mint, to John Locke, perhaps to Fatio—not to the bishops and
archbishops of the realm who sought out his company and later
left testimonials to his piety. But his style had changed. The break
between the public and the private man is now sharp; more than
ever he leads a double life.

During one of the annual elections of officers of the Royal
Society, John Chamberlayne, a Fellow who was a court official
under Queen Anne, wrote Newton surrendering to him his vote

for members of the Council and voicing a desire to see him made "Perpetual Dictator" of the Society.[1] This sentiment was shared by many others. Disciples dedicated their books to the "divine Newton," and the man who married his niece, John Conduitt, wrote that if Newton had lived in the ancient world, he would have been deified. Fatio de Duillier, Genevan bourgeois that he was, yearned for an extra hundred thousand *écus* to raise statues and a monument to him, and Edmond Halley proclaimed in Latin verse that no mortal could more nearly approach the gods.[2] Such adulation was more than mere baroque extravagance, for Newton did indeed become the "dictator" of the English scientific establishment, and standing on that solid base, he was apotheosized into the symbol of western science. With more than a soupçon of envy, Laplace later remarked that since there was only one universe, it could be granted to only one man to discover its fundamental law. When one remains attuned to the religious as well as the scientific meaning of a law in a Christian society, one begins to understand how those of his contemporaries, especially the young ones, who could read the hieroglyphic tablets of his law divinized the new Moses. If the hunger of Newton for recognition could ever be appeased, this was the moment.

A multiplicity of factors contributed to the making of the Newton image—it was not only the work of the later eighteenth-century popularizers of his philosophy. In large measure, it was created by Newton himself during the quarter of a century that he ruled the Royal Society. Longevity can be, as we have observed in contemporary politics, an important element in leadership, and Newton lasted long enough to institutionalize himself and his system. Such duration is not, of course, an unambiguous good. When the founder of a scientific movement lives on for decades after the spark in him has been extinguished, he may harden and even fossilize the system. His spiritual sons grow up in the shadow of an ancient oak and their own capacities are often stunted.

The creation of the headship of science may involve acts akin to the processes of winning political, military, or religious leadership. But while primacy in war, politics, and religious movements has been studied critically ever since the Greeks and the Romans, rising to titular hegemony in science—a more recent phenomenon —has in the nature of things been the subject of relatively little scrutiny. Qualities essential for scientific leadership are not the same in all times and places. The historical situation of Isaac Newton was unique, and in some respects his performance was idiosyncratic. But the later Newton, who is usually only of anecdotal interest, emerges from an examination of his doings as the first of a new type in European history—the great administrator of science. An exploration of this phase of Newton's career suggests analogies and may throw light on a historical subject of wide scope—the changing role of the man of science in western society.

Scientific truth can speak for itself, but requires an agency through which it may be amplified and diffused. As part of a larger study of the social and psychological forces at play in the creation of the "Newtonian world view," it may be worthwhile to observe the actual practices and instruments with which Newton operated in the scientifically less creative part of his life. His triumph was furthered by a complex of circumstances that did not obtain for either Galileo or Descartes in the previous generation nor for Leibniz who was his contemporary. The grandeur and genius of the Newtonian synthesis are here taken for granted, as is its emotional appeal to a monotheistic culture not yet divested of the religious swaddling clothes that had protected it in its early period. It has been noted often enough that the growth of a commercial society in a centralized state like England and its consequent concern with the products of "mathematicall magick," the affinity between the precise, methodical behavior of the experimental scientist and the comportment of the self-disciplined, puritanical Protestant helped fashion a general social environment in which science could flourish. The interaction of Protestantism, nascent capitalism, and the new philosophy can be recognized without the establishment of mechanical historical relations of cause and effect among them. Even the most refractory English scientists had been able to survive the Civil War: no Bruno had been burned, nor had a Galileo recanted and been sequestered.

An organized university system had evolved with professorships in mathematics and astronomy, and no major victims among the scientists had been claimed by the purges of the Commonwealth and early Restoration. Moreover, under the Restoration there was a curious royal court which at least played with science and to which its practitioners had access. The very insularity and provincialism of English scientists provided them with a foundation on which to build a scientific structure, an opportunity denied to those wanderers and exiles, Descartes and Leibniz, without roots in any soil. But when all of the auspicious economic, religious, and social factors are weighed—and there are many more that overdetermine English precedence—it still remains to inquire into the methods pursued by Isaac Newton in attaining a position of leadership in his own country and in the European world, after the heroic age of the founding fathers of the Royal Society had passed, as had the peak of his own creativity. If one descends from the realm of grand generalizations about the relationships of English science and religion, or English science and social structure, a description of how the first scientific "establishment" in the modern world was organized under Newton's governance may be of more than parochial interest. There is little likelihood that Newton deliberately set himself the task of devising a strategy to capture the Royal Society and transform it into his creature. Viewed retrospectively, however, his tactics and maneuvers show an underlying purposiveness and reveal the functioning of an organizational will.

To secure the ascendancy of his philosophical principles and to establish his unquestioned pre-eminence, Newton recruited a group of scientific adherents—younger men of varying degrees of talent—joined in absolute loyalty to his person and his doctrine. There were intrigues among the followers and inevitable ostracisms from the group; but his scientific supremacy was accepted by every one of them. It was a relationship of master and disciples, with all the complexity inherent in that bond. To make the Royal Society a worthy institutional vehicle for the propagation of Newtonian science, over the years he perfected administrative methods to bolster the Society through better housekeeping and closer supervision of its operations. Its unique personality was affirmed through a physical structure, a new building all its own. In the hope of insuring continuity in its scientific work, Newton even drafted a scheme for the introduction of an order of paid pensioners. He was also responsible for weaving a sacred and aristocratic aura around science through the development of ceremonials.

Newton's personal ties with the Whig politicians made him the ideal figure to work out a pattern for the role of science in a loose parliamentary regime, a pattern whose traces have not completely disappeared even in recent years. Science and government came to use and promote each other, but, in contrast with some continental models, English science retained a large measure of autonomy.

Finally, since no major creation is achieved without negation, Newton waged fierce battles to consolidate his scientific empire and destroy competitive or insubordinate rivals both within and outside the Royal Society. The bitter quarrels with the English Royal Astronomer John Flamsteed and with the cosmopolitan philosopher Leibniz, which punctuated the first decade of his presidency and in which he was spectacularly victorious, forcefully demonstrated his authority within the English establishment and in the international scientific world. In the presentation that follows, the acts described are representative rather than comprehensive; it is of course possible here only to set forth the lines of his policy and to show its wholeness.

THE GATHERING OF THE FOLLOWERS

For the first half century of its existence, the Royal Society had been a rather loose fellowship. Its central figures tended to be the secretaries, who served as a clearinghouse for scientific correspondence. The presidency was largely an honorific office, and though the chair was occasionally occupied by scientists, many of the incumbents were aristocrats and politicians, mere amateurs of science who often failed to attend either the meetings of the Council or the general sessions at which experiments were presented and papers dicussed. After the fifteen-year tenure of William, Lord Viscount Brouncker, from 1662 to 1677, there followed a succession of ten presidents, each of whom occupied the office for only a few years. They were intelligent men like Pepys, Montague, and Somers, but with no pretensions to science. No one man dominated the institution until Newton took control. (If any single figure had been outstanding, it was Robert Hooke, who had been a mainstay of the Society for forty years, but by the 1690's he was ailing in body and spirit.)

Though Newton was a member of the Council in 1697-98 and 1699-1700, he did not participate too frequently in the administration of the Society until he had a clear field, and he would not accept the presidency so long as his old enemy Robert Hooke was alive. From his earliest childhood, he feared and shunned competition. He either dominated a situation totally or refused to play. Immediately upon Hooke's death, however, Newton took over, and he reigned for the rest of his life. Isaac Newton had a way of recasting any office he occupied in his own image. During his years as president, he changed the character of the Royal Society, as he did the Mint's, and shed upon it the luster of his own pre-eminence in the world of science. "The very title was justly rever'd, both at home and abroad. . . . Infinite were the encomiums they received from foreign countrys; in a great measure owing to the superior capacity and unbounded merit of so illustrious a president," wrote one of the younger Fellows, Dr. William Stukeley.[3]

When Newton assumed the presidency in 1703, at the age of sixty, his genius was universally recognized though his great work was understood by few men and the continental reception of the *Principia* did not measure up to the admiration of the English. Virtually the whole generation of the Society's founding fathers and the second generation to which Newton belonged had died. Of the original group, only Christopher Wren was still alive (he died in 1723 at the age of ninety-one), and he continued to grace committees with his venerable presence—but he was no longer very active. Of Newton's contemporaries there remained Flamsteed and Francis Aston—the latter a compliant agent of no particular distinction, the former, the stiff-necked Royal Astronomer, the only major internal threat to Newton's authority. Thus sheer longevity, combined with political favor and towering achievement, made Newton's position almost unassailable.

Since the Royal Society was Newton's base of operations, the composition of its membership has an intimate bearing on his use of men in the furtherance of his ends. For Newton, persons were usually objects, not subjects. The Society's hundred-odd members over whom he presided were divided roughly half and half between men with some professional competence in science and aristocratic or gentlemanly amateurs. The scientists, in turn, were concentrated in two major groups—the medical doctors and physiologists and the mathematical-astronomical contingent. The doctors prominent in the Society—men like Hans Sloane, John Arbuthnot, and Richard Mead—were prosperous and influential court physicians who had easy entry to the palace and the aristocratic houses of the realm. Whenever Newton needed something at court, the doctors could serve as convenient bedside intermediaries. Sloane, whom Newton had inherited as secretary of the Society, had begun to resuscitate it after the Glorious Revolution, and he had a penchant for keeping matters in his control during the early years of Newton's tenure. Newton chafed at his behind-the-scenes direction, a hangover from the traditional pattern in which the president was a changing figurehead and the secretary was the effective officer, and he could be provoked into denouncing Sloane as unqualified, and further as a villain, a rascal, and a tricking fellow.[4] With the same persistence with which Newton had secured actual, not merely nominal, control of the Royal Mint, he moved into the Royal Society. Though he used Sloane when he needed him, by 1713 Sloane had been persuaded to withdraw to his house in Chelsea and devote himself to his famous collection of natural curiosities and manuscripts. With Sloane's departure, Newton chose as secretaries two men who were of his own creation, Edmond Halley and John Keill. Sloane did not return to the center of activity until Newton's death, when he succeeded him as president. His disappearance was no great loss to science, since he was an old-fashioned gatherer of nostrums and a purveyor of traditional remedies who stuffed the *Transac-*

tions of the Society with his questionable discoveries. Mead was a doctor of more philosophical bent and was Newton's personal physician during his last years. Arbuthnot, one of the numerous Scots who made good in the London scientific world, was close to the Prince of Denmark, Queen Anne's husband, and a great wit as his satirical writings show. He occupied a pivotal post as physician extraordinary to Queen Anne. When Newton cannily appointed him to committees in both the Flamsteed and the Leibniz contests, he does not seem to have taken his functions too seriously, casually performing in the manner expected of him by the president. The medical men in the Society gave Newton no serious trouble, and one of their number, Dr. Stukeley, a young man from Lincolnshire, became a favorite of his old age and his first biographer—though when Stukeley, against Newton's will, ran for office in the Society after Halley's resignation, he was punished with exile from the presence for several years.[5] As men of independent means, the doctors were not so beholden to Newton as the young mathematicians and astronomers, but so great was the prestige of his person and his system that they obeyed him and aligned themselves with him in any controversy.

The earnest young men upon whom Newton relied for the energetic building of his fame were the astronomers and mathematicians, who had come to the *Principia* as to a new revelation. They eagerly accepted the role of apostles. A few he had known and favored before he assumed office; others he continued to recruit through the decades of his long tenure, and he even outlived some of his earlier protégés. By the time of his death, the academic map of England and Scotland in the mathematical-astronomical sciences had been completely Newtonized. Year by year, as a professorship or a royal office to which a scientist could be appointed became vacant or a new chair was created, he filled it with one of his candidates. They became the king's men in Newton's realm, for there was a secular as well as a spiritual side to his sovereignty. The ties which bound these professors to him were often affective as well as scientific. For the young men, Newton was the father of the clan. The president who had lectured to empty halls during his Lucasian professorship now found him-

self the head of a scientific family. The old man who had never
known woman acquired sons.

David Gregory, who had been one of the first to teach the
Newtonian philosophy at Edinburgh in the 1680's, was appointed
Savilian Professor of Astronomy at Oxford in 1692, largely through
Newton's intervention. Roger Cotes, a mathematician and another of Newton's protégés, became Plumian Professor of Astronomy and Experimental Philosophy at Cambridge in 1706, when
he was only twenty-four years old. Newton, who had defined the
terms of the new chair himself, as an administrator of science
took a very different attitude toward publication than he had in
his youth: the Plumian Professor would be required to publish
regularly either at Cambridge or in the *Philosophical Transactions
of the Royal Society*. The handsome Cotes was a dearly beloved
disciple, and Newton lamented his premature death in 1716,
saying: "If he had lived we might have known something." [6] William Whiston, who as an undergraduate had heard a few lectures
by Newton, first made his acquaintance in 1694. On Newton's
nomination, he became Lucasian Professor of Mathematics at
Cambridge, after having substituted for him when he went up
to London. John Keill, one of David Gregory's students, was
named Savilian Professor of Astronomy at Oxford in 1712 and
gave courses on the new philosophy there. He also served as
"decypherer" to Queen Anne. Keill was a warhorse whose ardor
was so intense that Newton sometimes had to pull in the reins.

The one major scientist who remained by Newton's side
throughout the whole period of his tenure was the astronomer
Edmond Halley, and the nature of their bond may some day be
more fully defined if the Halley papers on Newton—which existed
at one time—ever turn up. A strange event marks the beginning
of their relationship. In 1684, when the twenty-eight-year-old
Halley first visited Newton at Cambridge and received from him
the fundamental propositions of the *Principia*, his father had been
found dead on the banks of a river near Reading. The coroner's
verdict was murder, and a wild insinuation was later made by
the academic gossip Thomas Hearne that Halley was implicated
in the crime. According to the same Hearne, Newton's death was

hastened by a violent scene between him and Halley.[7] But for more than forty years Halley behaved toward Newton with great circumspection. He knew how to mollify him when he was in a wrath, and in the great wars with Newton's enemies, he made himself indispensable as chief-of-staff. In the fight with Hooke, he was a reporter and an agent whose primary function was to see the *Principia* through the press and keep Newton from destroying the third part in his anger at Hooke's accusation that the law of gravity had been stolen from him. When Newton needed an astronomer to finish and force publication of Flamsteed's star catalogue, Halley was appointed editor. And when, in 1712, the Royal Society's *Commercium Epistolicum* against Leibniz was to be printed, Halley ran the editorial committee and did much of the paper work. Newton protected him and, though his reputation for religious skepticism was an impediment to his advancement, secured him an appointment as deputy comptroller of the Chester Mint in 1696. After a series of scientific voyages, through Newton's assistance he became Savilian Professor of Astronomy at Oxford in 1703, Secretary of the Royal Society in 1713, and Royal Astronomer in 1721.

Nicolas Fatio de Duillier, an erratic young genius from Switzerland, was another of the elect. Toward him Newton had had a strong emotional attachment back in the early 1690's, the feelings of a man of fifty toward his replica aged twenty-five. By the time Newton had become president of the Royal Society, however, Fatio had fallen into disfavor, though he lingered on the sidelines for a while. Samuel Clarke, who had been converted to the Newtonian philosophy in Cambridge about the same time as William Whiston, had refused a post at the Mint that was in Newton's grant and served as chaplain to the Princess of Wales, a vantage point from which he became the expositor of the philosophical and religious conceptions of the Newtonian philosophy in his famous correspondence with Leibniz—but only after careful consultation with Newton himself. Colin Maclaurin, Henry Pemberton, and John Stirling were of the second generation of disciples in the 1720's, àfter Fatio de Duillier was swallowed up by the Prophets of London, Whiston was estranged, and Gregory and Cotes had died. Maclaurin became Professor of Mathematics at the University of Edinburgh through Newton's sponsorship, and Henry Pemberton ultimately was made Professor of Physics at Gresham College.

Thus were the young mathematicians and astronomers rewarded with chairs in Oxford, Cambridge, and the Scottish universities. Few academic appointments in this field were made without consulting Newton, and his advice was almost always heeded. Sometimes he gave his protégés munificent gifts as well: five hundred pounds went to Clarke—one hundred pounds for each of his children—for his translation of the *Opticks* into Latin. When a minor and rather unreliable disciple, George Cheyne, refused his bounty, he was peremptorily dropped.

Newton usually dealt with people on the basis of "commutation," except on those rare occasions when his feelings became involved. He distributed academic posts and royal offices, and the beneficiaries acquitted their debts to him through service and loyalty. There is something feudal as well as paternal about his ties with these younger men. They fought his battles, and he awarded them university professorships as their fiefs. This formidable man sometimes inspired love—surely in Fatio, perhaps in Halley and Conduitt. More often, it was his masterful authority that gave the group of his adherents cohesion.

There was work for the protégés that related directly to Newton's writings. Before his London period Newton had timorously allowed certain of his mathematical papers to be shown only to a few elders, like Isaac Barrow and John Collins, but once he had stopped creating, he granted a number of younger men among his followers freer access to his private mathematical hoard. John Craig, David Gregory, John Raphson, Edmond Halley, Fatio de Duillier, William Jones, John Keill, Henry Pemberton, Abraham de Moivre, and Nicholas Bernoulli were among those who enjoyed the occasional privilege. Corrections and emendations of the *Principia* were begun soon after it was published, primarily by Newton himself, who in characteristic fashion blamed all but one of the errors on his ignorant amanuensis. Fatio de Duillier had thought of himself as the only disciple worthy to prepare the second edition. When he went off into the wildnerness of religious enthusiasm, the mantle fell on Roger Cotes, whose long preface became an integral part of the work and in popularizations of Newtonianism was usually cited as proof positive that the structure of the universe as revealed by Newton presupposed an infinitely good and wise architect. The third edition a decade later was the labor of Henry Pemberton. Throughout this period, the disciples also busied themselves with teaching the doctrine in the universities and with popularizations—usually with Newton's blessing, though sometimes accompanied by an underground rumor that the new renderings were endangering the prestige of the original, because they might become more widely diffused than Newton's work, whose grandiose architectural quality and elegant proofs few contemporaries were capable of understanding thoroughly. Whiston, Gregory, Cheyne, Clarke, Maclaurin, Pemberton, Keill, and Desaguliers all wrote books on Newtonianism during the Master's life or immediately after his death. Even the doctors and the divines in the Royal Society exerted themselves to show the application of the Newtonian philosophy in their respective fields of endeavor—the physicians often producing a literature bordering on the absurd, like Cheyne's proposal for a "Principia Medicinae Theoreticae Mathematica." The men in holy orders, who illustrated the religious nature of the Newtonian philosophy, used its principles as a laudation. The tendency that Dr. Richard Bentley initiated in the Boyle lectures for 1692 was brought to a climax in William Derham's lectures for 1711 and 1712, published as *Physico-Theology, or a Demonstration of the Being and Attributes of God from His Works of Creation,* which saw twelve editions by 1754. John Craig's *Theologiae Christianae Principia Mathematica* (1699) is perhaps the most outlandish example of the Newtonian fashion in religion. The first commentaries of the Newtonian movement were thus written under the watchful eye of the Master, and he allowed its ramifications into the strangest areas without dissent.

Although Newton protected his young men and fostered them, he demanded absolute obedience; the father would brook no criticism, opposition, nor actions that might reflect upon him and jeopardize his position as a crown official and luminary of the realm. He insisted upon social conformity in their public behavior. William Whiston proved to be an incautious man who could not restrain his tongue nor mask his views. Differing from Newton over matters of Biblical interpretation and chronology, in which he believed himself superior to his patron, he could not withhold his criticism, and such contumely did not sit well with the Master. When Whiston openly expressed Arian convictions that in reality were not very dissimilar from Newton's own secret faith, the lack of prudence was punished. Newton did not lift a finger when Whiston was ousted from the university for religious heterodoxy. And there is anecdotage to the effect that he kept him out of the Royal Society on grounds that he was a heretic, threatening to resign if Halley and Sloane went through with his nomination.[8] Whiston suffered deeply from this rejection and, like a lover denied, vented his spleen against those still in the entourage and against Newton's intolerance. He settled accounts in his *Memoirs*: "But he then perceiving that I could not do as his other darling friends did, that is, learn of him, without contradicting him, when I differed in opinion from him, he could not, in his old age, bear such contradiction." [9] Fatio de Duillier was excluded when he became involved with the seances of the wild Prophets of London and served as their secretary. When Fatio, whom Newton had once invited to live close to him in Cambridge, stood in pillory, Newton went about his business at the Treasury seemingly unconcerned. Fatio did not easily free himself of his hero-worship of Newton, and for years after Newton's death, he considered himself the only true disciple and interpreter of the system, until in his very old age, stricken with illness, he began to murmur that the Newtonian philosophy without Fatio's explanation was meaningless.

There was one other group in the Royal Society whom Newton befriended by supporting them in more modest positions than university professorships—the Huguenot émigrés. Though he seems to have recovered from the more violent seizures of anti-Catholicism which possessed him and his contemporaries in the eighties and nineties, he retained a deep sympathy for the victims of Louis XIV's laws against Protestants, who took refuge in England in a flight reminiscent of the movement out of Germany in the twentieth century. Most of the exiles sought security and respectability in their new home and were dismayed by the scandal of the Prophets from the Cévennes in which Fatio de Duillier had become enmeshed. Newton helped the reasonable ones— the mathematician Abraham de Moivre, the translator and compiler of scientific letters Pierre Des Maizeaux, and John Theophilus Desaguliers, who had been brought to England as an infant and became an occasionally paid experimenter of the Royal Society.

Newton kept in close touch with his disciples and his favored Huguenots, meeting with them regularly. David Gregory has an account of a session with Fatio, Halley, and himself at which Newton unfolded his publication plans.[10] Ralph Thoresby in his diary describes the agreeable Fellows he encountered at the Royal Society and afterward accompanied to the Grecian Coffee-house —President Isaac Newton, attended by the two Secretaries Halley and Keill, both his protégés and both professors at Oxford.[11] On many evenings, Newton picked up de Moivre at the coffeehouse he frequented, Slaughter's in St. Martin's Lane, and brought him to his own home nearby for philosophical conversation. There was a gentle side to the man that manifested itself in some of these relationships, but their function was primarily to nourish a scientific movement organized around a set doctrine.

Virtually nothing was done in behalf of the Newtonian philosophy without the Master's surveillance and permission. His manuscript legacy shows that in the great controversies in which he engaged, he supervised and usually corrected with his own hand the drafts of whatever the disciples wrote in his defense, but there was a tacit understanding among them that he was never to be exposed. An official portrait was being created of the calm, majestic genius who was above worldly concerns, a paragon of all the virtues of Christianity and the Enlightenment. Keill would send a piece to his friend Edmond Halley, inviting him and Newton to make changes as they saw fit. Cotes asked Newton to write anything he chose as the polemical, anti-Leibniz preface to the second edition of the *Principia* and offered to put his name to it and defend it as his own. The famous "review," or *Recensio*, of the *Commercium Epistolicum*, published in the *Transactions of the Royal Society*, every bit of which Newton himself composed, was passed off as Keill's. In Clarke's philosophical interchange with Leibniz, the manuscripts make it abundantly clear that Newton's is the guiding hand. And in Des Maizeaux' collection of documents, Newton permitted himself the license of final revisions of his disciples' letters, even after they had been sent. The Newtonians in the Royal Society—and the collective name had begun to be used—were really what Leibniz called them, Newton's *enfants perdus*, his reconnaissance patrol.

A BEING OF THEIR OWN

During his tenure as President of the Royal Society, Newton adopted a series of measures intended to introduce sound administrative procedures and firm discipline among the members. The meticulous, puritanical scientist could not tolerate slipshod ways, and the Society would be a mirror of his personality. While previous presidents had attended irregularly, according to count he was present at 161 out of 175 Council meetings.[12] And in order to participate in the general assemblies, he shifted the weekly session of the Society from Wednesday to Thursday, a day when he was not occupied at the Mint.

The last decades of the seventeenth century were an especially trying period for the Society as an institution: The membership fell off, dues were in arrears, and changes of officers were unusually frequent. The Society had not been able to afford the printing of the *Principia*, having exhausted its treasury on Willoughby's history of fish, and the publication of the *Philosophical Transactions* had been suspended for a time. The Society was on the verge of bankruptcy when Newton took over, and he attempted to make it solvent through a reorganization of its finances. In 1706, the Council ordered that every newly-elected member should pay his admission fee before his official induction and give bond that he would make regular weekly contributions. Nobody could become a member of the Council if his dues were in arrears. In 1723 Newton invested Royal Society funds, along with his own, in the South Sea Company, in order to profit from an enterprise whose stock was rising spectacularly. This was one occasion, however, when his manipulations were less fortunate— though he did not live to see the total debacle.

Newton's psychic owing was boundless, and he could not endure to be obligated or indebted to any man. Whenever he could, he tried to substitute paid for volunteer services. He was uncomfortable with anything but a *do ut des* arrangement. In 1720, he had a stipend fixed for the two chief secretaries of the Society as well as for a foreign secretary. When Desaguliers was appointed a curator of experiments, Newton allocated special funds for his work. But, in return, he insisted that every order of the Council be scrupulously obeyed. When he felt that Desaguliers was not performing a sufficient number of experiments, he had him reprimanded, much to the scientist's dismay.[13] At the last Council session that Newton attended, a few days before his death at the age of eighty-five, he bawled out Halley, then a mere seventy-one, for not transmitting astronomical observations from Greenwich to the Society with the annual regularity stipulated by royal order.

One of Newton's plans of institutional reform was a *Scheme for establishing the Royal Society*, of which six drafts in his hand are extant. Though the plan did not come to fruition, it tells us a good deal about the authoritarian direction in which he was moving. "Establishing" in this context meant giving the Society's projects a sound financial and organizational frame, though one is tempted to read his meaning as re-establishing the society anew under his aegis. Newton envisaged a system of appointed learned pensioners who would be obliged to attend all sessions of the Society and, if they wished to retain their positions, to produce inventions and discoveries on schedule. The plan classified science into five divisions, into each of which a pensioner would be fitted. Newton's early sense of the fluidity of science and the fantasies of the youth who dabbled freely in all forms of knowledge have vanished with age. Science is now organized and structured. In this document, the divine consecration of science is conspicuously absent, as he describes its mission in purely institutional terms. The ultimate goal is secular: to make the Society "famous and lasting"—in one draft he had written "perpetual," the language of the French Academy.[14] The recluse of Trinity turned administrator was moving along the path of the academies that were agencies of the French crown.

Before Newton's incumbency, the Society had fallen to such low estate that Sloane's "unfit entertainment" became the subject of a public satire.[15] Newton devoted himself to the moral as well as the financial renovation of the Society. He made a ceremony of the sessions over which he presided, the first high priest of modern science officiating at its rites. Dr. Stukeley, a hushed witness, has left a description of the performances:

> Whilst he presided in the Royal Society, he executed that office with singular prudence, with a grace and dignity—conscious of what was due to so noble an Institution—what was expected from his character. . . . There were no whispering, talking nor loud laughters. If discussions arose in any sort, he said they tended to find out truth, but ought not to arise to any personality. . . . Every thing was transacted with great attention and solemnity and decency; nor were any papers which seemed to border on religion treated without proper respect. Indeed his presence created a natural awe in the assembly; they appear'd truly as a venerable *consessus Naturae Consiliariorum*, without any levity or indecorum.[16]

If the solemnity was fractured, the culprit was ousted. In 1710, a famous fracas occurred between the notoriously choleric geologist and physician John Woodward, Professor of Physic at Gresham College, and Dr. Hans Sloane, who was reading a communication about bezoars, secretions found in the intestines of goats in Persia and India, which he called a kind of gall-stone and used as an antidote against poison. Woodward kept interrupting him with the remark that "no man who understands anatomy would make such an assertion." Upon Sloane's complaint to the Council that he had been insulted, Woodward countered with the charge that Sloane had been making grimaces at him. When Woodward refused to apologize, Newton had him removed from the Council to the accompaniment of reflections that he was a good natural philosopher, but not a good moral one.[17]

Newton's dread of disorder and tendency to ritualize his own behavior, along with a desire to imitate the elaborate manners of the great, led him to assign specific places to the officers who attended him at meetings, like the members of a royal court. The president was to sit at the head of the table, with the secretaries at the lower end, one on each side. The sacred configuration could be altered only to accommodate some "very Honourable Stranger." A liveried servant installed at the door and carrying a staff that bore the arms of the Society set the tone of the weekly meetings. Only when the president occupied the chair could the mace be laid, no lesser dignitary being permitted to enjoy this distinction.

Whenever Newton was identified with an institution, it became an extension of his person, and he sought to protect its position with the same zeal that he would his own. The feeling of identification with Trinity College that he had had during the Alban Francis case, with the Mint in his fight with the Lord of the Tower, he now transferred to the Society. His fierce sense of independence made intolerable the location of the Royal Society —with its museum, meeting room, and library—in the building of Gresham College, where it was subject to the will and desire of the Mercers' Company. Moreover, there were intimations that the Society might be asked to vacate. Newton first tried in vain to obtain a royal grant for a new house, then toyed with a plan for a union of the Queen's Library, the Cotton Library, and the Royal Society—a proposal which Halifax supported in the Lords, but which came to naught. Newton's final solution was to give the Society "a being of their own," as he phrased it, and he proceeded to find another site—a Dr. Brown's house at 2 Crane Court. Once Newton had made the decision to move, he perfunctorily called together a meeting of the Fellows on short notice, arrogantly refused to explain the reasons for the impending change, "which he did not think proper to be given there," and went ahead despite opposition and in the face of general perplexity as to why the members had been assembled.[18] Like many a modern administrator, he sought democratic assent to his decisions and was outraged when it was not forthcoming. In abandoning the old quarters, there was also a desire on Newton's part to break completely with the epoch during which Robert Hooke had controlled the Society. As it happened, in the process of transferring from Gresham College, Hooke's portrait—the only one in existence—and many of his instruments seem to have disappeared forever.[19] Newton wanted the Society to have a being of its own, but he equated that being with *his* being.

SCIENCE AND THE GOVERNMENT

When, in 1705, Queen Anne knighted the yeoman's son Isaac Newton in a formal ceremony at Trinity College, the first scientist to be so honored, the bond between science and the Crown was given symbolic representation. For Newton, this was a great personal triumph, staged in the College where he had once performed menial duties as a subsizar. In issuing a charter to the Royal Society and in founding the Royal Observatory, Charles II had expressed an interest in the advantages that might accrue to the kingdom through the promotion of scientific discoveries. Under Newton, Master of the Mint and dominant figure of British science, a much closer link was forged between science and the government than had ever existed before. Since he was frequently summoned by the Lords of the Treasury in his capacity as Master of the Mint, the leading scientist was looked upon no longer as a closeted Cambridge experimenter, but as a part of the governmental mechanism. Though his fixing of the gold standard in 1717 was a function of his office at the Mint, it was not alien to his long metallurgical experiments and even the alchemical ones which had continued until the eve of his departure for London. Newton always managed to capitalize on his past experience, however remote from current concerns it might appear; nothing seems to have been lost. Once a member of the government, he began to appear at court. He was consulted by Caroline, the Princess of Wales, about the education of her children, and to her he gave the first copy of his revision of chronology. Scientific events became matters of national interest. Even if his purpose

was *méchant*, the intrusion of George I into the Leibniz controversy—in one case reviewing a reply of Newton to Leibniz before
it was sent off—is indicative of the new status of science.

The Leibniz controversy brought the Royal Society and its
president before the eyes of European aristocrats. Those who
could not understand Newton's works were at least able to enjoy
the exchange of insults. The very notoriety of the quarrel gave
prestige to science, as the King, his mistress, Princess Caroline,
and the whole diplomatic corps took part in reviewing the documents in the case, expressing their opinion of the appropriate
tactics to be employed in its settlement. When science and the
Royal Society became fashionable, foreign ambassadors sought
membership in the Society as one might in an exclusive club, and
many more were admitted in Newton's day than ever before. The
snob in him was not averse to their presence. On occasion the
yeoman's son presided at Royal Society meetings surrounded by
European ambassadors, like a monarch holding court. The Journal
Book describes the occasion when Signor Grimani, the Venetian
Ambassador, Signor Gerardini, Envoy from the Grand Duke of
Tuscany, and the Duke d'Aumont, Ambassador Extraordinary of
France, were there together, entertained with experiments on "The
productiveness of light by friction; The mutual attraction of the
parts of matter; . . . preparations . . . of the veins and arteries
of a human liver."[20] Newton became a major source of national
pride among important segments of the upper classes. In hundreds
of eulogies while he was still alive, he was hailed as the glory of
the English nation, and his science was saluted as an exemplification of the national genius.

If in the previous generation the religious nature of scientific
inquiry had been given fervid expression—and to the very end
science remained for Newton a worship of God—the utility of
science was now recognized not only in philosophical works like
Bacon's and formal apologiae like those of Sprat and Joseph Glanvill, but in practical state measures. As if Marx had been stood on
his head, Newton, having devoted the first half of his creative
years to the development of a magnificent intellectual superstructure, turned in his latter days to its substructure. In 1709, he

accepted offices in the societies of the Mines Royal and the Mineral and Battery Works.[21] Having already given advice on curriculum reform of the Mathematical School at Christ's Hospital in 1694,[22] he turned to plans for reorganizing university education, with greater emphasis on science and upright conduct.[23] The Royal Society became royal not only in name, but in fact. It was represented on any governmental body which might remotely be involved with a scientific question. And its advice was sought on any parliamentary bill that concerned invention. As Stukeley wrote: "The Government, the great Council of the nation, paid a distinguished regard to their judgment in all matters of public utility." [24] The relations between the Society and the state were reciprocal. On February 7, 1713, Bolingbroke informed the Fellows that henceforward Her Majesty's envoys to foreign parts would promote the design for which the Society was founded by gathering information and answering inquiries that might be addressed to them by the scientists. (Among the first fruits of this union of science and the state was the dispatch to the Society of a giant's tooth discovered near Albany on the Hudson.[25]) Honorific appointments to the Society could serve the simple economic interests of the nation and its traders in foreign parts. Prince Alexander Menzicoff, an adviser to Peter the Great, was elected a Fellow on July 29, 1714, at the request of English merchants who sought concessions in Muscovy. And Newton in his own hand carefully prepared three drafts of the letter in response to the Russian nobleman's acceptance, a correspondence that is florid with love for science and humanity.[26]

It is well known that Charles II was moved to found the Royal Observatory because Flamsteed, in criticizing a charlatan's solution to the problem of longitudes, had pointed out how faulty existing star catalogues were. To say that the growing British Empire was anxious over safe navigation and the prevention of losses at sea is to labor the obvious. The Royal Navy, the merchants of London, and the ship's captains themselves were all vitally concerned. In May 1714 a petition was presented to Parliament asking that an award be offered for the discovery of the longitude, and a vast committee was appointed with the power to send for persons, papers, and records. Newton appeared at the hearing, as might a scientific administrator in a present-day inquiry, flanked by his scientists Clarke, Halley, and Cotes. The event presaged hundreds of similar confrontations between parliamentary committees and the new elite of science. The aged Newton was especially honored with a seat near the Committee chairman, and though he would have preferred to limit himself to the meticulous scientific analysis of alternative ways of proceeding with the discovery of the longitude, which he read from a prepared paper, neither the chairman nor the Committee, it seems, would move the bill until the oracle of science would say that one of the methods currently proposed was likely to be useful. William Whiston, among many other longitudinarians—as Arbuthnot satirized the profusion of inventors—had a plan of his own about which Newton was unenthusiastic; and it was only with great reluctance that he permitted a few words to be extracted to the effect that Whiston's method might be useful near the shores. Whereupon a bill passed the Committee and the Parliament offering £20,000, a huge sum, for a practical method of determining longitude within half a degree, and a Board of Longitude was established to sit in judgment on the various proposals and to allocate the awards for a full or partial solution. Newton was, of course, appointed a member of the Board.[27]

Though prominent Fellows of the Society like Arbuthnot had written about the manifold uses of mathematics for military as well as civil affairs and had stressed the need for more widespread mathematical education among officers, Newton himself seems to have been ambivalent about the scientists' participation in the development of military machines. David Gregory reports Newton's proposal to "cure the Bucking and wideness of touch-hole of great Gunns" by means of a new metallurgical mixture, another use of his chemical experiments with alloys,[28] but there is a contrasting story to the effect that Newton was hostile to the application of science to warfare. When the disciple's father, also named David, made an invention to improve artillery, Newton urged his son to destroy it on the ground that it would soon become known to the enemy and that it tended to the annihilation rather than the preservation of mankind.[29]

If scientists aided only sporadically in perfecting military weapons, they gave the government direct assistance in preventing public disorders. The comet of 1680 had generated a wave of terror and superstition. In 1715, Halley published a description and a map of the precise path of the eclipse before it happened on April 22, and public tranquillity was maintained. The utility of science to civil authority thus was dramatically demonstrated.

In the 1670's, John Evelyn dined with Flamsteed and referred to him with veneration as "the learned *Astrologer & Mathematician*, whom now his Majestie had established in the new *Observatorie* in *Greenewich* Park, and furnish'd with the choicest Instruments . . . ," as if he were a magus at an Eastern court.[30] By the second decade of the eighteenth century, such individual scientific positions of prestige and influence were virtually eliminated. Newton had systematically consolidated science in one body and under one head and had curtailed the independence of separate scientific agencies. Around him, a corporate scientific establishment with an authority of its own had taken shape. It did not enjoy munificent gifts from the crown, and its leading members were fairly independent economically, being supported by university posts, lucrative medical practices, or ecclesiastical appointments. Despite its relative autonomy, however, the activities that involved science with the government were being constantly multiplied.

THE WARS OF TRUTH

Of the events that established Newton's hegemony, the conflicts with Flamsteed and Leibniz were the most dramatic and the noisiest. The institutionalization of the Newtonian philosophy, like the victory of any great historical doctrine, required the slaughter of enemies both at home and abroad. The quarrels with Flamsteed and Leibniz, though they had earlier origins, flared up in earnest during the period of Newton's presidency. By defeating Flamsteed, Newton established his unquestioned supremacy in the

English scientific world, and thereafter no competitor dared raise
his head during Newton's lifetime. Before he was through with
Flamsteed, Newton had invoked the power of the secular arm
of the state to have himself and the Council of the Royal Society
appointed overseers of the formerly independent Greenwich Observatory and to publish as he saw fit and over Flamsteed's strenuous objections the Royal Astronomer's observations made at
Greenwich during a period of more than three decades. The Leibniz quarrel was the vindication of English science against the
"continentals." The enemy from without was routed, and Newtonian science could reign supreme and uncontested, except for
the rear-guard actions of the French Cartesians. By the time
Voltaire, the great propagator of the new faith, arrived in London, the issue was settled, and he wrote the famous eulogy of
Newton in the *Letters Concerning the English Nation*, which
perhaps more than any other single document popularized and
universalized Newton's image. In *Elements of the Philosophy of
Newton*, Voltaire became the Paul to Newton's Christ, though
it may well be doubted whether Christ or Newton would have
been satisfied with his respective apostle.

In the years after 1704, the president of the Royal Society
was in prime shape for personal and scientific infighting, and he
engaged simultaneously with Flamsteed on one flank and Leibniz
on the other. There was a difference in the nature of the contests.
Though the battle with Leibniz struck at his vitals, the com-
batants never confronted each other in person, nor did they exchange accusations except through intermediaries. Baroque pomp
and circumstance presided over the conduct of the war, and
grand secular potentates witnessed the fray as amused spectators.
Wrangling with Flamsteed—hardly an equal struggle, for the
Royal Astronomer was generally regarded as an eccentric—was
of a different order. The conflict between the two officers of the
English crown had a corrosive family intimacy, and their vocif-
erous quarrels at the Royal Society, in the Greenwich Observatory, and in Newton's house afforded Newton an opportunity for
the direct release of brutal rage upon another human being. After
the turn of the century, intoxicated with power and authority in

his dual capacity as Master of the Mint and president of the Royal Society, he allowed his angel of destruction, mightily armed, free rein. While the wearisome mutual recriminations of Newton and Flamsteed over a period of more than two decades are by no means an unprecedented example of science in the service of aggressive needs, Newton's vindictive pursuit of Flamsteed is perhaps more thoroughly documented than most. Unfortunately, as is usually the case, it is the victim who chronicles the story of his sufferings over and over again, finding a modicum of relief in the obsessive recapitulation of his persecution.

At the height of his power, Newton behaved toward Flamsteed, four years his junior, his younger brother in the Royal Society, as though he were a menial, and he made no effort to hide his condescension, if not his contempt. Newton looked upon Flamsteed as nothing more than a convenient source of data for his theories, a tool. And yet this was no schoolboy who was being maltreated, but a member of the Royal Society's Council, with an extensive correspondence among European scholars, the author of more than two-score papers in the *Philosophical Transactions*, a man who had devised novel methods of observation and was among the first to use an accurate timepiece and optical means for determining stellar coordinates. Flamsteed was as arrogant as Newton, and he dared to talk back to the president of the Royal Society, even to criticize the *Principia*—unpardonable sins.

Both Newton and Flamsteed were profoundly religious, and their works were dedicated to God as a worship. Both believed themselves to be of the elect, but they were also deeply concerned with what men thought about them, since they lived in a hostile world rendered even more nasty and brutish by their imaginings. The two troubled creatures—one the son of a tradesman, the other the son of a yeoman, now great officers of the crown and rivals for world fame, each believing that he was divinely ordained —were almost fated to clash. The confrontation of several Christs in one asylum has been studied by clinicians. Newton and Flamsteed, though neither of them was psychotic, enacted a similar tragicomedy on the broader stage of the English scientific world.

Our most detailed consecutive account of the quarrel from

1704 to 1716, when it blazed in the open in the scientific and political world, is the "Original Preface" that was suppressed by the editors of Flamsteed's *Historia Coelestis* when the work appeared posthumously (1725). The preface, written by Flamsteed in February 1717, concentrated on Newton's unjust and unremitting harassment of the author; one did not cast such aspersions upon the character of the divine Newton with impunity, and censorship was invoked.[31] The preface presented a lurid picture of Newton as a power-lusting, lying, conniving, treacherous monster, using his influence at court and his intimacy with Lord Halifax to do Flamsteed out of his star catalogue, his money, his independent position as Royal Astronomer. Flamsteed depicted himself as a long-suffering martyr whose devotion to science and the revelation of God's works would not allow him to issue an imperfect star catalogue, a man who was the object of a conspiracy in which hypocritical Newton and atheistic Halley were the prime movers. They had vied for the favor of the Prince of Denmark, and through chicanery had forced Flamsteed to surrender his manuscripts, making arrangements with booksellers that robbed him of his due, for the Prince had donated £1200 for their publication. Flamsteed was the righteous man of God pursued by a political manipulator and a band of adulators constantly singing his praises. Since Flamsteed would not join them, he had to be crushed, and each move in the long, drawn-out story of official intrigue was, in Flamsteed's reconstruction of events, consciously planned by the arch-villain.

Despite Flamsteed's obvious exaggerations, the account carries some conviction and cannot be dimissed as nothing more than paranoid confabulation. Newton would brook no opposition and was quite capable of destroying a man who crossed him. Flamsteed's version of 1717 is, in much of its detail, corroborated by letters that he wrote to friends at the time the events were taking place, so that if he fantasied, he at least clung more or less closely to the frame of his original imaginings. Nothing in Newton's correspondence contradicts the facts presented, and extant manuscript drafts of agreements and royal orders, in Newton's hand, bolster Flamsteed's central contention that it was always Newton who was pulling the strings. In modern bureaucracies, scientists have often been adept in the art of the cabal, which they quickly learned from their political colleagues when the skill did not come naturally.

Newton's mechanics were astute. He operated through a Committee of Referees who, though members of the Society, were appointed not by it, but by the Prince of Denmark on Newton's recommendation. He lied, used guile, and intimidated his victim with threats that he was guilty of *lèse-majesté* when he refused to surrender his observations. In a bewildering scene in Crane Court after the Society was installed in its new building, Newton—supported by Sloane and Mead—excoriated the victim and called him names—puppy was the least of them, according to Flamsteed.[32] In the end, Newton won—the first British star catalogue was published in 1712 without Flamsteed's consent and under the editorial direction of Edmond Halley whom he loathed. Flamsteed had been persuaded or forced to surrender to the Committee of Referees a record of his original observations and an incomplete set of star-places. Some of the papers had been put under seal in Newton's possession, and Flamsteed charged that he had broken the bond and released them. The printing proceeded haltingly until Prince George's death, when the Committee gave Halley—the cruelest cut of all—the task of publishing whatever was in their hands and then filling out the volume with his own observations. The 1712 edition that was pulled out of this chaos is a veritable hodgepodge, because there were numerous unresolved problems of identification when Halley assumed control. In addition, Halley's introduction to what was essentially Flamsteed's lifework made brutal reflections about the Royal Astronomer's capacities and accuracy.

Because of his relationship with the government, Newton had thus been able to force Flamsteed to surrender his observations and to have them printed not as the isolated astronomer would have had them appear, but as Newton the administrator dictated. Though he received a salary from the government, Flamsteed still thought of himself as the lone, autonomous servant of God and of his work as an offering. Newton, in the name of the superior interests of organized science and the kingdom, treated him like a rebellious clerk whose peculiarities would not be tolerated. The novelty of this act of intervention and command has been ignored by commentators, though it presaged a new form of scientific organization and control.

While dealing with Flamsteed as an internal threat to his authority, Newton managed at the same time to grapple with a foreign menace. In a published series of Latin documents— mostly translations of letters about the calculus to and from John Collins in the 1670's—known for short as the *Commercium Epistolicum* (1712), a committee of the Royal Society adjudicated a contest over priority in the invention of the calculus in favor of its own president, aged seventy, against one of its oldest foreign members, aged sixty-six.

In a joust over precedence in the new philosophy, the Knight from Woolsthorpe and the Freiherr from Leipzig had abided by no known set of chivalric rules. At the height of the contest, after repeated letters from Leibniz to Hans Sloane, Secretary of the Society, complaining that Dr. John Keill, a fellow member, had insulted him, Newton the president formally brought together his adherents under the guise of what he grandiloquently called "a large committee of distinguished persons of several nations expressly assembled by order of the Royal Society," to judge the merits of Leibniz' accusation. The nations represented on this much-touted impartial committee turned out to be English, Scotch, and Irish, with a Prussian ambassador and a Huguenot émigré later thrown in for continental flavor. The decision of the Committee insinuated plagiarism on the part of Leibniz, though its report was required only to exonerate Keill from the charge that he had injured Leibniz during a polemical exchange, or to confirm it.

Newton was so well protected that publicly the affair appeared to be a Keill-Leibniz controversy; he operated exclusively behind the scenes and with consummate skill. There is only one document in which he took specific personal responsibility for what was said—his reply to the Abate Conti in 1716; for the rest, he was the grand strategist who refused to be revealed. And when he deigned to answer Leibniz through Conti on that one occasion, it was by *force majeure*; for Conti, a Venetian aristocrat sojourning in England, and Princess Caroline of Anspach had playfully decided to act as intermediaries in a reconciliation attempt, and Newton had no choice but to go along with their efforts.

The exchange of letters between Leibniz and Newton through Conti in 1716 only brought into the open a war that had been waged clandestinely since the turn of the century. Two of the greatest geniuses of the European world—not only of their own time, but of its whole long history—had been privately belaboring each other with injurious epithets and encouraging their partisans to publish scurrilous innuendoes in learned journals. In the age of reason, they behaved like gladiators in a Roman circus. Here were two old bachelors—Leibniz not far from death, Newton with a decade more of life—each fighting for exclusive possession of his brainchild, the right to call the invention of the calculus his own and no one else's. The contest transcended the specific issue of priority of invention to embrace rival conceptions of the nature of matter, substance, the cosmos, God's providence, time, space, miracles. Their views of all things in the heavens and on earth became polarized as they stalwartly assumed opposite positions, exaggerating their differences, grossly caricaturing each other's opinions like schoolboys in debate. Their common commitment to advancing the new philosophy was totally forgotten.

For many years, others had perpetrated the hostile acts for the principals, who sedulously avoided an open confrontation—though the manuscripts now betray the extent to which they supervised the verbal assaults of their hangers-on when they did not themselves compose them under the cover of anonymity. Newton had a more numerous troop. He was in London, president of the Royal Society, embattled defender of the English nation in a war where world scientific prestige was at stake. Though Leibniz, too, had been president of an academy, it was in backwoods Berlin, and his last years were spent as a lonely old man in Hannover writing dynastic history for the head of the House of Brunswick who had become King George I of England. Leibniz had his adherents among the great continental scientists—Johann Bernoulli,

Christiaan Huygens—but they were leery of engaging with Newton and only reluctantly allowed themselves to be drawn into
the fray.

Leibniz was no innocent, and when he attacked Newton for
his revival of scholastic philosophy and his belief in occult qualities, he knew the barbs would sting.[33] Like an envious school-
master, Leibniz boasted, almost pathetically: "I am surprised that
the partisans of Mr. Newton produce nothing to show that their
master has communicated a sound method to them. I have been
more fortunate in my disciples." He smugly assured Conti that
Wren, Flamsteed, and Newton were all that remained of the
scientific *"Siècle d'or d'Angleterre"* and that their day would soon
be done.[34]

Of the scores of documents that Newton prepared on the
Leibniz controversy, the review, or *Recensio*, of the *Commercium
Epistolicum* which he himself wrote and published anonymously,
"An Account of the Book entitled Commercium Epistolicum Col-
linii & aliorum, De Analysi promota; published by order of the
Royal Society . . . ," reveals the lengths to which he resorted to
annihilate a foe. All but three pages of the *Philosophical Transactions* for January and February 1715 are devoted to this jejune
recapitulation of the quarrel, beginning with proof of Newton's
first discoveries in the sixties. Its text, interspersed with Latin
quotations and mathematical proofs, was hardly likely to have
great popular appeal, but the sharp edge of the polemical passages and the bite of the attack could be understood by anyone
who perused the volume. While the piece is unsigned and purports
to be a rectification by an editorial "we" of imperfect summaries
published abroad, at one point near the end where a solemn warning is issued to Leibniz, the author of the review lapses into the
singular personal pronoun. His identity is unmistakable. "And in
the meantime I take the Liberty to acquaint him, that by taxing
the Royal Society with Injustice in giving Sentence against him
without hearing both Parties, he has transgressed one of their
Statutes which makes it Expulsion to defame them." [35]

Newton's subtle and eminently persuasive structuring of Leibniz' intentions, the uncovering of a monstrous plagiarist plot, tells

us far more about Newton than it does about Leibniz, for papers have since revealed that Leibniz' method was actually inspired by reading some Pascal writings in Paris, as he had testified.[36] Newton hoarded a great part of whatever he wrote and always lived in a circumscribed geographic area, while Leibniz roamed from royal court to royal court—from Muscovy to Berlin, Vienna, Hannover, Paris—in quest of personal preferment and support of his grand projects for the unification of mankind and the promotion of knowledge. In his hour of need, he was caught without written proof, and at the very moment when he hoped to be invited to England as a royal historiographer by the head of the House of Brunswick-Hannover, George I, for whose glory he had labored day and night in the archives, he found himself accused of a flagrant falsification of scientific history.

Reading the indignant peroration of the *Recensio*'s charge to the jury, one almost forgets that Newton himself is delivering the verdict, that he appointed the Committee of the Royal Society, that he edited the documents of the *Commercium*, adding his own footnotes and sometimes selecting for publication extracts rather than the full texts, that he interjected numerous unsupported inferences, and that he would in 1722 republish the *Commercium* with further emendations that were not signaled in any preface or introduction.[37] On occasion, Newton's cold cruelty assumed unbelievable proportions. In his *Historical Memoirs of the Life of Dr. Samuel Clarke*, William Whiston reports in passing: "He [Mr. Jackson] heard Sir Isaac Newton also pleasantly tell the Doctor [Clarke] that 'He broke Leibniz's Heart with his Reply to him.' " [38]

The republic of science had become too small for both Newton and Leibniz, as the Royal Society had once been for Newton and Hooke. A quarrel which had its origins in a classical priority fight had been fanned into a great conflagration. Leibniz could sometimes look away and jest about the struggle, but he was nonetheless devoured by it. This, rather than the noxious potions he took for gout, may have killed him. During his lifetime, he stood a condemned plagiarist, for who would gainsay the verdict of the Royal Society of London in a judgment that Leibniz himself had demanded? He died alone, and nobody of consequence attended his funeral. Newton regurgitated the case repeatedly in Latin and in English, ungallantly pursuing Leibniz even beyond the grave—witness the five hundred-odd folios of manuscript devoted to self-vindication and attack in the University Library in Cambridge, in addition to the stray papers at the Mint, into which his great wrath poured itself. His obsession lasted for a quarter of a century, and nowhere are the destructive forces in his character more visibly on the rampage than in this vendetta.

By the early-eighteenth century, Newtonian science had acquired many faces, and it showed them all: for the young scholars, it was a scientific philosophy; for the bishops, it was a proof of the existence of God; for the merchants, it offered the prospect of reducing losses at sea; for the King, it was an embellishment of the throne; for aristocrats, it was an amusement. Thus, it could be assimilated in many different forms—not excluding "Newtonianism for the Ladies" [39]—a protean quality that is almost a prerequisite for universalist doctrines. In order to secure itself, the science of Isaac Newton used certain of the mechanisms of a conquering new religion or political ideology. It triumphed, a truth in its day, but it seems to have availed itself of the same apparatus as any other kind of movement. Followers were assembled and bound to an apotheosized leader with ties of great strength. An internal institutional structure was fortified. The word was propagated by chosen disciples. Since the doctrine was rooted in a national society, its relations with the government gave it special privileges and emoluments. It became the second spiritual establishment of the realm, and at least in its origins presented no threat to the primary religious establishment that it was destined to undermine and, perhaps, ultimately to replace. As in many militant doctrinal movements, the truth was not allowed to fend for itself, and on occasion the sacred lie and the pious fraud became means to a higher end.

The content of Newtonian science might have prevailed without the personal force that Newton exerted. But with his extraordinary genius and energy, he was able to impose on the western world a personal scientific style and a movement that reflected his character. There was perhaps something valid in Leibniz' prognostication of the imminent decline of English science, for Newton's grip on the establishment did, in fact, stifle inventiveness for a time: the immediate followers were mere epigoni. Newton's great power as both the creator of a closed scientific world view and the organizer of its institutional framework has had analogies in both earlier and later generations and in other fields of endeavor —with similar consequences.

NOTES

1. The Royal Mint Library, Newton MSS., II, fol. 334, John Chamberlayne to Isaac Newton, November 25, 1713.
2. See John Ball Keill, *Introductio ad veram astronomiam*, 2nd ed. (London, 1721), p. vi; Cambridge, King's College Library, Keynes MS. 130, autograph drafts of portions of John Conduitt's intended life of Newton; Edmond Halley in the introduction of the *Principia*; Bibliothèque publique et universitaire de Genève, MS. français 602, fol. 58, minute of a letter from Fatio de Duillier to Jean-Robert Chouet, November 21, 1689.
3. William Stukeley, *Memoirs of Sir Isaac Newton's Life*, ed. A. Hastings White (London, 1936), p. 81.
4. Sir David Brewster, *Memoirs of the life, writings, and discoveries of Sir Isaac Newton* (Edinburgh, 1885), II, p. 246.
5. Cambridge, King's College Library, Keynes MS. 136, Stukeley to Conduitt, June 26, 1727.
6. See J. Edleston, ed., *Correspondence of Sir Isaac Newton and Professor Cotes* (London, 1850), p. lxxvii.
7. Thomas Hearne, *Remarks and Collections*, VI (Oxford, 1902), p. 231, September 25, 1718; IX (Oxford, 1914), p. 293, April 4, 1727.
8. William Whiston, *Memoirs of the life and writings of Mr. William Whiston*, 2nd ed. (London, 1753), I, pp. 249-250.
9. *Ibid.*, pp. 250-251.
10. W. G. Hiscock, ed., *David Gregory, Isaac Newton and their circle; extracts from David Gregory's memoranda 1677-1708* (Oxford, 1937), p. 14.
11. Ralph Thoresby, *Diary*, ed. J. Hunter (London, 1830), II, pp. 111, 117.
12. Sir Henry Lyons, *The Royal Society 1660-1940* (Cambridge, 1944), p. 121.
13. Cambridge, University Library, Add. MS. 4007B, fol. 669, Desaguliers to Newton, April 29, 1725.

14. Cambridge, University Library, Add. MS. 4005, foll. 1-7.
15. Brewster, *Memoirs of the life, writings, and discoveries of Sir Isaac Newton*, II, pp. 243-244.
16. Stukeley, *Memoirs of Sir Isaac Newton's Life*, pp. 78-81.
17. Brewster, *Memoirs of the life, writings and discoveries of Sir Isaac Newton*, II, pp. 245-246.
18. Charles Richard Weld, *A History of the Royal Society* (London, 1848), I, pp. 391-393. Weld quotes an anonymous contemporary report of the meeting, *An Account of the late Proceedings in the Council of the Royal Society, in order to remove from Gresham-College into Crane Court, in Fleet-Street* (1710).
19. A foreign visitor to the Society, the Frankfort traveler Zacharias Conrad von Uffenbach, still noticed the portrait in 1710; see *London in 1710, from The Travels of Zacharias Conrad von Uffenbach*, tr. and ed. W. H. Quarrell and Margaret Mare (London, 1934), p. 102.
20. Quoted by Weld, *A History of the Royal Society*, I, p. 419.
21. D. Seaborne Davies, "The Records of the Mines Royal and the Mineral and Battery Works," *Economic History Review*, VI (1936), pp. 209-213.
22. Isaac Newton, *Correspondence*, III, ed. H. W. Turnbull (Cambridge, 1961), pp. 357-366, Newton to Nathaniel Hawes, May 25, 1694.
23. Cambridge, University Library, Add. MS. 4005, foll. 14-15, "Of Educating Youth in the Universities," printed in Isaac Newton, *Unpublished scientific papers*, ed. A. Rupert Hall and Marie Boas-Hall (Cambridge, 1962), pp. 369-373.
24. Stukeley, *Memoirs of Sir Isaac Newton's Life*, p. 81.
25. Weld, *A History of the Royal Society*, I, pp. 420-421.
26. Brewster, *Memoirs of the life, writings, and discoveries of Sir Isaac Newton*, II, p. 257.
27. Great Britain, House of Commons, *Journals*, XVII (1711-1714; reprinted 1803), pp. 641-642, May 25, 1714; pp. 677-678, June 11, 1714; p. 716, July 3, 1714; p. 721, July 8, 1714. See also Brewster, *Memoirs of the life, writings, and discoveries of Sir Isaac Newton*, II, pp. 258-262, 265-266; Louis T. More, *Isaac Newton. A Biography* (London, 1934), pp. 562-563; William Whiston, *Longitude Discovered* (London, 1738), Historical Preface, p. v.
28. W.G. Hiscock ed., *David Gregory, Isaac Newton and their circle*, p. 25.
29. Charles Hutton, *A Mathematical and Philosophical Dictionary*, 2nd ed. (London, 1815), I, p. 557.
30. John Evelyn, *Diary*, ed. E. S. de Beer (Oxford, 1955), IV, p. 98, September 10, 1676.
31. The preface was printed in Francis Baily, *An Account of the Revd. John Flamsteed, the first Astronomer-Royal* (London, 1835), pp. 71-105.
32. *Ibid.*, pp. 228-229.
33. Leibniz, *Die philosophischen Schriften*, ed. C. J. Gerhardt (Hildes-

heim, 1960-1961; reprint of 1875-1890 ed.), III, pp. 328-329, Leibniz to Thomas Burnet, August 23, 1713.

34. Pierre Des Maizeaux, *Recueil de diverses pièces sur la philosophie. . .* (Amsterdam, 1720), II, pp. 70-71, Leibniz to Conti, April 9, 1716, *apostille*.

35. *Philosophical Transactions of the Royal Society*, XXIX (1715), no. 342, p. 221.

36. J. E. Hofmann, *Die Entwicklungsgeschichte der Leibnizschen Mathematik während des Aufenthaltes in Paris, 1672-1676* (Munich, 1949), pp. 194-205.

37. John Collins, *Commercium epistolicum. . .ou Correspondance de J. Collins et d'autres savants célèbres du xviie siècle, relative à l'analyse supérieure. . . .* ed. J. B. Biot and F. Lefort (Paris, 1856). Biot and Lefort collated the texts of the 1712 and 1722 editions, indicating additions, suppressions, alterations, and interpolations in what purported to be merely a new edition of the old *Commercium*.

38. William Whiston, *Historical Memoirs of the Life of Dr. Samuel Clarke* (London, 1730), p. 132.

39. Francesco Algarotti, *Sir Isaac Newton's philosophy explain'd for the use of the ladies*, trans. Elizabeth Carter, 2 vols. (London, 1739; original Italian version, 1737).

8

THE INTELLECTUAL IN POLITICS: LOCKE, NEWTON, AND THE ESTABLISHMENT

While I have never been opposed to quantification techniques in history on philosophical grounds, hitherto I have had an unmistakable predilection for a sample of one. This paper represents a new departure: I am now well on the way to aligning myself with the massive quantifiers as I embark upon a sample of two, a hundred percent increase in one fell swoop.

Labeling Locke and Newton "intellectuals" requires immediate justification. For most of his life Newton would have identified himself in public as a professor of the mathematics. Once he came up to London he was known alternatively as Warden, then Master, of the Mint or President of the Royal Society. In private he stood in a rather special relationship to God, and in one of his manuscripts took notice of the fact that *Jeova*

Delivered before a joint meeting of the American Historical Association and the Conference on British Studies, Washington, D.C., December 29, 1969.

sanctus unus was an anagram for Isaacus Neuutonus. Locke enjoyed a respectable status as a medical doctor with a fashionable, if highly restricted, clientele. After 1688 he was called "the philosopher" among political leaders and bureaucratic colleagues on the Board of Trade and Plantations. The epitaph he composed for himself resolved his identity crisis with finality; he was "a scholar." In the decadent west of the twentieth century, a penchant for the aesthetic in morals and style of life has often been regarded as a distinctive earmark of the intellectual. Judged by this criterion, Locke and Newton would hardly qualify as intellectuals. They had no use for poetry and literary conceits; Newton walked out on the only opera he ever attended; and Locke measured rather than appreciated the great works of architecture he saw on his journey through France. Both were, in theory at least, committed to the matter-of-fact and the commonsensical. The term intellectual is apt with respect to Newton and Locke only if we adhere to the dictionary definition, a person having the capacity for the higher forms of knowledge or thought.

The "establishment" as a description for the general order of the elective monarchy, more inclusive than church or war establishment, originated in the official documents of the Glorious Revolution, and soon became popular in polemics of the period. My usage is therefore not anachronistic, despite the recent revitalization of the noun as a pejorative universal among the youth of England and America.

The coupling of Locke and Newton is an old one, though their relationship did not draw the attention of English contemporaries. It took a foreigner to point out that England had brought forth two men who together were the founding fathers of a fresh world view. Successive chapters in Voltaire's *Philosophical Letters on the English Nation* (1733) probably did as much as any single work to fix them in the mind of literate Europe as the gemini of the new order. By the end of the century they had become inseparably paired symbols in England and America. And in 1807 Henri de Saint-Simon, writing an imaginative—really imaginary—history of science, fancied a conversation between them at the University of Oxford in the course of which they agreed to divide the whole field of knowledge between them, Newton pre-empting physical science as his province and Locke taking the science of man as his.

Actually, though both had been members of the Royal Society for many years, it was only after the Convention Parliament had been convoked and Locke had returned from exile that they became intimates. Locke was about fifty-six, Newton ten years his junior, and their major creative work had already been accomplished when they ventured upon full-time careers in active politics. Newton had seen the *Principia* through the press in 1687; the optics and the calculus had long since taken shape, even though they were not yet published in final form. Locke's writings on epistemology, government, money, education, toleration were still in manuscript, but the later printed works were mostly an updating of earlier versions, or perhaps a settling into definitive positions where once there had been some vacillation. Thus for Locke as for Newton politics did not crowd out the creative life of the mind, but filled a vacuum after its zenith had passed. Neither of them was capable of inactivity, and politics was in some ways a godsend.

In recent decades both Locke and Newton have become the subjects of large-scale, international, scholarly industries that may well be threatened by imminent crises of overproduction. New Lockes and new Newtons have emerged from a study of their manuscripts and a close examination of their writings—portraits that would not have been recognizable in the eighteenth and nineteenth centuries. Beyond occasional gleanings from the Locke papers, I have no important new data to contribute to the findings of the specialists.[1] To the vaster Newton industry, whose captains are far too numerous to catalogue, I have added my share—some members of the cartel in this field would probably say, a mite too much.

I aim to proceed this afternoon more in a Lockean than a Newtonian manner. Their connection with the establishment will not be defined in terms of postulata and lemmata, but rather in the loose manner of the *Essay Concerning Human Understanding*, by dwelling upon the same argument and expressing it in different ways with quite different designs. "Some objects had need be turned on every side," as Locke wrote.[2] The relationship of Locke, Newton, and the establishment has at least three sides, as I perceive it. This paper will therefore treat of the administrative and political roles that Locke and Newton filled in the government, or Locke and Newton as bureaucrats; of the part that the establishment played in their psychic economies, or Locke and Newton and their need for public status and recognition; and finally, of the influence that Locke and Newton came to exert in the formation of the spirit of the British establishment, conceived in broader terms than the particular governmental establishment they served, or Locke and Newton as intellectual superstructure.

Locke had followed Shaftesbury into exile, and narrowly escaped extradition from Holland. Mystery shrouds the details of his early involvement with William of Orange, though it is known that he was active in his behalf. Locke did not sail to England with William and the first contingent of glorious revolutionaries, but charily drew up the rear with the ladies on a safe conveyance. He was no Lenin fatefully boarding the sealed train. Once settled in London, he reaped tangible rewards for his allegiance to the Happy Revolution. Time and again he was offered foreign embassies, which he declined for reasons of ill health and an incapacity for drinking enough to ferret out intelligence. He finally did accept membership on the Board of Trade, which was the effective agency for administering the colonies.

Newton, too, was a minor hero of the Revolution. While still a professor at Trinity, he had come out of his academic shell long enough to help organize defiance of King James's attempt to insinuate Catholics into the University of Cambridge with a view to their ultimate domination. He had stood his ground before the bullying of bloody Lord Jeffreys and his ecclesiastical commission, had sat in the Convention Parliament as a representative of the University, and with lawyer-like logic had manoeuvred the University through the moral and religious crisis of oathbreaking to the old monarch and oath-taking to a new one. His rewards were slow to materialize, and the delay in securing a place was an element in his psychic crisis of 1693. But the appointment he eventually secured as Warden of the Mint was only the first of the honors that were heaped upon him for three decades—mastership of the Mint, knighthood, presidency of the Royal Society, and interment in Westminster Abbey.

These two middle-aged bachelors, Locke and Newton, who met at the time of the Revolution, had much in common. Both had been born in small towns near a great road not too far from thriving commercial centers. They were roughly of the same economic status—Locke the son of an impecunious lawyer who was a clerk of the local justice and related to a Puritan tradesman family, Newton the son of a man who still called himself a yeoman but had come into the possession of a small manor, and of a woman who was the daughter of local gentry that had seen better days. There were divines in their families and at least one knight in a collateral branch. Locke appropriated the arms of an ancestor, and Newton had fantasies about his noble origin. But at school they were the "poor boys"—Locke a *peregrinus* at Westminster, Newton a subsizar at Cambridge. The notebooks in which Locke and Newton preserved meticulous records of their paltry expenditures are virtually interchangeable. They were close enough to the rich and the powerful to aspire to join them; yet their roots were in classes that sustained themselves by work in a respectable calling.

For both Locke and Newton the new establishment afforded dignities and material satisfactions that they had never derived from their intellectual labors. Newton's post in the Mint brought in about 500 pounds a year and Locke's on the Board of Trade and Plantations about 1,000—handsome emoluments for those times. They died in prosperity, Locke leaving an estate of about 20,000 pounds, Newton 37,000. A part of their income came from the tenants on lands they had acquired, and they were quite strict in the collection of rents. Newton pressed hard for his share of the enclosures in Woolsthorpe. Both played the stock market. Locke, like Voltaire after him, was even involved in the slave trade at one time, and Newton unfortunately was caught in the South Sea Bubble with his own and the Royal Society's funds. While maintaining a firm base in the lands of their native counties, they

were constantly drawn into closer relations with the commercial interests of the capital. In the government their hunger for the
palpable symbols of power and status found appeasement. The
peregrinus of Westminster and the subsizar of Trinity became
great men of the realm. On the Board of Trade Locke sat with
new and old nobility. At the Royal Society Newton presided in
a ritual he himself developed with aristocratic ambassadorial guests
at his side. He was a caller at Kensington Palace who advised
Princess Caroline on the education of her children. Whether
knighthood was meant to reward the Master of the Mint or to
elevate the scientist, Newton became the man he had always
fantasied himself to be—an aristocrat of sorts. He even had himself painted with a sword. In his last years he gave thanks to the
establishment, which had treated him so munificently. How
grateful he was to have been born an Englishman, he once told
John Conduitt, for he lived in a land of liberty, unlike unfortunate Descartes and Galileo.

As servants of the crown, Locke and Newton worked for the
new regime primarily in the equivalent of ministries of economic
and colonial affairs. And once these major figures were installed
in the bureaucracy, they infused a new spirit into their agencies.
Searching questionnaires about the state of the colonies drafted
by Locke resulted in some of the best reporting on local conditions in America. The appraisal of Virginia at the close of the
eighteenth century by John Blair and John Locke is believed by
one commentator to have effected a new allocation of power in the
structure of the colony. Employment of the English poor, Irish
linen, pirates, Harvard College, oath-taking in Maryland, rice in
Carolina, naval stores, bureaucratic intrigue among colonial officials were typical problems with which the wide-ranging Board
grappled. The empirical philosopher put his doctrines to practical
use. Newton and the astronomer Edmond Halley, whom he
brought with him into the government, had their troubles with
subordinates used to more easygoing ways, for Newton behaved
in office with the same severity and rigor that had marked the
conduct of his scientific experiments. Doubtless Charles Montague had gotten Newton the Mint as a sinecure, but Newton

turned out to be a veritable Javert in pursuit of coiners and clippers. Hundreds of interrogations in the Tower which he attested in his own hand bear witness to his assiduousness. I have elsewhere hazarded a guess on the role that these prosecutions played in Newton's psychic economy, affording a temporary release from a dangerous aggressiveness that had once turned inward; but in the economy of the realm he was an effective civil servant, remaining at his post until his dying days. His last known letter gave approval to the hanging of a counterfeiter.

Locke and Newton composed memoranda on the recoinage, on rates of interest, on the founding of the Bank of England, on dealing with the poor, and on the control of navigation with the colonies. They were the experts who could advise about the complex relationships of gold and silver and paper money. Newton fixed the gold standard, which lasted just about as long as his views of absolute time and absolute space—an arresting synchronism. As ruling economic theorists of the 1690's, Locke and Newton did, of course, keep secret their alchemical interests and pursuits. One shudders to think of the reaction in the City if it had leaked out that Locke was toying with Boyle's legacy of recipes involving transmutation of metals through the agency of a "red earth" brought from the East, and that Newton the new Warden of the Mint had conducted his last dated alchemical-chemical experiment only weeks before the delivery of his patent of office. But intellectuals in government, like most people, usually have a few skeletons in their closets.

While Newton the civil servant concentrated primarily on matters directly related to coinage in England, Ireland, and the New World, because of his intimacy with Charles Montague dating from his Cambridge days he was involved in the mechanisms of winning elections and was privy to court secrets. Through his special relationship to Somers, an old acquaintance, Locke became a general mentor in politics whose counsel was frequently solicited and implicitly followed. A century later James Madison at the Federal Convention still joined the names of Somers and Locke as exemplars of political wisdom. Locke had personal ties with the King, with the Whig ministers, and with a pivotal par-

liamentary group of his close friends organized in a club called
the "College." Of the manner in which, through them, he shaped
policy in both domestic and foreign affairs we have detailed accounts in the correspondence with his friend Edward Clarke,
though I understand that official papers in this field are still
being worked on.

The roles played by Locke and Newton enhanced the prestige
of men of the mind, and changed the image of the philosopher as
an incompetent, impractical dreamer. One of the masters of the
rival literary culture, Jonathan Swift, a minister of propaganda
in search of a place, tried to perpetuate the caricature of the scientist as an abstruse idiot in *Gulliver's Travels*. But far from being
a man with his head in the clouds, Newton, regularly waiting on
the lords of the treasury, showed himself to be an able administrator. Nor was he a slouch in defending his little empire from
fellow-bureaucrats who crossed his path, men like the Controller
of the Mint, or the officer in charge of the soldiers in the Tower,
who molested *"his* workers."

From dependents on the favor of politicians, Locke and Newton themselves became dispensers of favors. Locke was directly
involved in the distribution of important colonial posts and he
received fulsome thanks from those he patronized. Newton revived the moribund Royal Society and elevated it to the status
of the scientific establishment of the realm. There he ruled supreme. And through this agency he came to control the major
university and school appointments in the physical and mathematical sciences and positions on government boards that were
in any way concerned with scientific matters. Parliament would
not agree to offer a prize for the discovery of a method to determine longitudes at sea until the exalted Newton, flanked by his
favorite disciples, appeared in person before a committee and
gave his assent to the idea. He ruthlessly crushed the autonomy
of the Royal Observatory and brought it under the Royal Society's
supervision, despite the towering rage of the Astronomer Royal,
John Flamsteed. The Royal Society was identified with Newton's
very being. Ultimately he became the symbol of British science,
and his victories over the "continentals"—Leibniz and the

French *monsieurs*—were hailed by contemporaries as a national triumph.

As Newton and Locke hobnobbed with the rulers of England, their style of life changed. Once the scholarly recluse of Cambridge, Newton was seen more often in coffee-houses after meetings of the Royal Society. Carried about the city in a sedan chair he grew quite corpulent; and on occasion he graced great dinners at which a galaxy of aristocrats were present. In the bloated, choleric features of his last portrait it is difficult to discern traces of the sensitive face Godfrey Kneller painted in 1689. As prominent bureaucrats, men of the world, Locke and Newton lost the protection of academic obscurity, and both had to endure attacks against their persons from enemies of high and low station. The coiners and clippers whom Newton imprisoned swore they would have his blood if ever they were released. A theological polemicist denounced the "seraglio at Oates," the country seat of Lord and Lady Masham where Locke would take refuge from the London climate. For myself, I am today prepared to vouch for Locke's chastity, as once I did for Newton's. To some unfriendly observers there was a flagrant incompatibility between the life of the mind and politics and administration. One of Locke's more vituperative critics asked rhetorically how a member of the Board of Trade could possibly be a just writer on philosophical questions. And the Royal Astronomer, the Reverend Flamsteed, was provoked into taking swipes at the scientist Newton who had been seduced from his calling by the poisoned fruits of power.

Newton and Locke made an effort to maintain private intellectual existences without shirking their responsibilities in the government. The backsides of Newton's Mint papers are scribbled up with notes on theological controversies in the early church and on world chronology. Newton tried to keep up with the moon problem, though he flew into a rage when Flamsteed gossiped about his interest, lest there be some imputation that he was dabbling in science instead of devoting himself wholeheartedly to the King's business. Locke managed to compose answers to criticisms of the published treatise that he avowed, while he kept complaining how little leisure he had for his philosophical work, deriding himself as "a man of trade concerned with coal, fuller's earth, lamp black and hob nails." But the attractions of power were not to be resisted. Dolefully lamenting the burdens of office and yet refusing to relinquish a toehold on power is not an unfamiliar phenomenon in this city of lost professors.

But the significance of Locke and Newton for the state transcended their successful operations as government functionaries, for they came to represent a philosophical view of the world which, in part at least, rubbed off onto the establishment. Doubtless the Whig Party bosses cared little about their higher mental systems, concerned as the politicians were with immediate practicalities. But Locke and Newton, who had in fact partitioned the universe as Saint-Simon supposed, provided the reconstituted English society of the late seventeenth century with a formalized new outlook. It was oriented around the empirical, that which could be touched with the hand and seen with the eye, suspicious of the grand a priori hypothesis, committed to the industrious, denigrating excessive luxury, worshipful of the trinity of science and commerce and liberty—albeit the definition of the new triplex was sometimes as difficult as that of the old.

In their relationship Locke always looked up to the "incomparable Mr. Newton" as the ideal of intellect, and he struggled heroically with the proofs of the *Principia*, though he may have understood more of it than has sometimes been supposed. Locke's popularization of Newton's achievement was probably a key document in the transmission of the Newtonian model of the world to posterity. The Newtonian system embodied the true knowledge of which man was capable, exclusive of the world of faith. Locke stood in awe of Newton both as a man of science and as a reader of Scripture, and he was quick to overlook the temporary aberrations of his psychic crisis, when Newton thought him a Hobbist, a man who tried to sell him a place and embroil him with women, and when he wished Locke were dead.

Though in their theology Locke and Newton had a profound attachment to what they fancied was the simple Christianity of the primitive church, their doctrinal position was coupled with a fundamental sense of distance from the "people." The people were the heart of darkness. Popular superstition took many forms, worst of all "papism," "enthusiasm," and "fanaticism," grave sources of disorder. Both men considered the lower classes outside their main concern. For Locke, laborers could not live a full, rational life. They managed to survive on a subsistence level and were not really a part of the political process. Newton had contempt, rather than sympathy, for ordinary people, whose intellectual limits were fixed. He would converse with an elite of scientists; for the rest, he would hold himself aloof and write as abstrusely as he could in order not to be troubled by "smatterers in the mathematics."

Men were by original nature equally rational and capable of acquiring property, Locke believed. Those who did not were deficient in some sense, like minors, lunatics, and the shiftless rabble. While all men *could* be illuminated by reason, they were not so in fact. In regulations he drafted for the control of the poor, the lazy, able-bodied ones were to be impressed into the navy, and begging minors were to be whipped. It would never have occurred to Newton to allow a voice in the polity to the clippers and coiners, the molls and the cheats—characters out of Gay's *Beggar's Opera* with whom he dealt as Master of the Mint. Nor would Locke tolerate as citizens the Catholic relic worshipers and the cardinals with mistresses and fine boys he saw in France and commented about in his private journal.

Locke's attitude toward property finds a parallel in Newton's feeling toward his great inventions. Newton's terror of deprivation, which had its origins in childhood traumas, was a psychological reality that in the course of his life was fortified by a Lockean sense of property in his inventions. In his historical fantasy Newton believed that there was a pristine body of knowledge in which the wise and learned of all ages participated, even as in Locke's thought God had originally endowed all men with access to common property. But ownership, mine and thine, was a matter of individual labor and appropriation. And intellectual appropriation involved toil, even as did the appropriation of land from the American wilderness. Newton had not merely propounded a loose hypothesis about gravitation as Robert Hooke had, but had done the actual work, had sweated through the proofs. Property belonged to those who came by it first, not later claimants. An invention belonged to the one who discovered it first; second finders of the calculus, like Leibniz, had no rights. And such second finders probably stole from other people's gardens.

Were I to use the language of Karl Marx to define the relationship of Locke's and Newton's philosophy to the establishment, I would say that for their historic moment they were true consciousness. They provided a magnificent, coordinated outlook for Whiggery *before* its political triumph in 1688. Were I to describe the relationship in psychological terms, I would say that they were geniuses who had foreknowledge, prevision, prescience, universal solutions which suited a type of ruling society that was coming into being. There is a fittingness between their personal life experience and the historical moment. In the privacy of their closets, they had been preparing the new spiritual framework while the old one was still standing. In this sense they were authentic philosophers because they came *before* the fruition of the event, unlike the owl of Minerva who flies at dusk. They conform to Marx's image of the philosopher, not Hegel's. Locke and Newton were the philosophical superstructure for the commercial classes who came to dominate England, but they were a superstructure that ante-dated the substructure, though not by long. Though they did not bring the substructure into being—I hold to no such one-way ideological causation—they were form-creators, and this is one meaning of their genius and their relationship to the polity.

It might be said that Locke and Newton laid the intellectual foundations of British smugness. For what did a maritime Protestant power need after their collective revelations? It is true that Locke did not realize his hope to demonstrate mathematically a system of morality; nor did Newton find a common element in all matter that would end the alchemical quest. But there was not much else left to be done by posterity. From Locke the British had at least the rhetoric with which to solve all conceivable moral problems, if not an impregnable set of consistent arguments, and a language of psychological motivation that made most overt human behavior comprehensible; from Newton, a system of the world that could only have epigoni for about two hundred years. All of this gave their compatriots a sense of assurance about God, man, and the universe that Locke and Newton may never have enjoyed themselves.

For it would be a distortion to identify Locke and Newton totally with the tone, the attitudes, or the mores of the establishment. They were independent men of genius, who cherished secret interests and beliefs that did not dovetail neatly, or even loosely, with the new regime. They serve the historical moment, but are not encompassed by it. The systems of Locke and Newton, while they could be used by their contemporaries, surely transcended them. An area in which they were truly alienated from the run of their political associates was religion. Their devotion was in no sense of the same order as that of their colleagues. Great intellectuals are always two-faced: they look backward and forward. Newton and Locke were profoundly religious men, and to a great extent their Irenic theology and intense. religious experiences remained beyond the reach of their contemporaries. They tried to observe Bacon's formula for the separation of religious and scientific concerns, but in practice found this untenable. When their discoveries were adapted by others to bolster religious faith they applauded, and when irreligious implications or consequences were drawn by their enemies from their intellectual positions, they reacted with sharp counterattacks. Newton had been wounded in many sensitive psychic areas by Leibniz' accusations, not the least telling of which was the charge that in the Newtonian system the power of the Creator was diminished. Newton responded by violating his own dicta on the separation of religion and science and appending to his scientific works queries and scholia that are impassioned professions of religious faith. Locke answered even the most boorish attacks on the *Essay Concerning Human Understanding* if they touched on his faith.

In matters of religion Locke and Newton often resorted to Aesopian language or sought the cover of anonymity. Members of the establishment were allowed to see only the surface of their religious faith. For one thing, their deep commitment to some form of Maimonidean unitarianism had to be concealed. By dissembling they found a place for themselves in a latitudinarian Anglican establishment and managed to live in peace under a religious statute that expressly excluded from toleration those who did not believe in the deity of Christ. In general they behaved like conformists. Locke took the sacraments in the Anglican Church when required by his office; Newton was carried to his grave by bishops as well as peers of the realm, and no one voiced doubt about his orthodoxy.

The popular philosophical triumph of Lockeanism and Newtonianism is another thing. The establishment could have true religion and science too; latitudinarian Anglicanism and a discreet measure of doubt about the deity of Christ; government by consent of the people and yet no interference from the rabble; a doctrine of absolute property sanctioned by the abstraction that labor was the special quality which made it a right, while the actual toilers, the day-laborers, were disenfranchised. The establishment could maintain an insular suspicion of Papists, atheists, and foreigners, all those who did not have the mental capacity to assimilate the foregoing august and righteous principles and their ambiguities. Finally, the establishment seemed justified by its national philosophers in preserving a comfortable, commonsensical distance from excess of passion, enthusiasm, and the aesthetic way of life. When William Blake at the turn of the eighteenth century declared war on Newton and Locke and the Romantics in his wake took off after the empirical philosophy, they knew whose fathers they were killing.

> Thus the terrible race of Los & Enitharmon gave
> Laws & Religions to the sons of Har binding them more
> And more to Earth: closing and restraining:
> Till a Philosophy of Five Senses was complete
> Urizen wept & gave it into the hands of Newton & Locke.[3]

NOTES

1. See, for instance, the work of James L. Axtell, Maurice Cranston, Kenneth Dewhurst, John Dunn, Peter Laslett, Wolfgang von Leyden, John Lough, Leo Strauss, John W. Yolton.
2. John Locke, *An Essay Concerning Human Understanding* (1690) (Chicago, 1956), p. 4.
3. William Blake, *The Song of Los* (1795), in *Poetry and Prose*, ed. David V. Erdman (New York, 1965), p. 66.

9

HENRI SAINT-SIMON ON THE ROLE OF THE SCIENTIST

It was reported by the eighteenth-century memoir writer Mathieu Marais that Saint-Simon's maternal grandmother, who engaged in strange chemical experiments to find the philosopher's stone and prepare medicines for the poor, had died asphyxiated in her laboratory with an assistant who was also her lover. Other accounts have described his parents in attendance at amateur chemical courses where the wonders of the new science were displayed to while away the hours of the bored aristocracy. Henri Saint-Simon's own technical training in science had probably not advanced far beyond that of his ancestors. He may have acquired an interest in engineering at the military school in Mézières, and he showed some practical knowledge of the art while he served as the Marquis de Bouillé's aide-de-camp during the Revolutionary War in America, but none of his writings betray more than an elementary or autodidact's knowledge of any science. Under the Directorate, when he was wealthy with the monies acquired through speculating in national properties, he settled down in Paris in the vicinity of the great schools and invited the famous scientists of the day to his table; he acted as a Maecenas to young geniuses like Poisson and Dupuytren, and he even established a free scientific institute. At most he achieved a smattering of science through osmosis.

But though he knew virtually no science, in all his writings he had a great deal to say about scientists and their unique role in modern society. In one of his autobiographical fragments he confessed that an understanding of the character of men of science was always his paramount interest in listening to their conversation. During the quarter century of his creative intellectual life, from 1802 to 1827, he adopted a wide variety of changing attitudes toward them, many of which were doubtless colored by the individual reactions of scientists and the dominant scientific schools to his person and his doctrine. Nonetheless his conception of the role of the scientist may be a fruitful vantage point from which to examine the whole body of his writings. It is one of the most persistent motifs recurring time and again with variations. The isolation of this theme and a treatment of its historical development in his works highlight the prescience of this bizarre genius.

The very first work Saint-Simon ever published, the anonymous and erratic letter *A la société du lycée* (1802), posed a momentous scientific question. What was the key to the historical progress of mathematics from the quantitative judgment of the first animals through Newton? Primitive man's mentality was not far above that of the animal directly beneath him on the scale of intelligence, and yet man had made such impressive strides in this science. Perhaps if the secret of the history of mathematics were unraveled, then the whole future of science would be within man's control, subject to acceleration at will. Nobody bothered to answer the great query since Saint-Simon was generally regarded as a scientific buffoon.

In the *Lettres d'un habitant de Genève à ses contemporains* Saint-Simon discussed the problem of the role of the scientist as the crux of the contemporary social disarray in France. His class analysis of the French Revolution and its aftermath, an essay whose originality Friedrich Engels admired and perhaps exaggerated defined the underlying development of the whole epoch

as a conflict between the propertied and the propertyless. A third
element in the struggle, the scientists, were a floating elite with
no natural class alignment. They were mobile and could be recruited to one or the other side of the dichotomic conflict.
Though numerically weak the scientists held the balance of power
and could therefore throw victory in the class war to the con-
testant they favored. In the French Revolution, Saint-Simon
maintained, the scientists had sided with the men without property and the consequence was upheaval, bloodshed, and chaos.
Actually it was to the interest of both hostile social classes to put
an end to the crisis of the times, but this could be achieved only
by neutralizing the political power of the scientists. Blandly Saint-
Simon advised both rivals that the best way to achieve this reasonable solution was to raise the scientists to the apex of the
social structure and to subordinate themselves to their rational
commands. If scientists organized the spiritual world, social conflicts would cease and men would attain terrestrial happiness.

The immediate intellectual origins of this conception are not
hard to identify. They derive from Condorcet, from Cabanis, and
from the *idéologues*, who prior to their fatal political miscalculation
in sponsoring Napoleon probably dreamed of such a hegemony of
science under the benign tutelage of a modern Marcus Aurelius.
Condorcet's view had been set forth in great detail in his commentary on the New Atlantis of Chancellor Bacon, and though
it was not published until 1804 the ideas were common enough
in the Cabanis circle. Saint-Simon went a step further than the
idéologues when he explicitly summoned all classes in world society to establish a new universal spiritual power in the form of
the scientific priesthood of the *Religion of Newton*. Aside from
the synthetic character of the ceremonials he proposed—rather
creaky contrivances after the manner of theophilanthropic cults—
his founding of the sacerdocy of science was based upon a number
of rationalist and historical considerations which were current
at the time: the widespread consensus that a people had to have
some religious beliefs and institutions in order to preserve order
and that even if atheism was an ideal for the elite there had to be
an exoteric religious doctrine for the mass of the people. The

theory of Charles Dupuis, propounded in his *Origine de tous les cultes*, that all ancient religions were really codifications of scientific knowledge was adapted by Saint-Simon for practical religious purposes. The new religion, which he at one point dubbed Physicism, was merely a modern application of respectworthy time-honored usages among mankind.

The rule of the priest-scientists would end the moral crisis of the age and would give impetus to a vast expansion of scientific knowledge. New scientists would become "positive" in an appropriate hierarchical succession from the less to the more complex, culminating in the science of man. As a consequence of the creation of this elite the men with the greatest energies and capacities would no longer pour their efforts into wars of destruction, but would become productive scientists, an idea which Condorcet had already suggested in one of his manuscript elaborations of the tenth epoch of his *Esquisse*. "No more honors for the Alexanders! Long live the Archimedes!" [1] was Saint-Simon's hortatory way of predicting this inevitable ideological metamorphosis. In the *Lettres* he naively expressed confidence that both social classes would not fail to subscribe to the fund rendering scientists absolutely independent of the temporal powers—the men of property in order to be reassured about what they were most interested in, possession of their property and freedom from revolution; the propertyless in order to be saved from becoming cannon-fodder in war.

Saint-Simon's attitude toward the scientists is sometimes an ambivalent one in the *Lettres*; he seems at moments to parallel Diderot's description of genius in *Le neveu de Rameau* (still unpublished at the time, of course). The scientist held the key to the salvation of mankind in his power of discovery and he should be supported and granted complete liberty for the development of his precious talents. Many passages bewail the lot of the neglected and impoverished young scientist in a romantic phraseology usually reserved in the early nineteenth century for the depiction of the sufferings of poetic genius. And yet Saint-Simon is equally aware of the destructive potential of the scientist, his demonic quality. The superhuman power of scientific genius must be harnessed for social peace and progress, is Saint-Simon's ominous warning to the propertied and the propertyless alike.

Once Saint-Simon fell into penury under the Empire, his bitter personal experiences with the official scientists of the Napoleonic hierarchy roused him to a frenzy of violence against them. In his paranoid state he fixed on Laplace and Bouvard of the Bureau of Longitudes as his arch-enemies, the men who were preventing the sublime truths of his *Introduction aux travaux scientifiques du xixe siècle* from being recognized. His conception of the scientist's role became more complicated. On the one hand he still held firm to the idea that the individual scientist was the seminal historical force, a thesis he demonstrated in numerous truncated *aperçus* on the history of world science; in fact, historical epochs were definable primarily in terms of their scientific geniuses. But almost simultaneously in his scattered unfinished works of the Empire he adumbrated a kind of scientific historical determinism. According to his formula the historical process of science, like all fundamental movements both physical and spiritual, required an alternativity of analysis and synthesis. Thus in the development of modern science the age of Descartes synthesized, Newton and Locke analyzed, and now a new synthesis was to follow; a synthesizing man of science had to arise. "Indeed, are the constitutions and conceptual power of men like Lagrange and Laplace inferior to those of Newton? I do not believe it at all. But I think that they are subject to a law of circumstances which has left them no other use for their powers than the improvements which we owe to them. At the end of the sixteenth century they would have been Bacons, at the beginning of the seventeenth Descartes, at the beginning of the eighteenth Lockes and Newtons; and if today these same men were no more than twenty I would vouch that before having finished half their careers they would alter the course of the School [of Science]." [2]

This scheme for the history of modern science was the rational kernel in his otherwise pathological attacks against the contemporary Napoleonic scientists. Instead of proceeding with the new synthesis, which was their historically ordained mission in accordance with the law of alternativity that he had propounded, the school scientists were continuing to act like *epigoni* of eighteenth-century science and were becoming mere particularizers, detailists. "You gentlemen are anarchist scientists. You deny the existence, the supremacy of the general theory," he charged in a series of violent letters.[3] The great Napoleon had summoned them for a report on the needs and mission of science, and they continued to conduct their individual experiments oblivious to historic duty, in fact in open defiance of the true destiny of nineteenth-century science. They were thus at once traitors to science, to history, and to Napoleon. The science of the nineteenth century had to develop a unified plan, to construct a new view of the world, to oust old-fashioned religion and purge education of residual elements of superstition. Scientists had to cooperate and join in the production of a new encyclopedia based upon a principle of synthesis that would replace Diderot's merely destructive encyclopedia. They had to fit their individual studies into an organic whole and then to crown their labors with social physiology, the newest of the sciences in which was hidden the secret of man's salvation. Instead, scientists were piddling away their time egotistically on their own petty, disordered experiments. "The philosophy of the eighteenth century was critical and revolutionary, that of the nineteenth will be inventive and organizational," was the motto of his new encyclopedia.[4] Saint-Simon knew that the synthesis of the coming century would have to have a single principle and he divined *a priori* that the principle would be Newton's law of gravitation, an idea which was by no means limited to physics but could be extended to chemistry, physiology, and the science of man. What he desperately needed was the aid, the collaboration of technicians and other scientists —the men who spurned him. This fixation upon an interpretation of Newton's laws of motion as the clue to the human sciences was not unique with Saint-Simon. After all, that rival genius who wrote his first important work precisely in the same year 1808, Charles Fourier, had independently discovered the application to the social world of Newton's laws in the *Théorie des quatre mouvements*.

During the period of Saint-Simon's gravest psychic crisis, in 1812-1813, when the slaughter in Europe was at its height, his rage against the indifference of the scientists mounted to a frenetic violence. At first he distinguished between the mathematical and the life scientists. He had quickly become disillusioned with the *brutiers*, for unlike Condorcet he saw no prospect for the solution of the social problems of mankind through the application of the calculus of probabilities. Many fragments directed against the mathematical and physical scientists hiding behind their "ramparts of X and Y," coldly indifferent to the fate of man, serving in the destructive corps of all the armies of the continent, have a contemporary poignancy. With sarcastic contempt Saint-Simon ordered the inhuman *brutiers* from the height of the scientific eminence. He demoted them in esteem. For a while the only hope lay in the biologists, physiologists, and social scientists. A Dr. Burdin, a surgeon in the armies of the Revolution, had once told him that the new science would be born when someone synthesized the writings of Vicq-d'Azyr, Cabanis, Bichat, and Condorcet, and Saint-Simon long clung to this expectation as the hope of Europe. But there were times when even the life scientists seemed to have been engulfed in the general chaos. In his madness he cried out for the creation of a scientific Papacy, for the summoning of great international councils of science to save mankind. And the official scientists did not deign to cut the pages of the writings addressed to them.

Saint-Simon's recuperation from his breakdown coincided strangely with the end of the Napoleonic wars and the respite of Europe. When he emerged into the light his attitude toward the scientists underwent a drastic change. In the early years of the Restoration, as he gave ever greater prominence to the organizing role of the *industriels* in society, the scientist lost status by comparison. There are a number of different versions of his shifting sociological approach, but they all have this in common, a uniform devaluation of the role of the scientist in society. At times he thought of an ideal duumvirate, with more or less equivalent status for scientists and industrialists, the one representing the spiritual, the other the temporal power. He refashioned his whole philosophy of modern history along the lines of a novel pattern: the replacement over the centuries of the medieval priestly and military ruling classes by the scientists and the bourgeois. This historical conceptualization had many dialectical turns of thought: the new scientific elite did not succeed the old priesthood in a mechanical manner; in the very bosom of the medieval sacerdotal class the modern scientists occupied strategic positions from which they were able to carry on their destructive warfare against religion.

But despite this rather traditional dualism in which the scientists seem to represent a growing independent spiritual force, in the early Restoration writings Saint-Simon tended more and more to subordinate them to the *industriels*. Sometimes he tried to use old projects, like his encyclopedia, as a device for the forging of a common militant consciousness between the scientists and the *industriels*, but on many occasions he forthrightly proclaimed that it would be best for society as a whole if the *industriels* would in the last analysis become the final judges of the worth of what the scientists accomplished. When he was most deeply under the influence of the French liberal economists such as Dunoyer and Jean-Baptiste Say, he found no objection to considering the achievements of the scientists as mere commodities whose worth was to be estimated by the *industriels* in terms of their practical needs and desires. His disappointment with the official scientists was so profound that he could no longer conceive of them as playing a role of primacy in society. They were not heroic leaders, but mere followers. Most of them lived on sinecures and emoluments from the state and it was too much to expect of them any overt opposition to the retrograde Bourbon aristocracy. They were timid and pusillanimous. Their intellectual achievements were substantial—and they were not to be classed with useless bureaucrats, generals, and priests—but often as not Saint-Simon came to see them as underlings. In some writings he grouped them along with other useful persons such as entrepreneurs and workers under the general rubric *industriels*, which came to be an overall category of productive people in every conceivable occupation, contrasted with the *fainéants*, the do-nothings.

Unfortunately for his material well-being, try as he might Saint-Simon could not long rest content with his limited role as a moderately successful propagandist for the bourgeois. As soon as he broke loose and propounded the crucial need for a terrestrial morality in *L'Industrie*, he was thrown back into the problem of the competitive roles of the scientists and the priests. One of his solutions, during the period when he was still eager to retain the financial support of his non-revolutionary Restoration business-men, was to propose a transitional stage for society during which the priests of the old religion would be taught more and more science in the seminaries, so that those who in fact controlled education would thus promote the ideology of science while still wearing clerical garb. To avoid the horror of revolution and the evils of precipitous change, Saint-Simon would advise the priests to become scientists—or he would have the Papacy order them to do so. Existing conditions in the spiritual world of the Restoration were morally intolerable because the great learned organizations were in the hands of scientists, while the educational system was still under the control of priests who knew no science, a fatal division that resulted in chaos. Perhaps if the priesthood could be converted to science no class revolution in the spiritual realm might even be necessary since a mere transition would suffice. Of one thing Saint-Simon was certain: the scientific ideas of the elite of savants were penetrating all elements of the population, even the lowest classes, and the ultimate expunging of existing ortho-dox religious ideas was inevitable.

In the final stages of Saint-Simon's doctrinal development, roughly after 1822, the scientists had to share their elite position not only with the administrative directors of society, but with a third ruling group, the moralist leaders of the New Christianity. Religious and scientific functions were conceived of as distinct, requiring different capacities. This was the period when Saint-Simon realized the full social implications of an idea which he had first discovered in the writings of the physiologist Bichat. There he found a separation of all men into three natural classes, psycho-physiological types so to speak, in each of which one quality pre-dominated—the motor, the rational, or the emotive. During his last years Saint-Simon adopted this triadic division as the ideal social structuring of human beings in the good society of the future, as contrasted with the existing unnatural roles into which men were cast by the status of their birth and by haphazard. In the new world of Saint-Simon men would engage in motor activity either as administrators or workers, in pure rational research as scientists, or as moralizers and inspirers of mankind by appealing to human emotions through preaching and the arts. Since under this "industrial system" each man would be fulfilling his natural capacity to the utmost, there would be no misfits and no class conflicts. Each "capacity" would labor in its respective branch and would evince no desire to encroach upon the province of another. Perfect harmony would prevail, the power state would disappear, and men would be directed to the exploitation of nature instead of exercising dominion over one another. While Saint-Simon tended to conceive of the three capacities of acting, thinking, and feeling as mutually exclusive of each other, he did make exceptions; in one of his works he even had a prophetic insight into the future central role of the engineer in the industrial system. In Saint-Simon's classificatory order the engineer combined the characteristics of both the administrator and the scientist, and he could therefore serve as an ideal intermediary in the implementation of the grandiose projects of the new society. A substantial portion of Saint-Simon's writing in his final years was devoted to the drafting of blueprints for the administrative organization of the future world. Their detail is often tedious and obsessive, but they have one constant element: all organs of administration—he eschewed the term government—were so arranged that each of the three fundamental natural classes was always represented in what he called the "high administration of society" in the fulfillment of its special capacities. As a rule, under the new division of labor the emotive or moralist branch tended to initiate projects, the scientific to criticize and evaluate them, and the administrators to execute them. In these ideal constitutions the scientist was thus cast in a rather uncreative, rationalistic role; he was more often the emendator than the original inventor. The scientist seemed to represent the analytic spirit more and

more, as Saint-Simon came to appreciate the originality of the
poet and the moralist above the talent of the scientist. In principle the three capacities outlined by Bichat were equal in worth,
but if the spirit rather than the letter of Saint-Simon's latter-day
writings is considered, the scientist has somehow become the least
preferred of the three brothers, and the religious leader who taught
men to love one another was awarded ever greater prestige. The
cynic of the Directorate was on the way to becoming a Saint-
Simonian.

It was probably over the respective role of the three elites
of the good society that the relationship between Saint-Simon
and Auguste Comte foundered—this at least was the intellectual
dispute which aggravated a host of personal differences. In a famous preface to Comte's brilliant youthful essay entitled *Système
de politique positive,* Saint-Simon accused the disciple from whom
he was becoming alienated of favoring the Aristotelian capacity,
their private language for the scientist, over the Platonic, by which
they meant the poet-moralist. Comte denied the accusation, insisting upon equality among the elements of the triumvirate. In private letters Comte at one point went much further in his criticism
of Père Simon, accusing him of a plan to make all members of
society, including the scientists, mere lackeys of the bourgeois.
The issue was not merely academic, for it involved the question
of where the main effort of a reformer's activity should be directed. Paradoxically enough, the Auguste Comte of the *Cours de
philosophie positive,* with its emphasis upon the primary necessity
of consolidating an overall theory of science—by implication the
world of affairs was subordinate—was reverting to Saint-Simon's
position under the Empire, when scientific system was the overriding preoccupation, and only in the end of the days when he
proclaimed the Religion of Humanity did Comte, as if recapitulat-
ing the life of his master, assume the moralist position of Saint-
Simon's last work, the *Nouveau Christianisme.*

The final article in a collection Saint-Simon published in
Paris in 1825, the *Opinions littéraires, philosophiques et industrielles,* was a discussion among representatives of the triumvirate
who were destined to direct the future society entitled *L'Artiste,*

le savant et l'industriel. The mission of his profession set forth by the scientist was precise: it was another plea for a general theory to encompass all the sciences rather than allow each of the sciences separately and in isolation to achieve a high degree of abstraction; but there was also a new emphasis in this work upon the relations of theoretical science to "practice." As a consequence of the new social philanthropic tendency of his lifework he insisted upon a reorganization of both science and education for practical purposes, which meant the speedy increase of the production of goods. The scientist's utilitarian and even "proletarian" goals were set forth with simple frankness. "What are the general applications of mechanics and of all the other sciences by means of which the most numerous class of producers will be able to increase its comforts and diminish its physical exertions, with the result that the price of human muscular labor will rise in direct relationship with the perfection of scientific processes. In a word scientists will undertake a series of works directly intended to perfect industrial arts." [5] While the scientists as a corps retain their dignity they are forced out of their isolation—pure theory in any particular science is thrust aside—and all their works are specifically applied to the needs of technology which alone is able to bestow a new worth upon the manual laborer. According to this dialogue it is the function of the artist, the man of imagination, to inspire mankind with the desire to see this industrial-scientific union put into practice as soon as possible. The "great trinity" [6] can direct mankind to happiness by the subordination of all political power to their administrative leadership. In the *Nouveau Christianisme*, his last testament, these ideas received their final formulation: all men belonged to the "classe des travailleurs" whose "natural chiefs" were artists, scientists, and the heads of industrial operations. Their common goal was the rapid increase of the social happiness of the poorest and most numerous classes.

As for the general method and spirit of science in the world of the future, Saint-Simon brought up to date his theory of a scientific *Zeitgeist* to which individual practitioners had to subordinate themselves on the pain of being useless. In a brief though provocative schematization of the history of thought which Saint-

Simon introduced into the *Nouveau Christianisme*, he defined the middle ages as an epoch devoted to generality, the period from Luther to the nineteenth century as an age immersed in particularity, and then announced that mankind stood on the threshold of a new society in which men would be capable of both generality and particularity at the same time. The passage is too crude to be identified with a "higher synthesis," but its parallel to Hegel should not be entirely overlooked.[7]

Two hundred years after Saint-Simon's birth his system of natural classes based upon capabilities seems to be acquiring more realistic significance than it enjoyed during the intervening period. Relations between scientists and administrators are now among the crucial internal problems of organization of the more complex civilizations, whatever their economic systems may be. The third element in the Saint-Simonian triad hardly seems to have held its own with the other two. Neither has Saint-Simon's conception of the mutual exclusivity of the three capacities been borne out by time. If few administrators have awakened to discover themselves endowed with rare scientific talents, the scientists, at least in the American economy, have been constrained to accept administrative responsibilities of a complexity never dreamed of before. The subordination of science to technology, military and civilian, is now taken for granted despite an undertone of protest in the name of pure science. Science is now controlled, directed, and administered by scientists themselves and by bureaucrats to a degree inconceivable in Condorcet's and Saint-Simon's wildest imaginings. The "anarchist scientists" have given way to the totally organized scientists, with results yet unforeseeable in productivity or, who knows, perhaps in sterility.

NOTES

1. *Lettres d'un habitant de Genève*, in *Oeuvres de Saint-Simon et d'Enfantin* (Paris, 1865-1878), XV, p. 22.
2. *Oeuvres choisies* (Brussels, 1859), I, p. 141.

3. *Lettres de C.-H. de Saint-Simon, Première correspondance* (Paris, 1808), p. 74.
4. *Esquisse d'une nouvelle encyclopédie* (Paris, n.d.), p. 5.
5. *Opinions littéraires, philosophiques et industrielles* (Paris, 1825), pp. 374-375.
6. *Ibid.*, p. 392.
7. *Nouveau Christianisme,* in *Oeuvres,* XXIII, pp. 184-185.

REFLECTIVE HISTORY

IO

FROM EQUALITY
TO ORGANICISM

One of the crucial developments in modern intellectual history is the reversal from the eighteenth-century view of men as more or less equal, or at least similar, in nature and hence in rights, to the early nineteenth-century emphasis upon human uniqueness, diversity, dissimilarity, culminating in theories of inequality and organicism. The transition can be traced in representative French thinkers from Rousseau and Helvétius and Condorcet through Cabanis, Bichat, de Bonald, and Saint-Simon, punctuating the novel elements introduced into the general climate of opinion.

The majority of eighteenth-century moralists derived from the Lockean postulate that differences among mature men as they were observable in society were the direct consequence of early education and the play of individual circumstances and experiences. While conceding that gross physical defects at birth might account for cases of monstrous intellectual deformity, it was an article of faith that, apart from such exceptions, all men were born free and equal and were molded into somewhat different shapes by their environment. The very posing of the question by the Dijon Academy in 1753—"What is the origin of inequality among men, and is it authorized by natural law?"—which Rousseau answered with his thunderous discourse, implied that inequality was a phenomenon in the history of man which had to justify itself and had to be explained. Though Rousseau's brief commentary on natural and unnatural inequalities, like many of his theses, could be developed in a number of contrary directions, the moral drawn by contemporaries from the total work was clear and simple: men were once equal in the state of nature and they could be at least semblances of real men in their unfortunate present social state only insofar as they remained more or less equal. Otherwise they became slaves and corrupt lackeys. This was the way revolutionaries read his writing and in this form its message was embodied in the great American and French political documents.

The eighteenth-century theorists were almost unanimous in their acceptance of the psychological principle that all men were equal in their natural faculties, hence in their capacity to receive impressions of the external world; and if they were given identical educations they would all have the same rational concepts.[1] Essentially the capacity to receive impressions was, had been, and was likely to be the same at all times and in all places among all men.

On the problem of whether men were really identical—not merely similar—in the strength of their organs, the French followers of Locke, such as Helvétius and Condillac, came pretty close to a theory of absolute equivalence at birth, while Rousseau's distinction between natural and unnatural inequalities early in the *Second Discourse* seemed to imply a contradictory theory, that there were substantial natural inequalities, based on health, bodily strength, and powers of the intellect and the soul.[2] However, the overall reading of the *Discourse* makes it abundantly evident that even the natural inequalities are natural and significant only in the present civilized state of society. In the early scenes of the idyllic state of nature the primitive savages were not remarkably distinguished from one another in physical or mental prowess; the natural differences so striking in society were really the consequences of the corruption and decadence of a substantial portion of the human species under the vicious influences of the societal state. The process of civilization, in other words, had by now introduced inequalities at birth which originally, in the state of nature, were not there—or at least were minimal. It is difficult to discern natural inequalities among Rousseau's torpid savages who wake from time to time to eat an acorn or copulate with a woman. Thus in Rousseau one can distinguish few if any natural inequalities in the state of nature; these increase in number in the state of civilization; and soon even they are overwhelmed by the flood of inequalities which he designated as unnatural, primarily inequalities of wealth and status and power. *La Nouvelle Héloïse* was the century's most passionate plea for the right of all men to love, and the *Contrat Social*, whatever germs of absolutism recent critics have discovered in its pages, was in its day a proclamation of the principle of equality in the social state.

All *philosophes* were agreed in allowing men equality of natural civil rights, though they might differ about their precise definition. Few *philosophes* went so far as to posit equality in wealth and property as a natural and necessary form of equality. While Morelly, Brissot de Warville, and a minority of radicals did adopt the extreme view that since property did not exist in the state of nature, it was theft and had to be abolished in society,[3] the overwhelming body of opinion took the position that the maintenance of civilization required the preservation of inequalities of wealth and perhaps even of social status in order to make man who was by nature indolent submit to the discomforts of work. This was Voltaire's viewpoint in his paradoxical article on equality in the *Dictionnaire philosophique*; and this was the attitude of the economists who wrote about the new laws of true political economy. Even Voltaire, however, who was no sufferer of the pretensions of cooks and lackeys, held to the theory that "all men are equal in the possession of their natural faculties" and agreed that inequalities of wealth had probably been exaggerated in contemporary society.[4]

Condorcet made the establishment and preservation of "absolute equality," by which he meant equality in law, the heart of

his *Déclaration des Droits* pamphlet published in 1789;[5] moreover, he was fully aware that his constitution might ultimately
result in juridical "inequality in fact" unless society instituted
measures to render men more or less equal in other respects. This
is the dominant spirit of his final testament. The *Esquisse d'un
tableau historique des progrès de l'esprit humain,* in which the
ideology of the French eighteenth century found its climactic
expression, exalted equality as the primary aspiration of the human
spirit, a goal to which mankind was inevitably progressing. Though
absolute equality might never be attained, the essence of progress
was the movement toward a social state in which all nations on
earth and all individuals within these nations approached as near
as possible to a status of equality, material, moral, and intellectual.[6]
If the universal "social art" properly fulfilled its function, all men
would really become capable of enjoying a more or less equivalent
level of prosperity, for there was no basis in nature for such
extreme variations of man's estate as the condition of barbarism,
of a colonial master's opulence, and of the pauperized lower
classes of European civilized society.

The unique quality of genius and the problem of his role
in society was perhaps the one disturbing element in the calm
of this egalitarian conception. Condorcet and other *philosophes*
before him had indeed wrestled with that anomalous—to Diderot
almost demoniac—character who gave impetus to the progress of
the whole species. Like the deformed monster at the other end
of the scale, genius was a flagrant violation of the idea of natural
equality. And yet the future ascendancy of man depended so
heavily upon him, upon his creativity, his discoveries. In his
commentary on Bacon's *New Atlantis,* Condorcet solved the
dilemma of genius by placing the whole of society under the
direction of the preeminent scientists.[7] Since the key to universal
happiness lay in the cumulative discovery of scientific laws, laws
of human behavior as well as laws of nature, the exceptional
gifts of the scientist-genius had to be nurtured and his position
of absolute independence safeguarded. Beneath the scientists who
were philosopher-kings all others were about equal.

Despite the apotheosis of the scientists, general equality of the human condition persists as the ultimate social end, for the new inventions and the new social laws, created by the scientists and embodied in legislation, tend to eradicate the twin plagues of misery and ignorance, universalizing rational behavior, drawing the whole of mankind up the mountain, ever closer behind the vanguard of scientists who are eternally forging ahead. In each succeeding generation, as the mass of mankind approach nearer to equality with one another, they are simultaneously raised from one plateau of scientific and moral excellence to another. This is the true progress of the human spirit: the virtual achievement of that equality in rationality of which men are capable. But however pervasive the egalitarian ideal, the final reflection is inescapable that the dramatic recognition of the natural superiority of genius does leave the portals open for the antinomic idea of inequality and the construction of an elitist theory.

While the Declaration of the Rights of Man did not adopt a philosophical position on the nature of human equality and explicitly limited itself to the pronouncement that "Men are born and always continue free and equal *in respect of their rights*" [italics mine], loudly trumpeted egalitarian slogans became a vital, intrinsic part of the revolutionary myth. As the Revolution progressed many variations on the theme of natural equality were sounded. The most notorious, perhaps, was Babeuf, who in the name of Rousseau proclaimed in his Manifesto that men had to be equal in property even as they were equal in the natural enjoyment of the sun in order to be truly free. Among the *enragés* and the lunatic fringe of Jacobinism, equality in the possession of women was included on occasion in a latitudinarian interpretation of the natural rights doctrine founded upon an affirmation of man's polygamous nature.

However sharp the divergences in tone and temper, extremists and sober citizens alike defined the issue in the same terms—how equal were men by nature and how equal should they be in society—and always resolved it in the general direction of equality. For all the justifications of wealth and *bourgeois* declamations against the sloth of the *canaille*, there was a widespread consciousness at the height of the Revolution that men were interchangeable in most of their social roles. Property restrictions excluded some men from the status of active citizens even after the abolition of all other distinctions of class and occupation, but all men were capable of attaining that status by the acquisition of a minimal amount of property. Uniform costumes and uniform laws were imposed by the Revolution, enduring symbols of equality. The new political society offered equality of civil rights and through its educational system it was opening up the avenues of equality of opportunity. The Spartan ideal of continence made conspicuous display of wealth suspect. True Jacobins were in fact becoming more or less equal in dress, in consumption, in devotion and service to the state.

Strangely enough, the *volte-face* from an emphasis on man's potential, if not actual, equality, both of knowledge and of condition, to the acceptance of human inequality as the cornerstone of the good society was executed in the very heat of the revolutionary turmoil.

A cogent expression of the idea of inequality can be found in a passage of a National Assembly committee report, prepared by Talleyrand, in which an analogy is drawn between a well-organized state and a great national workshop.[8] The image, which he could well have derived from any number of economists of the seventeenth and the eighteenth centuries, was doubtless nourished by the realities of English and French industrialization. The novelty lies in its incorporation into a government report on education. Men are born with a variety of different faculties, Talleyrand asserted—the Lockean concept is banished—and these diverse faculties lie dormant until the national system of education comes along and arouses them. A wise educational system takes cognizance of the differences among men and fosters the development of special faculties. The real secret of the social art is the placement of individual men in the most appropriate positions in the national workshop in accordance with their native talents.[9] The analogy of the workshop, which presumes acceptance of the Smithian idea of the division of labor, involved a new emphasis on the dissimilarities among individual men and on their natural inequalities, which it became salutary to preserve.

Within a few years after the publication of Talleyrand's report with its stress on the creation of schools and institutes for the education of specialists in all branches of knowledge, the *idéologue* scientists who took possession of French thought under the Directorate drew attention to another aspect of inequality, the broad physiological and psychological divergences among men. Their ultimate goal remained the egalitarian society unveiled by Condorcet, but the new medicine was leading the *idéologues* to momentous philosophical conclusions about the nature of man. The intellectual revolution was generated not so much by the discovery of hitherto unknown scientific data as by a new interpretation of empirical facts which doctors and life scientists had been accumulating over the century.

In the Years IV and V Doctor Cabanis read before the Class of Moral and Political Sciences of the Institute a series of papers on the interconnections between man's physical and moral being, in the course of which he developed a complete typology of character, as well as a series of generalizations on how men were affected by sexual differences, age, temperament, states of morbidity, regimen, and climate. He concluded that even rational men did not behave the same way at all stages of life, that their minds showed not minor but substantial differences in performance when assailed by crisis in their sexual nature, by illness, by senescence. Different men seemed to react differently to crucial transformations in human nature during the course of the life cycle. The emphasis throughout was on the physiological and psychological variations among men, not their similarities, which the legislator would have to take into consideration.[10] Cabanis here modified the sensationalism of Locke, Helvétius, and Condillac at its very source, their presupposition that in general all human beings received identical impressions from nature. This simply was not in accord with his experience, the Doctor found. The differences in sensory perception among men were greater than their similarities and gave rise to "different turns of mind and soul."[11] The subject of inquiry was not a Condillac statue which was endowed with the capacity to feel, but men living in different climates, men with different native temperaments, obeying different patterns of conduct, men subject to the exigencies of sexual change, age, and sickness. There was no "type common to the whole human species."

The doctors whom Cabanis quoted were dwelling upon the fact that men were born physiologically unequal, that the organs of their patients were far from being equally strong, that different patients reacted in diverse ways to the same doses of drug. The scientific study of pathological conditions of the body and Pinel's pioneer inquiries into the nature of madness, free from religious prejudice, were revealing wide disparities in human reactivity and capacity. Cabanis' psychology, anchored in the accumulation of physiological data and medical experience, cast a powerful light upon the dissimilarities among men and broke with the philosophical psychology of Helvétius and Condillac which in the previous generation had served as "scientific" underpinnings for the doctrine of equality.[12]

Since the Condorcet ideal of equality was still dominant, his friend Cabanis was studying human distinctions with the lodestar of a perfected man before his mind's eye. The purpose of medicine as he conceived it was not restricted to curing individual ailments; its higher objective was the perfection of the species.[13] The study of natural human frailties or inferiorities should lead to their elimination through time, a feasible prospect since he firmly believed that acquired characteristics were inherited.[14] Cabanis still had an eighteenth-century faith in the extraordinary malleability of human nature and his aim in focusing upon congenital and environmental differences was not to utilize distinctions as Talleyrand wished but to narrow their range. He studied human pathology in order to make men equally healthy and rational and he trusted in the power of science to achieve the general perfection of the human species. Nonetheless, *idéologue* psychology was turning sharply away from Master Locke when it took to studying distinctions—it was a momentous departure.

The same interest in the investigation of disparities was reinforced by numerous lesser eighteenth- and early nineteenth-century researches in physiognomy and phrenology, divergent as were the hypotheses of a Lavater[15] and a Gall.[16] Men were distinct from one another and their differences were written on their faces or in the convolutions of their brains. The mystical and astrological elements which sometimes were intermingled with these character studies only served to widen the breach between them and the common sense interpretation of human differences upon which Helvétius had insisted to the rigid exclusion of occult influences and vague concepts such as humors and tempers.

A key figure expressive of the new scientific attitude toward human nature was the physiologist Bichat, whose works were known throughout the civilized world at the turn of the century. In his *Physiological Researches upon Life and Death* he divided men into three physiological categories. While such classifications had been made often enough before in antiquity and in early modern times on the basis of dominant humors and temperaments, the importance of Bichat lies in the fact that his writings were picked up and read by one of the seminal social theorists of the age, Henri de Saint-Simon. And it was in the form expounded by Bichat that the physiological doctrine of inequality first penetrated social theory and became part of a new general conception of the nature of man and society.

Bichat distinguished among three major types—a trinary division has always communicated itself most readily in western society—a brain man, a sensory man, and a motor man. In each type one particular dominant faculty was capable of great development, while the other two were destined to remain feeble.[17] Bichat's vitalist theory allowed for only a given quantum of energy in each individual; and no man, with the rarest of exceptions, could develop all three major faculties to an equivalent degree. Physiologically men were born limited and restricted— either brain, or sensory, or motor—and vital energy invariably tended to channel itself into one receptacle rather than the two others.[18]

The consequences of this theory for education and human progress, if accepted as a new definition of human nature, are manifold. Cabanis had still concentrated upon the flexibility and easy educability of any human trait through laws and medicine; Bichat's iron law of physiology dictated that only one of the

major capacities could and should be trained. It was the responsibility of society to identify a man's major faculty and to develop
it to the uttermost limits of his capacity, to the neglence of the
other two faculties, since it was futile to attempt to fashion what
was not by nature educable. Perfectibility lay not in an identical
Spartan education for all men, but in the stimulation of uniqueness, in specialization. This led to the conception of an organic
society based upon differentiated functions.

The physiological theory of inequality merged at the turn
of the century with elements which for want of a better term
one must still call Romantic—the new emphasis on the "genesis"
of national character as revealed by Herder, the new image of
the unique personality as drawn by Goethe and Sénancour, the
general climate of opinion that fostered a new sensibility for
diversity and plenitude rather than universality and oneness.

The Romantic spirit became so all-pervasive that it is point-
less to relate its diffusion to individual poets or philosophers. It
discovered a new man with a complexity, with expansive dimensions, that the popular theorists of the previous generation had
not dreamed of. Man was capable of an acuteness, a variety of
sensations, and an extravagance of behavior that the rationalist
egalitarians of the eighteenth century would have curtly dismissed
as an aberration of nature. Men can have equality in reason, particularly if, as with Turgot and Condorcet, there lies ahead the
prospect of a complete mathematicization of all knowledge; but
if the floodgates of emotion are opened and men become religious
mystics, poet-seers, if they delve into the lower depths of their
bestiality and ascend the heights of the ethereal, if they roam
the world in search of new feeling in exotic lands, if they resurrect
all past history to find new colors and forms of expression, the
abstraction of virtuous men behaving in more or less similar fashion
in accordance with the dictates of their equivalent, enlightened
natures becomes a lifeless scarecrow. Romanticism cannot abide
the *philosophe*'s image of egalitarianism either as a description
of man's inner nature or as a future ideal. The early identification
of the Romantic poets with the philosophical theocratic reaction

was not fortuitous—they had a common abhorrence for the *phil-osophe*'s man of universal, facile reason, so self-evident and so readily accessible to all in equal portions. The eighteenth-century *philosophe* turned his head away from the monster with repugnance; Romanticism made him its hero. The idea of natural equality could not survive in a Romantic world of convulsion and prodigy.

The impact of the French Revolution upon the philosophical minds of Europe is the most potent political factor in the repudiation of the concept of equality. It was not necessary that the Revolution become a personal trauma, as it was for men like Saint-Simon and Fourier (both imprisoned by the Jacobins) and for the *émigrés*, to make men recoil with revulsion and fear before the bloody deeds of the Terror. The identification of the chaos and sheer destructiveness of the Revolution with the ideology of the *philosophes* had been made by Edmund Burke in the early years of the Revolution and his thesis had swept the continent. Egalitarianism had been a central proposition in the armory of the "literary cabal"; the revolutionaries had paraded *Egalité* upon their banners, the *enragés* among the *sans-culottes* had propounded doctrines and suggested conduct in the name of equality that profoundly shocked the sensibilities of Christian Europe. Equality was an explosive idea that had inflamed the Paris mobs with a violent passion and had implanted illusory hopes in the breasts of "ignorant proletarians." Equality had brought European society to the brink of annihilation. To consider the idea of equality—however it was interpreted—as a dangerous heresy was the instinctive reaction of the conservative thinkers of the continent, and its extirpation became a spiritual necessity for anti-revolutionary theorists of every stripe. Burke's invective against the leveling spirit had sounded the clarion call to battle against the "barbarous philosophy" of the equals. In 1793 when Necker in exile sat down to contemplate the meaning of the Revolution, in which he had been a major actor, one of his first projects was the writing of *Réflexions philosophiques sur l'Egalité*.[19] If man wished to associate himself with the spirit of the Divine Creation, he had to mirror in the social order he established the diversities of the natural order. "Inequalities in a state of harmony, that is the rule of the universe." [20]

The concept of inequality as translated into political-religious terms by a group of traditionalists, foremost among them de Bonald and de Maistre, was a major new intellectual force in European thought. They created the image of an anthropomorphic medieval society as the last good society, in contrast with the conflict-ridden, atomistic, egalitarian eighteenth-century world whose bloody climax was the Terror. They revalued status, the virtues of the nobility, the corporations, and the jurands, and they conceived of the social order as an organic unity. These men were polemicists of stature and they knew how to excoriate the preachers of equality with a vehemence, a subtlety, and a philosophic universality that no Christian apologist had achieved in more than a century. The theocratic school was less absorbed in attacking the scientific validity of the idea of natural equality than in contrasting this "sterile" political conception with the Christian moral rules of behavior imposed upon one man in his relations with his "neighbor," his "fellow-man," his "likeness." De Bonald stripped the idea of equality of that sense of human dignity which it had acquired among the *philosophes* and revealed it as a naked political relationship in contradiction to the Christian commandment of brotherly love.[21]

But while the spirit of the counter-revolution gave forceful impetus to the anti-egalitarian onslaught, enemies of the abstract principle of equality had also sprung up in quarters that were far from hostile to the regime in France after Thermidor. Paradoxically enough, in the weakening of the ideal of equality there was a confluence of pressure from opposite directions, both from the atheistic doctors of the Institute—the *idéologue* scientists who were the official philosophers of the state until they were ousted by Napoleon—and from the *émigré* theocrats.

Henri de Saint-Simon was influenced by all these waves of doctrine, perhaps most of all by Condorcet, Cabanis, Bichat, and the Traditionalists—an odd assortment of antecedents for his organismic view of society rooted in the concept of natural inequalities. In Saint-Simon's doctrine the scientific elite of Condorcet, the findings of the new physiology of Bichat, the new psychology of Cabanis coalesced with an appreciation of the organic social order of the theocrats.

Saint-Simon has one underlying preconception which is identical with the outlook of the philosophical egalitarians, the conviction that the ideal forms of the good society must be congruent with what is natural in man. From a cursory reading of the physiologists, however, Saint-Simon came away with a different version of the natural: the natural was inequality. He inveighed against philosophism for its ignorance of the simple physiological facts, positive scientific facts, which had since been set forth by Cabanis and Bichat. Confirmed in the belief that physiology was the only sound foundation upon which to construct a social theory, after numerous experiments with variant schema of social classification in the final phase of his thinking he devised a plan that was a direct adaptation of the Bichat typology.[22] There were three social functions and three mutually exclusive social classes, which corresponded to the physiologist's three human types.[23] First, society needed scientists to discover positive laws, which in turn could be translated into guides for social action. This scientific capacity—the brain type—which he sometimes called the Aristotelian capacity, if given free play would fulfill the mission that Condorcet had proposed for the leading scientific intellects. Bichat's motor capacity was transformed by Saint-Simon into the industrial class. In his latter days the term *"industriels"* was used to cover all men in whatever station in life who were engaged in production of material artifacts and their exchange. In the same category he bracketed a whole range of individuals from the director of a great industrial enterprise to its humblest manual laborer. Most of mankind, whose primary aptitude was the motor capacity, were destined to remain manual laborers, though a small elite of this class with essentially the same kind of talent would become the administrators of the temporal affairs of society—the men who organized states and directed public works and engineered vast projects for the exploitation of nature. Saint-Simon's third class, which corresponded to Bichat's sensory man, were the artists, poets, religious leaders, ethical teachers, whom he sometimes identified with the Platonic capacity. In the last years of his life, when he emphasized the religious character of his doctrine, he endowed the sensory aptitude with special worth since he considered it capable of overcoming the atomist, egotist, egalitarian propensities of the contemporary world in crisis. The men of sentiment would give the new industrial society its quality and cohesive humanitarian spirit.

The good society thus represented a harmonious association or cooperation of men fundamentally dissimilar in their most essential natures, organized in three natural classes. Together they embodied the total needs of mankind—rational scientific, manual administrative, sensory religious. The eighteenth-century *philosophes*, even when they admitted human inequalities, had still insisted upon organizing the state and society around those elements that men had in common, their natural equalities and relatively equal capacity for governance and the holding of public office. Saint-Simon and all later organicist doctrines that derived from him may have taken for granted some of the equal rights of the *philosophes*, but they then proceeded to fashion society out of the different clays that were the raw materials of human nature. All men were not equally capable of participating in the administration of society. The new philosopher of society approached the whole problem with the initial preconception that the physiological and psychological differences of men were the very brick and mortar of his perfect social edifice. Fourier's theory of the passions, independently developed with an almost compulsive detail and a mania for the multiplication of psychological types, is only an exaggeration of the same tendency. The order of the phalanstery is a harmony of properly distributed human beings who perform social functions in accordance with the requirements of their personality types.

If mankind were organized on the basis of Saint-Simon's— or for that matter Fourier's—natural physiological classification, conflict and frustration would in time vanish from society. Historic conflicts of previous ages had their origins in the fact that class stratifications were not natural, and were for the most part mere groupings of rival interest corps, competing for power over one another. Past history had witnessed the attempt of single classes to dominate the whole of society. This had been true even in the last relatively organic social epoch, the Middle Ages, when despite the universal veneration of Christ, the temporal and spiritual estates, nobility and clergy, were engaged in a death-struggle for the totality of power. As long as classes remained expressions of the lust for dominion, chaos would reign forever, there could be no peace and no social harmony. Under the new organic system of natural classes the lust for dominion would be transferred from men and directed against objects. With time the very nature of this power lust would undergo a metamorphosis.[24]

The presumption is overwhelming that each man seeks to express his own and not an alien nature, that he desires to live and work in the classification where he has natural endowments, be they Saint-Simon's scientific, administrative, and poetic capacities, or any one of Fourier's multifarious dominant passion types. Saint-Simon here adapted one of the major contentions of the theocrats, who steadfastly maintained that men were not driven by a passion for equality with other men of higher status or greater wealth, but really had a profound desire to remain in their own traditional occupations and to continue to express themselves in the traditional roles into which they had been cast at birth. They wanted not equality but the expression of their true social natures. Saint-Simon merely translated this conception into scientific terms: men by nature desired not equality with others but the expression of their true social natures based upon their intrinsic and immutable physiological aptitudes. The Aristotelian idea that every being seeks a fulfillment of its essential character or nature has found an echo both in the theocratic and in the Saint-Simonian theories. It is a dogma that no man would be so monstrous as to desire to exercise administrative functions if he were born with a scientific capacity. At least, no good social order would allow such an anarchic misplacement of human talent. When a man operates in a social class to which he does not naturally belong, he is wasting his own talents and reducing the total creative potential of humanity. Among Saint-Simon's last words was a message to his favorite disciple that the quintessential goal of his new doctrine was the total development of human capacities and the arrangement of the social order so that these capacities might achieve their maximum realization.[25]

In the last analysis the validity of human life in an organic society derives not from the individual's relationship to his fellows, but from his relationship to the society as a whole. Inequalities of status and authority are as obvious as the physiological differences among men, but they are justified in terms of the society's total organization and purpose. A rationale for these inequalities clearly emerges in Saint-Simon's ideal industrial-scientific regime, where power is transformed into function and privilege into responsibility.

Saint-Simon's formula for the organization of society aims to eliminate the possibility of social maladjustment and friction. Within each class of aptitudes, of capacities, the course is always kept open to talent. Here again there is the presumption that among men with similar or identical aptitudes, superiority and excellence will automatically be recognized without jealousy and without conflict. Saint-Simon generalized to all aptitudes the apparent unanimity with which the foremost mathematicians, physicists, and biologists seemed to be appreciated by men of science.

In the good society a natural elite corps (he was directly influenced by the contemporary analogy of Napoleon's *troupes d'élite*), one with authentic, proved capacities, directed the various classes. Leadership was not, as the doctrine of popular sovereignty presupposed, a generalized capacity in which all men were more or less equal and which made it feasible and natural for offices to be elective. In the organic society, workers instinctively rendered obedience to their natural superiors, their "chiefs," in their own class.[26] The idealized image of the Napoleonic army, in which ordinary soldiers had risen to be marshals, in which rank was at least in theory the reward of merit, was a prototype for Saint-Simon's civilian class society.

Saint-Simon's anger against the nobility and the clergy, which he denounced as useless bodies of *fainéants*, was fired far less by their exclusive character than by their decadence, his awareness that in reality they had ceased to be functioning elites within the body politic. Unique excellence and attributes, what he called anomalies, in the Middle Ages had been the very basis for the constitution of elite corps such as the nobility and the clergy. The egalitarian *philosophes* had made the fatal error of proclaiming the abolition of all specialized corps merely because the existing elites in name had ceased to be elites in fact. In the Saint-Simonian world outlook, organic inequality among men, inequality in the social hierarchy, and difference of social function were natural and beneficent, wholly superior to the *égalité turque* of the Jacobin revolutionaries which was an equality of slavery beneath an omnipotent state authority.[27] Men who are born unequal in capacities require an organic society in which each is allotted a function "according to his capacity"—this is the true meaning of the famous slogan of the Saint-Simonian cult.

The organismic society, unlike the atomist egalitarian society, which functions like inanimate clockwork, requires a "vitalist" element—some pervasive emotion, feeling, or belief to give life to the organic body. Though the eighteenth century had developed the concepts of benevolence and humanity as characteristics of natural men of virtue, Saint-Simon in the romantic temper infused the idea of the love of humanity with an emotional drive that it had lacked in the minds of the *philosophes*. Love was the fluid that coursed through the body social, gave it movement and energy. In Saint-Simon's judgment the equal atoms of the eighteenth-century world view were always on the verge of strife; his ideal of love created an organic harmonious whole out of society's vital parts. Men hungered for this comfort on the morrow of a quarter of a century of world revolution which had loosened the very bonds of the social fabric. The need for the emotionalization of relationships if society were not to fall apart and disintegrate into its discrete elements had been dramatized by Burke and de Bonald and de Maistre. Saint-Simon by his own testimony was communicating the same urgent longing of men for a society in which they could feel themselves integral parts, an organic society, as contrasted with a state in which isolated units competed and fought with one another. Egalitarianism had come to represent the eternal struggle of equals in a world of cold and brutal competition.

Talleyrand's image of the national workship survives in Saint-Simon's writings, where the goal of the new society is maximum production through maximum utilization of individual capacities. In Saint-Simon's vision of the future golden age of plenty, the emphasis is placed upon ever more production and creation, rather than upon consumption and distribution. The banquet spread before mankind is so sumptuous that dwelling upon material rewards, so characteristic of a world of scarcity, seems to be beside the point. Saint-Simon's humanitarian doctrine thus incorporated the Condorcet principle that society could be so organized that misery and ignorance became accidents rather than the norm of human experience; [28] his theory had none of the crushing pessimism associated with later Social Darwinism, even though he too was inspired by biological analogies.

Perhaps the difference between the Saint-Simonian and the eighteenth-century conception has its crux in a new view of humanity. Instead of the man of reason as the most perfect expression of humanity toward which all men are striving, Saint-Simon thinks of man now and in the future as at once rational, activist, and religious, at once mind, will, and feeling. His ends are moral, intellectual, and physical, three major areas of human effort corresponding to the aptitudes of the artist, the scientist, and the industrialist. This is the whole man, whose being is paralleled in the organization of the healthy body social. If man is primarily a rational animal and the highest form of reason is mathematics, the Turgot-Condorcet egalitarian ideal of rational units behaving in accordance with mathematicized social rules is comprehensible. But if humanity is a composite whose various manifestations include the predominantly activist or religious as well as rationalist, the social structure, reflecting and embracing the variety and diversity of men, will be organismic, a harmony of complex, different, and essential parts.

NOTES

1. "Quintilian, Locke, and I say: Inequality among intellects is the result of a known cause and this cause is the difference in education." C. A. Helvétius, *De l'Homme* (1772), in *Oeuvres complètes* (Paris, 1818), II, p. 71.
2. Jean-Jacques Rousseau, *The Social Contract and Discourses*, trans. G. D. H. Cole (London, 1947), p. 160.
3. See especially Morelly's *Code de la nature* and Brissot de Warville's *Recherches philosophiques sur le droit de propriété et sur le vol considérés dans la nature et dans la société*. André Lichtenberger, *Le Socialisme au xviiie siècle* (Paris, 1895), is still the classical work on this group.
4. F. M. A. de Voltaire, *Dictionnaire philosophique*, in *Oeuvres* (Paris, 1835), VII, pp. 473-475.
5. M. J. A. N. C. de Condorcet, *Déclaration des Droits*, in *Oeuvres*, published by C. O'Connor and F. Arago (Paris, 1847-1849), IX, pp. 179-211.
6. Condorcet, *Esquisse d'un tableau historique des progrès de l'esprit humain*, in *Oeuvres*, VI, p. 238.
7. Condorcet, *Fragment sur l'Atlantide, ou efforts combinés de l'espèce humaine pour le progrès des sciences*, in *Oeuvres*, VI, pp. 597-660.
8. D. Talleyrand-Périgord, *Rapport sur l'instruction publique fait au nom du comité de constitution de l'Assemblée Nationale, les 10, 11, et 19 septembre 1791* (Paris, 1791), pp. 7-8.
9. *Ibid.*, p. 7.
10. "When one compares one man with another, one sees that nature has set up among individuals differences which are analogous to and correspond in a certain sense to those which can be recognized among species." P. J. G. Cabanis, "De l'influence des tempéramens sur la formation des idées et des affections morales," in *Mémoires de l'Institut de France*, Académie des sciences morales et politiques, 1st series, II, p. 230.
11. "But the impressions which the same objects make on us do not always have the same degree of intensity and are not always of the same duration. Sometimes they glide by hardly exciting our attention; sometimes they captivate it with an irresistible force and leave behind profound traces. Surely men do not resemble each other in their manner of feeling." Cabanis, "Considérations générales sur l'étude de l'homme et sur les rapports de son organisation physique avec ses facultés intellectuelles et morales," in *Mémoires de l'Institut de France*, I, pp. 65-66.
12. Cabanis wrote that his admiration for Helvétius and Condillac did not prevent him from recognizing that "both of them lacked phys-

iological knowledge, from which their works could have significantly profited." If Helvétius had known the "animal economy" better, he could not have "maintained his system of the equality of intellects." *Ibid.*, I, p. 63.

13. Cabanis, "De l'influence des tempéramens," pp. 283-284. In the same spirit Condorcet had said: "A well-directed system of education corrects the natural inequality of the faculties instead of strengthening them. . . . " *Esquisse d'un tableau historique des progrès*, in *Oeuvres*, VI, p. 251.

14. Cabanis believed that the inheritance of acquired charcteristics applied both to "physical disposition" and to "dispositions of the mind and propensities of the soul." "Considérations générales sur l'étude de l'homme," p. 93.

15. The classical work of Johann Caspar Lavater (1741-1801) was his *Physiognomische Fragmente zur Befoerderung der Menschenkenntniss und Menschenliebe*, 4 vols. (Leipzig, 1775-1778).

16. Franz Joseph Gall (1758-1828) wrote *Recherches sur l'anatomie du système nerveux en général et du cerveau en particulier* (Paris, 1809).

17. Xavier Bichat, *Physiological Researches upon Life and Death*, trans. Tobias Watkins (Philadelphia, 1809), pp. 112-113. The work was originally published in France in the Year VIII (1799-1800).

18. "You will seldom or never see the perfection of action in the locomotive organs co-incident with those of the brain or the senses, and on the other hand it is extremely rare to find the former very apt in their respective functions when the latter possess considerable energy in their's." *Ibid.*, p. 109.

19. These reflections were later appended to Necker's *De la Révolution Françoise*, 2 vols. (Paris, 1797).

20. *Ibid.*, II, p. 116.

21. L. G. A. de Bonald, *Essai analytique sur les lois naturelles de l'ordre social, ou du pouvoir, du ministre, et du sujet dans la société*, third ed. (Paris, 1836), pp. 214-215 and n. The work was first published in 1800.

22. While Saint-Simon was already struggling with this conception in the brilliant, though eccentric, fragments he wrote under the Empire, the full meaning of his organic conception of man and society did not emerge until after 1819, in *L'Organisateur, Du système industriel, Catéchisme des industriels, Opinions littéraires, philosophiques et industrielles*, and the *Nouveau Christianisme*.

23. The "immortal physiologist" Bichat was by Saint-Simon's own testimony the source of his conception of mutually exclusive capacities, a theory which in *Du système industriel* he called a law of human organization. *Oeuvres* (Paris, 1865-78), XXII, p. 56.

24. "The desire to command men has slowly transformed itself into the desire to make and remake nature in accordance with our will." Henri de Saint-Simon, *L'Organisateur*, in *Oeuvres*, XX, p. 127n.

25. *Notice historique,* in *Oeuvres,* I, p. 122.
26. The idea of the natural elite was developed by Saint-Simon in *L'Industrie* (1817), in *Oeuvres,* XVIII, pp. 142-145. The same conception had been adumbrated earlier in the fragment entitled "Sur la capacité de l'Empéreur," in the *Introduction aux travaux scientifiques du xixe siècle,* 2 vols. (Paris, 1808).
27. Saint-Simon, *Du système industriel,* in *Oeuvres,* XXII, p. 17n.
28. Condorcet, *Esquisse d'un tableau historique des progrès,* in *Oeuvres,* VI, p. 238.

II

TWO STYLES OF
PHILOSOPHICAL HISTORY

The title of this essay might lead to the suspicion that its author has himself succumbed to the *morbus philosoph-historicus*. Some reassurance is therefore required from the outset. Far from presuming to dichotomize philosophical history in all times and places, these reflections are limited to two traditions, one in France, the other in Germany, during the period that might be called the classical age of modern essays in philosophical history —roughly from the middle of the eighteenth through the middle of the nineteenth century. There appear in this brief time span a sudden self-consciousness about the problems, a thematic richness, and a creative originality which render it unique; by contrast, late nineteenth- and twentieth-century philosophies of history sometimes seem to be the work of industrious epigoni, whose voluminous writings have filled the old bins with the harvest of modern historical scholarship, the chaff and the wheat.

The French chain of intellectual transmission runs from Voltaire and Turgot through Condorcet, Saint-Simon, the Saint-Simonians, and Fourier, culminating in Auguste Comte; the German one, from Winckelmann, Herder, Lessing, and Kant, through Schiller, Schelling, and Fichte, culminating in Hegel. Two towering figures will be conspicuously absent from this presentation:

at the beginning, that lone Neapolitan, Giambattista Vico, and at the end, Karl Marx, with his synthesis of elements from both the German and the French schools. Vico is omitted because of my deep conviction that, despite his nineteenth-century translators in France and Germany and occasional quotations from his work, he had relatively little influence on either style. If Marx is looked upon as a great syncretic figure, his place is in another context.

As a body of literature the French and the German philosophies of history of this period have been examined from a variety of viewpoints. They have been used as prolegomena to action programs, often in conjunction with political movements of a nationalist or a social revolutionary character. They have been read devotionally as theodicies, or as descriptions of God's way among the nations, or as works of inspiration inducing an oceanic feeling which Freud thought kindred to religion and infanthood. In a paper a few years ago[1] I tried paradoxically to emphasize the empirical insights in these writings and their provocative juxtaposition of historical observations in a novel order. But these philosophies of history can also be considered in a different vein, not as things-in-themselves to be judged in their own terms, but as remarkable documents revelatory of something else—a general intellectual *esprit* prevalent in a given time and place. This is for me, moreover, not an isolated and discrete inquiry. A study of interpretations of ancient myth in eighteenth-century thought in 1959 has already presupposed that an investigation of a problem of this character (the nature of myth) can be fruitful in defining the mind and sensibility of an age.[2] Similarly, the rich modern cosmic and world-historical myths generally called philosophies of history can be studied as significantly expressive of mind and sensibility rather than as approaches to truth. They may be delusions to the positivistic historian, but what magnificent delusions! Almost as good as poetry. Finally, there is an even more pretentious, if less overt, purpose to my analysis: the philosophies of history in France and Germany in the classical period formed cultural personality as well as expressed it. Since they imprinted themselves upon national character, their mood outlasted the age of their composition; and sometimes their images persisted well into the twentieth century.

This is clearly a rash enterprise and ought to be undertaken only with the privileges of what the Germans call *Narrenfreiheit*. It involves riding rough-shod over the differenecs among the three Herders which Germanic learning has recognized, the young and the old Hegel, Saint-Simon before and after the insane asylum, Auguste Comte before and after his love for Clothilde de Vaux, and similar distinctions which have been made by laborious scholarship.

A word about the autonomous development of the two styles. The very idea of building a significant contrast between two schools of philosophical history in two late modern European nations which are divided by nothing more than the Rhine might well be questioned. But the facts are that the two styles did evolve in relative intellectual independence during this period. Of course many theoretical idioms are common to both of them, and one could profitably explore the resemblances; but this essay will concentrate on their distinctions. The two styles, while definable, are by no means absolutely pure, and some figures such as Diderot in France and Lessing in Germany do not fit very neatly into the categories; the polarity of the two types, in my judgment, is nonetheless illuminating.

In eighteenth-century Europe intellectual currents moved from west to east. That group of creative Germans in far-off East Prussia (Kant, Hamann, and Herder) read all the important French books at a time when French thinkers hardly deigned to peruse what any German was writing. Yet, though Herder and Hegel actually journeyed to Paris, their contact with French thought aroused in them only hostility, negation, and ultimate rejection. In one of his last lectures on the *Philosophy of History*, Hegel pontifically excommunicated all the Romanic nations: [3] "With them the inner life is a region whose depth they do not appreciate, for it is given over 'bodily' to particular absorbing interests, and the infinity that belongs to the Spirit is not to be looked for there."

Similarly, the impact of the German philosophers of history

on the French was negligible. By the time Herder, Lessing, and Kant were translated, the foundation and framework of the French structure had already been erected. Though Victor Cousin was a fashionable Parisian lecturer on German thought during the last years of the Restoration, it is highly dubious whether his much-touted transmission really "took" in the first half of the nineteenth century. Saint-Simon had made a brief trip to Germany early in the century, but he always spoke ill of the German romantic spirit. When the Saint-Simonians were forging their doctrine in dramatic closeted debates in 1829 and 1830, the term "Hegelian" was a scornful epithet hurled at metaphysical quibblers. If the Saint-Simonians borrowed the concept of Antagonism from Kant's essay on universal history, they grafted a completely different meaning on it. It is reported that Hegel said a few kind words about Comte to his friend Gustave d'Eichthal and that Comte reciprocated by including a Hegel Day in the Calendar of Humanity, but that was the extent of their communion.

There is one momentous exception to this thesis of autonomous development, however, and that is the ubiquitous Jean-Jacques Rousseau. His apotheosis by the French revolutionaries only superficially identifies him with the rationalist, activist, progressive spirit which that political event came to represent in modern history. Rousseau the pietist from Geneva belongs to the pietists of East Prussia; it was fitting that he should be repudiated by Parisian intellectuals and comprehended in all his profundity only by the Germans, by Kant and by Herder. If the *Emile* is a *French* treatise on education, based on principles of reasonable utility, natural virtue, benevolence, and fellow-feeling, the real tragic history of mankind depicted in the *Discourse on Inequality* and the nightmarish self portrait of a totally alienated man in the *Confessions* are documents whose essential meaning was understood above all by the Germans, and these are the works whose spirit informs their philosophies of history. Karl Barth has rightly claimed Rousseau for the German Protestants. The moments of illumination before the composition of the Dijon prize essay, which Rousseau has himself described in a letter to M. de Malesherbes, are in the character of a sudden conversion: [4] "All at once my mind seemed dazzled by a thousand lights . . . my head swam with a dizziness akin to drunkenness." Rousseau's discovery of man's secret inner nature was a religious experience, and by the same token it was foreign to the Baconian methods of acquiring and diffusing knowledge that were hallowed by Turgot, Condorcet, Saint-Simon, and the positivists.

First to the Frenchmen. By the time Voltaire invented the term *philosophie de l'histoire* in 1765,[5] Turgot had already delivered his famous harangues before the Sorbonne on the successive "progressions of the human mind," a title which was preserved by his protégé Condorcet in the famous *Esquisse* of 1795. As if in reply to Montesquieu's anatomy of the fall of Rome, these philosophers demonstrated that the values of contemporary French scientific and rationalist society would endure forever, growing in strength throughout all time: the modern Antonines would never decline. Because of the cumulative effect of scientific knowledge—in a Baconian sense—regression was impossible. The French had already reached a high level of intelligence, and there were still loftier summits ahead. Or, as Herder mocked the Encyclopedists in his first essay on philosophical history, "We are the top of the tree, swaying in the divine breeze." [6]

The problem of man had been solved; scientific method, now universally appreciated, had projected a roadway into infinity. Progress was irreversible and indefinite, by which Condorcet in his *Esquisse* meant that only from a greater height could one even conceive of the future prospects for mankind in terms of pleasure and power over nature. By wresting from nature its own secrets, its laws, he wrote in a manuscript, nature could be tamed. In the future man would enter the lists an equal in power with nature itself—one of the grandest expressions of hybris in an age not characterized by excessive humility.

Universal history was the record of man's steady conquest of the external world, beginning in a period when he was still weak and feeble and culminating in his present high estate. In the struggles of the past, victims had fallen by the wayside, but human action, always guided by the pain-pleasure principle, had kept fairly well to the road. Pleasure and desire had led man onward, and so had the mild but necessary irritability engendered by pain. The historical process could be represented as a series of needs, their appeasement, and the creation of new needs in the course of satisfying the old ones, ad infinitum.

An element of conflict had been introduced into history when wicked corps (tyrants, priests, cliques of philosophers) had monopolized the instruments of power, of knowledge, and of pleasure. The corps spirit had suppressed novelty, Turgot charged in the *Discourses*. But the stagnation periods had never endured very long: men broke the bonds of sameness, gathered fresh impressions, promulgated new ideas, and found adherents among the rulers themselves. For who could long reject the instrumentalities that promise power and pleasure? Occasionally there were barbarian irruptions from the heart of darkness, but the new peoples were quickly assimilated as they acquired the tools of knowledge.

Condorcet, writing at a pivotal moment in the history of the idea of progress, raised the momentous question as to whether the liberty and the free inquiry which in the past had been the guarantees of progressive development might not in the future have to bend a little before the new demands of scientific organization. The rate of the rather haphazard development of the past might in the future be increased to an undreamed-of degree if the practice of science by organized bodies rather than by freewheeling individuals were encouraged. Hence the impressive catalogue of world-wide controlled researches projected in Condorcet's *Fragment on the New Atlantis*. Since each scientific acquisition in the past had ultimately been transmuted into a quantum of pleasure distributed among mankind, what a harvest of well-being and happiness was in store if the accumulative process of science and technology could only be accelerated through coordination. Condorcet the doctrinaire liberal in politics was willing to accept the imposition of external discipline on the republic of science for the sake of human betterment.

The movement of future progress described by Condorcet can be likened to the advance of the whole of mankind on an open plain. In the front rank, ahead of their fellow men, the scientific elite are dashing forward at a speed which is continually being augmented; behind the main body portions of humanity lag because they have been duped by Machiavellian despots and their priestly minions. But the forward thrust of the great cohort of scientists is of such Herculean power that it pulls the whole of mankind along with it. And as they advance in time, men are ever healthier, happier, more acute in their sense perceptions, telescopically and microscopically, more precise in their reasoning power, more equal in wealth and opportunity, more humane in their conduct.

There was a break in the French tradition when, in the romantic spirit of the nineteenth century, their philosophers of history abandoned a concept of man in which mind was a supreme capacity to which all other talents were subordinate. Once the Saint-Simonians and Comte defined man as a feeling and willing being whose capacities for love and action were of equivalent, if not superior, worth to his reason, history had to be reformulated as the progress of love or the progressive actualization of all human capacities instead of the development of mind alone. Nevertheless, the basic model of progress as a measurable extension of human welfare over ever broadening areas, at an ever faster tempo, was preserved.

True, Saint-Simon and Comte introduced new motifs—especially the idea of the conflict of classes and the concept of crises. But in the French view of the historical process the crises are always readily resolved; the standard formula was the defeat or abdication of an old ruling class and its replacement by a new one. Historical crises were the consequence of a mechanical disequilibrium in the manifest organization of civil society, which had failed to take account of the vast accretion of power in what were formerly subordinate groups. The ideal historical solutions were largely institutional: the creation of a new hierarchy, a more reasonable division of labor and power reflecting the new realities, the elimination of contradictions between civil and political power. The legions of adherents to the problem-solving school of historical

interpretation who people our American universities are blessedly
unaware of the degree to which they reflect this simplistic progressive style of philosophical history.

In this French school the process of historical change is remarkably continuous—perhaps its most significant characteristic.
A stage or a period in Condorcet's *Esquisse* is merely a step on
the ladder of progress. And steps merely punctuate the continuous
progressions. The discoveries of genius are great moments in the
historical ascent, but they have been prepared by a long series
of little steps called gradual development. Historical movement
is so inherently continuous that all periodization is in the final
analysis arbitrary. One may recall that there are ten epochs in
Condorcet's *Esquisse*, a rational number. How convenient of
history to express itself in terms of the metric system! (In the
same tradition, American texts on Western civilization run to
fifteen or thirty chapters to fit the number of weeks in the school
schedule.) Condorcet's favorite analogy to the historical process
is a mathematical progression. Auguste Comte, who periodized
history into three states, was still anlyzing one long linear "social
series"—his term. This same sense of a continuous process (without leaps or real disruptions) holds true even after dialectical
elements were introduced by Saint-Simon, the Saint-Simonians,
and Comte. They may talk about the organic nature of society
(particularly the Saint-Simonians), but they really mean a clear
and distinct group of elements which define progression and rest.
Auguste Comte's sociological neologisms, Social Dynamics and
Social Statics, sufficiently characterize the essential nature of this
style; though Comte was learned in the new biology, he remained
the mathematics tutor and polytechnician to the end.

Across the Rhine one is immediately struck by a different
temper. The Germans who composed philosophies of history were
either pastors like Herder, sons of pastors like Lessing, or state-
university professors like Kant and Hegel. Germany was economically weak and politically divided, and despite the respectable
positions occupied by the pastors and professors in their isolated
principalities, they never presumed to affect directly the external
political world. At most, they were educators. Lessing's hundred

aphorisms were entitled *Die Erziehung des Menschengeschlechts*. The philosophies of history written by the Germans were educational treatises which, in describing how the human species was fashioned, were at the same time molding the inner beings of their students and their small, literate public. The Frenchmen who created the major themes of philosophical history were incorrigible activists—a king's minister, Turgot; a revolutionary leader, Condorcet; founders of movements and new religions like Saint-Simon, the Saint-Simonians, and Comte. For the Frenchmen the prospect of implementation was immediate; they themselves were bringing the new world into being, accelerating the projected historical series. Among the German pastors the militancy of a Luther had long since died. And in the university the distinction between the *vita activa* and the *vita contemplativa* was absolute. Kant never left Königsberg; and Hegel insisted that the owl of Minerva, philosophy's grey in grey, only takes flight at dusk. Contemplation *after* the event. To the traditional German academic of that epoch, the activism of the American professoriat and its direct manipulation of power would not be the least astonishing aspect of our way of life.

The German style of philosophical history mirrored the temper of these doctors of the inner life. In effect, the religious spirit of Luther—not his political style—informs virtually all the works of the Germans. While the French wrote a history of man's expanding capacities and his good works, the Germans composed a history of the inner man, a Protestant world history. The French systems were plainly sensationalist under the influence of Locke and Condillac; the Germans remained profoundly religious, whether their authors shunned the church building, as Kant did, or not. If religious residues remained in the French outlook, theirs was a vision of man triumphing through works. Cumulative progress is like a world treasury of merit to which the great scientific geniuses (the secular analogues of the saints) are all contributing their substance.

In the end, the French are therefore buoyantly optimistic, even when they are subject to moments of skepticism and doubt; the Germans are profoundly pessimistic, even though they may write about perpetual peace, the ultimate fulfillment of man's nature, and the conquest of Spirit. If the French school presents man's destiny as a utilitarianism temporalized or a history of pleasure and gratification, the Germans from Kant and Lessing down are writing a history of spiritual liberty and instinctual repression. Protestantism has taught them that illumination and knowledge of God were a long and arduous process which required extraordinary exertions, soul-searching, and the effort of will. The German philosophers of history have extended the history of individual God-seeking to the whole species. Even when they use words like *Fortgang* and *Fortschritt*, they do not mean what the French do by *les progrès*.

The Germans, at least Kant and Herder, felt that they were still living among Scythians, and their outbursts of despair and repugnance at the contemplation of their immoral contemporaries are frequent. "Everything in the gross is composed of madness, of childish vanity, and frequently of childish wickedness and the rage of destruction," Kant wrote disgustedly in *An Idea of an Universal History in a Cosmopolitical View*.[7] "Out of such cross-grained crooked wood as man is made of, nothing can be timbered quite straight."[8] For Schelling, history is a "tragic spectacle performed on the mournful stage of this world." If Hegel's spirit triumphs, it triumphs amid the death of cultures.

The French philosophers of history concentrate on the novelties; they revel in the material conquests and in the new acquisitions. They take a Baconian delight in sheer accumulation and in the variety of objects. They take pleasure in what Montesquieu called *le bonheur de l'existence*. For the Germans, who made world history into a *Bildungsroman*, the education of the human race was no lark. There is throughout these writings a sense of the pain and anguish of growth. They were dealing with a refractory pupil who kicked against the pricks and learned only through punishment. Man refuses to quit his minority, lamented Kant, anticipating Freud. The Germans were always conscious of the bloody travail of history, while among the French the philosopher's eye was focused on the growing ease and the new rationality.

The Germans, even the secularists among them, were weighted down by a sense of inborn evil. The baubles of French civilization they rejected with the moral righteousness of a Rousseau negating the arts and sciences. Herder could never accept the idea of perfectibility in terms of a mathematical increase of artifacts and powers. In the *Letters for the Advancement of Humanity* he posed the question rhetorically: "Or could perfection mean an augmentation in the number of tools and instruments for human force to use?" And he answered himself: "Were that so the question still would remain whether or not they were used for the good, since in the hands of malevolence greater instruments might signify greater evil." [9]

That simple reflection, which now strikes us so forcibly, obvious as it is, just never occurred to the French historians of the progress of civilization in the classical period. One should probably say "hardly ever," because there are inklings of this preoccupation in the last years of Auguste Comte. To the Germans it was the heart of the matter. Only moral *Innerlichkeit* counted, not objects. French enlightenment implied a progressive material increase in candle power until mankind, which had once been steeped in the darkness of superstition, would live in pure and clear, abstract yet distinct, ideas. For many Germans enlightenment meant metamorphosis, moral transformation, illumination in a religious sense, Paul at Damascus, a realization that to be man one must bear the burden of the categorical imperative.

When the Rousseauist conflict between natural man and societal man was resolved by the Germans, they invariably posited a giant leap into a new form of humanity. Historical time for them was discontinuous. It was expressed in Herder's image of the butterfly shedding the ugly worm-like skin of the caterpillar; in a pietist vision of the moment of sudden illumination, a breakthrough that metamorphoses man's moral nature, in a word, a religious conversion to morality with all the psychic appurtenances of new birth; in Lessing's prophecy of a Third Covenant.

The French philosophers were in one form or another writing histories of *bonheur* and *bienveillance*, and their happiness was a worldly one. The historical drama could be described as overcoming the impediments which mankind met in physical nature and in residual wicked instincts which had to be channeled or atrophied in order that *bonheur* might reign unchallenged. Fourier demanded a new social mechanism to attain *bonheur*, which for him involved nothing short of the complete abolition of repression and the proclamation of total instinctual gratification. "Pleasure is the perfect development of the existence of every living being," is an affirmation with which the French school—with the important exception of the later Auguste Comte—would have concurred, despite its tainted origin in one of the utopias of Restif de la Bretonne.[10]

With the Germans, the pursuit of happiness plays only a minor role in history, as in the last writings of Herder, or else it virtually does not exist. (Lessing's goal of *Glückseligkeit*, though nearer the French concept of happiness, is still far from *bonheur*.) Individual man may want happiness—he has desires and he has passions, *Habsucht, Herrschsucht, Ehrsucht*—but nature or the Providential plan has quite another end for its creature—the total repression of his animality, as Kant taught. The attainment of consciousness, Kantian or Hegelian, does not create the happy fellow of popular imagery. Kant has left us a sketch of the ideal consummation of nature in human form (almost a self portrait) in his essay *Observations on the Feeling of the Beautiful and the Sublime:* he is a melancholy man, anxious lest he fall from grace, lest he not obey the universal morality, which he has internalized; and conscious of all the possible consequences of all his actions all the time. He is necessarily worried that he will inadvertently sin against the categorical imperative. "He is a severe judge as well of himself as of others, and not seldom tired of himself and the world." [11] In Arcadia, in innocence, men might be sheep-like and contented, but not in history. "Man wills to live commodiously and contentedly, but nature wills that he shall quit the state of laziness and inactive contentment." [12]

After Kant has argued himself into what he called a "heroical belief in the future history of virtue," in one of his last essays, *The End of All Things,* he carefully distinguishes this prospect from happiness or contentment. Such an idea might be applicable to timeless heaven where there is a monotonous chanting of hallelujahs, but in this world it must be excluded. "For the state in which man is at present always remains an evil compared with the better in which he is ready to enter." [13]

Turgot talked of four progressions—moral, mechanical, scientific, and aesthetic; Condorcet still used the plural, *les progrès;* for Saint-Simon and his school there were three progressions—rational-scientific, moral-emotive, and physical. To the French the world of the future was full of many things in motion. A Saint-Simonian dithyramb by Charles Duveyrier communicates the temper of the whole school: [14]

> Celebrations, scientific and industrial inventions, works, on land and sea, in the air, everywhere movement, a crowd yet the most perfect order, monuments, convents, shops, wonders of art, a blaze of colors, perfumes, concerts, dances, religious performances; and moral well-being, social and individual, love which grows, grows, grows, always, always!

For the Germans history had one end: the hard-won battle for consciousness, which is Hegel's Spirit, or the struggle for liberty which even in the secularist Kant is not far removed from Luther's Christian liberty.

Meaningful history to Kant would have been a depiction of the antagonism between the forces of sociability and asociability, which somehow leads to the development of man's nature in all realms beyond the instinctual and to its expression in institutions such as those of a just civil constitution. But the Kantian historical world view, which at first glance seems most committed to the concept of progress, and was read that way by many Frenchmen, was shot through with doubts. What will keep mankind from falling asleep, once the stimulus of antagonism has vanished? Who shall guard the guardians, is a perplexing question in another section of the essay on universal history. To the degree that Kant's universal morality was an absolute and indivisible whole, the partial historical achievements of morality and civilization did not impress him.[15]

Rousseau was not far wrong, he wrote,

to prefer the state of savages, when this last step, which our species has still to ascend, is omitted. We are cultivated to the highest degree by art and science. We are civilized, to a troublesome degree, in all sorts of social politeness and decorum. But there is yet a great deal wanting to us to be considered moralized.

Condorcet's vicarious enjoyment of the future happiness of mankind merely through contemplation (this was his description of the philosopher's reward at the end of the *Esquisse*) was not the way for Kant. He could not be so readily compensated for the revolting spectacle before his eyes. There is more than mild disdain in the aged Kant's closing remarks in the second part of the *Disputation of the Faculties,* where he likened the contemporary wars of the nations to drunken brawling in a china shop.

If viewed mechanically and only in his lectures of the twenties, Hegel's history is a realization of consciousness and freedom and spirit in the world through time in a definable movement east to west; but it is hard to sense a triumphantly optimistic temper even in this work. Surely, if one accepts the centrality of the problem of bad conscience in Hegel's historical world view, as Jean Wahl does,[16] it is rather difficult to find the final dénouement of the historical drama convincing. The memory which lingers is the terrible contest of the individual and his collectives throughout time, inherent in the very split (*Entzweiung*) of being. In new birth, the pain and the torment predominate and become the essence of life.[17]

> Spirit will experience from nature not only opposition and impediments, but it will often see its endeavours fail because of nature, and often it will succumb as a result of the complexities in which it becomes entangled either because of nature or because of itself.

The Hegelian Spirit wrestling with itself is devoutly Protestant.

It is the state of contradiction that is creative, and for Hegel how miserably inadequate and superficial have been most past resolutions, especially the flat French eighteenth-century one. Is not Hegel's world history a history of the forms and self-tortured grimaces of alienation throughout time, as well as the victory of Spirit? In a few passages on the new industrial order and the psychological character of the alienated human relationships it was establishing, did not Hegel presage Marx's trenchant critique?

Seen through the eyes of the Germans, history is a holocaust. Hegel's Absolute Spirit has traveled from China to Germany, embodying itself temporarily in one world-historical state after another, nourishing itself on one national genius after another. Once a nation had reached its zenith, Spirit moved on to the next in order, leaving the soulless people to drag itself on through years of uncreative nullity, busied with politics and perhaps war, with a senile repetition of itself, until it finally died in the body, having long since been dead in spirit.

When history expressed itself in a world-historical figure, such a man trampled underfoot many a moral flower, because individuals had to be sacrificed to the course of Spirit. While hailing the triumph of the Idea and the Protestant German state in which it found its most complete expression, the final resolution of the conflict between objectivity and subjectivity, Hegel takes more than a nostalgic look backward to the Greek ideal of his youth; there is in him a longing for the image of spontaneous beautiful Hellas which he had once shared with his friend Hölderlin. No German of his century was ever completely consoled for the death of the youth of mankind that was Greece. Thus, even for Hegel, the education of mankind, the fashioning of Spirit, entailed a maiming loss as well as a gain, as it had in Herder's first essay on philosophical history, in which he abandoned himself to a rather stilted analogy between the ages of man and the succession of civilizations from that of the patriarchal Middle East to the present. The Germans' fascination with the myth of Greece has been described too often to require further commentary: it obsessed virtually all the philosophers of history— Winckelmann and Herder, Schiller and Hegel. The French admired the heroic figure of Socrates as much as their neighbors did, but they knew that they themselves had surpassed Greece in science and morality and civilization, if not in art.

French philosophical history has been generally rather democratic and cosmopolitan. Despite the unshakable conviction that
the French were in the vanguard of the historical process, the
bounty of civilization was universally communicable to all races
and peoples who were willing to assimilate and become a part of
progressive history. The Saint-Simonians proclaimed with outstretched arms: "All shall be called and all shall be chosen." [18]
For Comte, the whole of the past was embodied in the Great
Being. Not so the Germans. It is with some sense of shock that
we read Kant's summary dismissal of the black race as incapable
of reason [19]—passages, by the way, which are omitted from the
compendia by his devoted admirers.[20] To many Germans, meaningful historical activity was only the destiny of an infinitesimal
body of the elect. Hegel was more selective than the most hard-
bitten Calvinist. The actual living experience of most peoples was
doomed to oblivion, in so far as the world history of the Idea was
concerned. He wrote at the end of the *Philosophy of Right:* [21]

> Each of its stages is the presence of a necessary moment
> in the Idea of the world mind, and that moment attains its
> absolute right in that stage. The nation whose life embodies
> this moment secures its good fortune and fame, and its deeds
> are brought to fruition.

Yet at any given moment there is only *one* embodiment in
one particular world-historical nation; events in all other nations
at that moment of Idea are empty, devoid of meaning. All prehistory (life before the consolidated state) is without content;
similarly, life in a nation that has spent itself, after its world-historical moment is passed, is treadmill activity, repetitive; the
nation is a living corpse—it does not matter when it actually
perishes. Hegel's world history is really a history of rare moments of perfection in a succession of national cultures. There
are chosen moments in four or five chosen cultures. For the rest,
there is nothing but inchoate barbarism or else decay.

In Hegel's *Philosophy of Right* the awesome exclusiveness of
the Idea is expressed with a thunderous crash befitting a *Welt-
gericht* handing down its verdict:[22]

The nation to which is ascribed a moment of the Idea in the form of a natural principle is entrusted with giving complete effect to it in the advance of the self-developing self-consciousness of the world mind. This nation is dominant in world history during this one epoch, and it is *only once* that it can make its *hour strike*. In contrast with this, its absolute right of being the vehicle of this present stage in the world mind's development, the minds of the other nations are without rights, and they, along with those whose hour has struck already, count no longer in world history.

What happens when a nation is passé?

Perhaps it loses its autonomy, or it may still exist, or draw out its existence as a particular state or a group of states, and involve itself without rhyme or reason in manifold enterprises at home and battles abroad.

The debris of history—the Marxist concept, which the Russians have adopted to depict the losers in the struggle—is profoundly Hegelian.

Herder's *Volk* cultures, too, had only a fleeting moment of excellence. In each *Naturvolk* there is a form-giving period during which national genius and the environment coalesce to bring forth unique creations in myth, poetry, and music; but the *Volk* culture is doomed to seek dominion and through overextension to find its genius corrupted. The world has witnessed thousands of these cultures passing through their biological cycles, and, in accordance with the dogma of romantic plenitude, thousands more will be born and will die. Herder's historical world literally swarms with cultures dashing through their life cycles.[23]

No *Volk* has long remained and could remain what it was. Like every art and every science and what-not in the world, each *Volk* has had its period of growth, flowering, and decline. And each of these changes has lasted only the minimum period of time which could be afforded it on the wheel of human fate.

Of one thing, he asserts, you may be certain: the culture now at its apogee is about to fall—Herder's eye is cocked on the French as he foretells the doom; and the cultures that are still close to nature (perhaps the Germans' and the Slavs') are bound to flourish. In Winckelmann's history of Greek art, the prototype for all German genetic theories, absolute perfection lasted but an instant somewhere between the second and the third stages of the cycle. The rest was a descent to inevitable death in sterile imitation— *völlige Untergang*.

Since for the French man was endlessly malleable and his reason easily amenable to new truth, there was nothing inherently necessary in a long hiatus between the discovery of a truth and its implementation. The speed of change depended on the wills of men, which could be appropriately organized for maximum output. The French *philosophes* from Turgot down, with their geometric pattern of enlightenment—blocks of darkness which presented danger and of light which in time would penetrate the black—expected this conversion of superstition to scientificism to take place as fast as possible. Even Auguste Comte, the Frenchman most committed to a stadial theory, nevertheless argued in the *Positive Polity* that the contemporary savage world could be rapidly changed from fetishism to scientificism (under the appropriate tutelage of Parisians, of course), skipping the intermediary stages through which western Europe had passed.

Beginning with Herder, German philosophical history was bound to a slow genetic sense of time. Benign transformations in national genius had sometimes taken place through the penetration of its hard core, but only with the passage of ages. For each being, each *Volk*, for Mankind itself, there was an appropriately ordained time span of growth and decay, and there is nothing that organized wills can accomplish to affect genetic time. In Aphorism 89 of *The Education of Mankind*, Lessing, though paying homage to the genius of Joachim of Fiore and his prophecy of the third kingdom, chided his medieval predecessors because they were premature: "They believed that they could make their contemporaries, who had hardly outgrown their childhood, without enlightenment, without preparation, all at once into men who would be worthy of their third age."

In Hegel, World Spirit itself was obliged to suffer laboriously through cycle after cycle, in a whole series of cultures, from China to Germandom, and there was nothing which could have accelerated this tragic trek. From genetic time there is no appeal. To interfere in a life process, a nation's natural historical development, means to destroy its inner being. That is what the colonial powers have been doing to the savage and barbaric peoples of the earth, Herder charged in a summary of world-travel literature. That was the danger in a Frenchified king of Prussia addicted to *raisonnement* and orderliness and despotic rationality quickly imposed; he was killing the German spirit. That was the evil of even political freedom when it was imposed as a foreign yoke (Herder meant the French Revolution). "Therefore a history which justifies everything in all countries on the basis of this utopian plan [of the best governmental form] is a dazzling history of deceit." [24]

Perhaps in the contrasting sense of historical time we perceive the most fundamental difference between the French and the German philosophies—the one continuous and subject to rapid acceleration, the other profoundly discontinuous and beyond human will. In one the marking of divisions is extrinsic, in the other it is intrinsic. One is a history of events, the other a history of human nature. Though both use a terminology that betrays a common Christian origin—*esprit* as in *Saint Esprit* and *Geist* as in *Heilige Geist*—the French wrote a history of the *achievements* of the human mind (to amend Condorcet), the Germans a history of Spirit itself.

It would be supererogatory on my part to offer examples of the endurance of the French model of philosophical history in our time. It is the sea around us; from historical doctrine it has become official dogma. The German style, too, has persisted in twentieth-century philosophies of history—perhaps most of all in the writings of Protestant theologians educated in the German tradition. Even in Spengler, despite some of his disparaging references to the philosophies of history by Herder, Kant, and Hegel in his introduction to the *Decline of the West* and his different conception of historical morphology, one can still discern the same pervasive tragic spirit, the same genetic sense of time, and the same basic concept of cultural exhaustion. In my judgment he is deeply rooted in those thinkers of his culture whom he repudiated in his eagerness to appear the bolder innovator. Surely, his most fundamental analytic tool—the distinction between a creative moment called culture and a long decline known as civilization—is an echo of the German philosophies of history of the classical period.

By the second World War, one must admit, however, the national character of these two types of philosophical history no longer holds. In a strange spiritual transvestism, the two attitudes represented by the French and by the Germans have switched sides. The French have recently taken Hegel to their bosoms. Simone de Beauvoir reports somewhere that the day the Germans entered Paris she found herself reading him in the Bibliothèque Nationale—a double conquest. Conversely, it would appear that the Germans have had enough of *Innerlichkeit,* and that the break with their philosophical tradition is all but complete. The new West Germany has risen out of the ashes to a material acquisitiveness and practicality which seem to have brought heaven-on-earth to Frankfurt-am-Main.

NOTES

1. Frank E. Manuel, "In Defense of Philosophical History," *Antioch Review,* Fall 1960, pp. 331-343.
2. Frank E. Manuel, *The Eighteenth Century Confronts the Gods* (Cambridge, Mass., 1959).
3. Georg Wilhelm Friedrich Hegel, *Lectures on the Philosophy of History,* trans. J. Sibree (London, 1902), p. 439.
4. Jean-Jacques Rousseau, "Letter to Malesherbes," in *Oeuvres* (1797), XV, p. 389. According to *Les Confessions,* Pléiade ed. (Paris, 1933), p. 344, the mere reading of the announcement was overwhelming: "I saw another universe and I became another man."
5. Voltaire maliciously published a work by this title under the name of the Abbé Bazin.
6. Johann Gottfried von Herder, *Auch eine Philosophie der Geschichte zur Bildung der Menschheit* (Riga, 1774), p. 132.
7. Immanuel Kant, "An Idea of an Universal History in a Cosmopolitical View," in *Essays and Treatises on Moral, Political, and Various Philosophical Subjects* (London, 1798-1799), I, p. 412.

8. *Ibid.*, I, p. 421.
9. Johann Gottfried von Herder, *Briefe zu Beförderung der Humanität* (Riga, 1793), II, p. 102.
10. Nicolas Edme Restif de la Bretonne, *La Découverte australe, par un homme-volant, ou Le Dédale français* (Leipzig, 1782), II, p. 244.
11. Kant, "Observations on the Feeling of the Beautiful and Sublime," in *Essays and Treatises*, II, p. 25.
12. Kant, "An Idea of an Universal History in a Cosmopolitical View," in *Essays and Treatises*, I, p. 418.
13. Kant, "The End of All Things," in *Essays and Treatises*, II, p. 437.
14. Paris, Bibliothèque Nationale, MS. n.a.fr. 24609, fol. 457v, a canticle by Charles Duveyrier.
15. Kant, "An Idea of an Universal History in a Cosmopolitical View," in *Essays and Treatises*, I, p. 425.
16. Jean André Wahl, *Le Malheur de la Conscience dans la Philosophie de Hegel* (Paris, 1929).
17. Georg Wilhelm Friedrich Hegel, *Vorlesungen über die Philosophie der Geschichte* (Stuttgart, 1961), p. 130.
18. *Doctrine de Saint-Simon. Deuxième Séance*, ed. C. Bouglé and Elie Halévy (Paris, 1924), p. 178.
19. Kant, "Observations on the Feeling of the Beautiful and the Sublime," in *Essays and Treatises*, II, p. 73.
20. "The blacks are remarkably vain, but in a negro manner, and so loquacious, that they must absolutely be separated by the cogent and conclusive argument of caning" (*ibid.*, II, p. 74).
21. Georg Wilhelm Friedrich Hegel, *Philosophy of Right*, trans. T. M. Knox (Oxford, 1942), p. 217.
22. *Ibid.*, pp. 217-218.
23. Herder, *Auch eine Philosophie der Geschichte*, p. 47.
24. Herder, *Briefe zu Beförderung der Humanität* (1797), X, p. 165.

12

THOUGHTS ON GREAT SOCIETIES

Over two thousand three hundred and fifty years ago an Athenian aristocrat and philosopher undertook a long, arduous journey to Syracuse in Magna Graecia for the purpose of achieving "some marvelous overhauling" in that city-state in conformity with his already-published paradigm of an idèal society. The fundamental proposition to which he was committed is set forth in what became known as his Seventh Epistle, in a passage paraphrasing his own previous writings: "Wherefore the classes of mankind will have no cessation from evils until either the class of those who are right and true philosophers attains political supremacy, or else the class of those who hold power in the States becomes, by some dispensation of heaven, really philosophic." [1]

The tragic failure of his mission, thrice repeated, should serve to discourage any would-be philosopher with the hope of contributing significantly to the establishment of an ideal republic. It is surely not of Platonic justice that you would have me talk, and though the senses of Dionysius have become acute with new technological devices and capable of receiving messages at incredible

Lecture before the Arthur F. Bentley Seminar, Syracuse University, Maxwell Graduate School, March 25, 1966.

distances, I am under no illusion that men of power are likely to be converted to philosophy.

Without Plato's absolute before my mind's eye, I am nonetheless prepared to discuss various ideals of great societies in the past and possible ideals for the future, not excluding the fleeting company of the present. For while in a gloomy mood I might repeat Plato's reflection that "all the states which now exist . . . one and all they are badly governed," I have come to learn that some are immeasurably worse than others.

I do of course conceive of the Great Society as more of a wish than a fulfilled present reality, more of a hope than a fixed prospect. One of the ways in which I can examine our contemporary American civilization in historical perspective is by blurring the line between present and future and at the same time sharpening the line which separates us from the ideals and values of societies, once deemed great, that have passed away. This is both an un-Burkean and an un-Marxian exercise, entirely unbecoming to a historian. But perhaps we can the better define ourselves dialectically, by contrasting our visions with those that other societies, now dead, once lived by and that can no longer move us. For past history has set certain limits on the possible—and unless you are as obsessively committed to the cyclical conception of the world as the Stoic Chrysippus, the future *must* be different. My attempt will be a brash twentieth-century American undertaking, alien in spirit to the traditional form of self-examination in Western society that stressed, as a matter of course, the links with the past and that could understand the present only in terms of the generally recognized virtues and hallowed precepts of the Judeo-Christian and Greco-Roman societies.

My approach will be direct. I have selected a number of attributes of great societies of the past, and will try to see which, if any of them at all, could fit the Great Society. By attributes I mean qualities that great societies assigned to themselves as well as those that later reflective historians and philosophers foisted upon them. They have not always been the same.

Some periods of Western history have been peculiarly self-conscious about their own greatness—for example, Periclean

Athens, Augustan Rome, Florence of the Renaissance, Elizabethan England, the age of Louis XIV, the epoch of the French Revolution. The epithet "Great Society" which has been adopted by our President is, in its original form at least, not one of the noteworthy expressions of Christian humility. Despite the fact that the term was clearly meant to evoke an ideal image and not to label a current state of affairs, the notion is abroad that at some future date it might well serve as an appropriate chapter heading in a history book on this administration.

ATTRIBUTES OF GREAT SOCIETIES

Great societies have been praised for their military prowess, lawful orderliness and security, devotion to beauty, absolute commitment to a principle of religious transcendence, the prevalence of a warm communal feeling, their size, power, and grandeur, their opportunities for sensate or spiritual happiness, their harmony and justice, peacefulness, egalitarianism, freedom, duration in time, constancy and changelessness, their pursuit of excellence. No society with which I am acquainted has arrogated to itself *all* of these attributes, and some appear to be flagrantly contradictory. There is an old European idea, developed rather fully in the eighteenth century by Montesquieu in France and Herder in Germany, that societies, like individuals, have dominant passions. Without subscribing to the full implications of any such facile analogy between individual psychology and the underlying drives of nations, I should like to quote a famous passage from the *Spirit of the Laws* as the guiding text for this essay: "Though all governments have the same general end, which is that of preservation, yet each has another particular object. Increase of dominion was the object of Rome; war, that of Sparta; religion, that of the Jewish laws; commerce, that of Marseilles; public tranquillity, that of the laws of China; navigation, that of the laws of Rhodes; natural liberty, that of the policy of the Savages; in general, the pleasures of the prince, that of despotic states; that of monarchies, the prince's and the kingdom's glory." [2]

Examples of the magnificent virtues that societies of the past have claimed for themselves can readily be collected in any library.

Toynbee takes especial delight in the letter presented in 1793 by the philosophical Emperor Chi'en Lung to a British envoy of King George III on the very eve of China's dismemberment. "Our dynasty's majestic virtue," he wrote, "has penetrated into every country under Heaven, and kings of all nations have offered their costly tribute by land and sea. As your Ambassador can see for himself, we possess all things." [3] Such expressions of what Toynbee calls the egocentric illusion, the belief that one's own living society is the consummation of human history, which he finds rather general among mankind, must fill the philosophical historian with amusement, when they do not arouse in him a superstitious terror that he is witnessing a tragic spectacle of hybris, of sinful arrogance before a downward plunge.

We all remember Scipio's premonition of the fall of Rome as he watched the burning of Carthage, which he had set to the torch. The *Ubi sunt* theme is a stereotype of the medieval chroniclers, and one does not have to take literally every historical analogy in the works of Spengler, Toynbee, and Sorokin to feel one's tongue cleft to its roof in the utterance of the words Great Society. But though I probably believe in the mortality of all societies, I shall proceed to affirm the current potentialities of our Great Society, and shall deliver á eulogy of its emerging character.

It should be taken for granted that everything presented here is predicated upon an era free from nuclear catastrophe. Should this assumption prove to be entirely fallacious, I trust that if we meet some day amid fire and brimstone you will forbear adding insult to injury by reminding me of my indecent optimism. Moreover, my remarks may not be totally irrelevant to the indefinite postponement or even prevention of the holocaust. If we are truly committed to the greatness of this society in its peculiar virtues, we may conceivably find the strength to crush the serpents who would have us eat of the tree of unreality with its old and rotting fruit—calls to glory—when we might cause a tree of true knowledge and achievement to flower in our midst, perhaps not forever, perhaps not even for a thousand years, but for a while, a precious while. I will not be outdone by any man in my lack of faith. But

I am skeptical about prophecies of doom, as well as those of eternal paradise.

The difficulties inherent in any comparative study of the overriding drives of historical societies widely separated in time and place are obvious. What other civilizations meant by a state or a society is often so different from our daily usage that comparisons of this nature are at best impressionistic. The idea of greatness itself has changed radically—not merely the content that might be poured into greatness but the value of the thing in itself.

But then again, this may be one of the last periods when comparisons of this sort are possible. If there is validity to what will be my underlying premise—that the American model of a society presents a spectacle qualitatively different from anything known before in the tempo of its dynamism and changeability—then we, among the last generations with a historical sensibility, can still ask historical questions which in a while will be meaningless and incomprehensible. When and if the divorce from the past in our civilization becomes absolute, as Paul Valéry suggested in an essay on progress—a process that has been accelerating at a far greater rate of speed than even he imagined—then archeological comparisons of great societies may perhaps continue, but they will more and more be reduced to objective measurements totally devoid of feeling tone, to the size and quantity and shape of artifacts. History will present to future generations, Valéry prophesied, an indecipherable hieroglyph. "Everything that is not purely physiological in man will have changed, since our ambitions, our politics, our wars, our customs, our arts, are at present subject to the rule of very rapid replacement. They depend more and more closely upon the positive sciences and, thus, less and less on that which was. The *new fact* tends to assume all the importance that tradition and the *historical fact* have hitherto possessed." [4]

The attributes of great societies upon which I mean to concentrate will tend to be expressed in polar terms: we will probe for commitment to traditionalist constancy or relentless innovation, communal cohesiveness or loose individualism, religious transcendence or secular worldliness, ascetic self-denial or expansive gratification, harmonious beauty or esthetic indifference; aristocratic elitism or democratic egalitarianism, warlike aggressiveness or military restraint. My main function, as I see it, is to evoke images of other societies. For some these images may look like handwriting on the wall; for others they may arouse nostalgia or contempt; for me they will be highlighting the extraordinary uniqueness of the present historical moment.

CONSTANCY OR DYNAMISM

Nowhere is the contrast between our present conception of a great society and that of virtually all previous civilizations more striking than in the different attitudes toward constancy and change, toward an immutable, stable order and dynamic novelty. Most societies have been traditionalist to the point of extolling a changeless state of being as the highest good. In the ancient public documents of the Near East, a plea to the gods for an enduring order was the prayer of the king. When Messianism with its foretelling of a great transformation appeared in Judaic and Christian history, its promise of a radical metamorphosis was looked upon with suspicion by the rulers of society as a dangerous and disruptive idea. Even in war and conquest most societies aimed at the establishment of an immutable order. The ideals of Christian life expressed by the medieval scholastics centered around the concept of *ordo*, which implied fixedness in economic and social conditions. The ideal of *manu tenere*, the preservation of an existing governmental form and its maintenance against intruders, the reaffirmation or restoration of this pristine order when it became subject to decay, was ubiquitous in Renaissance political thought. In the midst of the vicissitudes of states and empires, of which the sixteenth-century *politiques* were so acutely conscious, the establishment of a lasting order was the common purpose of men as diverse as Thomas More and Machiavelli, Bodin and Contarini. The widespread sixteenth- and seventeenth-century myth of Venice as the most perfect society of all time was founded upon its supposed duration from the fifth century onward without any alteration whatsoever in its constitution. As late as Montesquieu, the end of society was to preserve the existing laws true to the national spirit. Rousseau's ideal society allows for few changes in the laws once they have been promulgated by the general will. When Edmund Burke wrote his famous defense of eighteenth-century English society, he boasted of England's stability in contrast with the fickleness of revolutionary France. If you want to know how different we have become, listen to Burke's self-appraisal: "Our political system is placed in a just correspondence and symmetry with the order of the world and with the mode of existence decreed to a permanent body composed of transitory parts, wherein, by the disposition of a stupendous wisdom, molding together the great mysterious incorporation of the human race, the whole, at one time, is never old or middle-aged or young, but in a condition of unchangeable constancy. . . ." [5] Carried away by his own rhetorical portrait of unchanging Britain, Burke proclaimed with pride that his countrymen had not "lost the generosity and dignity of thinking of the fourteenth century."

In hundreds of western European utopias written prior to the latter part of the eighteenth century, the explicit ideal of social life was calm felicity. The mood of the system was sameness, the tonus one of Stoic placidity, without agitation of the passions. One day was to be like the next, except that natural holidays related to the seasons and nuptial rites would punctuate the year with occasional festivals.

If we move halfway across the globe to China and India, we find that the same attributes of constancy were valued above all others by those civilizations. When Ssu-Ma Ch'ien, the historian of the Han, wishes to praise an imperial regime, he describes its adherence to the Taoist principles of non-action. Peace is an important element in this picture of constancy, but the purpose of peace is to allow for governmental inaction and the continuation of a natural rhythm of sameness in an agricultural society. "In the reign of Emperor Hui and Empress Lü," the Grand Historian concluded, "the common people succeeded in putting behind them the sufferings of the age of the Warring States and ruler and subject alike sought rest in surcease of action. Therefore Emperor Hui sat with folded hands and unruffled garments and Empress Lü, though a woman ruling in the manner of an emperor, conducted the business of government without ever leaving her private chambers, and the world was at peace. Punishments were seldom meted out and evildoers grew rare, while the people applied themselves to the task of farming, and food and clothing became abundant." [6] In Indian society the good rule of life is dharma, that which is established or firm, the steadfast decree, the law, usage, practice, customary observance, or prescribed conduct, the norm of social class in which a well-defined inalterable duty prevails.

In America we are committed to a rule of life so contradictory to that of these civilizations that at moments one seems to be dealing with another human nature. We are enrolled under the banner of Francis Bacon, who gave pithy expression to the new scientific and technological ideal in the New Atlantis. "The end of our foundation is the knowledge of causes, and secret motions of things; and the enlarging of the bounds of human empire, to the effecting of all things possible." [7] Short of the fulfillment of a Spenglerian prognostication of which there are as yet no signs—the engineer's flight from the machine for the sake of his soul—a rampantly dynamic industrialism and scientificism seem to be our destiny. Bacon is our prophet, a somewhat corrupt man who occasionally takes bribes, but he confesses the fact to himself and he has a genius for a certain type of reality. We in America have, in addition, become the primary heirs to an eighteenth-century conception embodied in the writings of two of Bacon's French followers, Turgot and Condorcet. For them sameness and repetition, attributes which men had once contemplated with admiration in nature and in societies that mirrored the cosmic order, became evil things in themselves. Constant inconstancy, eternal change and progress, the taming of nature, were for them the only distinctions of mankind. I single out these French theorists and their nineteenth-century followers as true prophets of what has in fact been happening in American civilization because they joined to Bacon's ideal two elements totally absent from his scientific-technological world view. These are egalitarianism and a sense of accelerating speed in change, elements which would have been utterly abhorrent to the Elizabethan aristocrat. Unlike Bacon and Newton, the French *philosophes* also had an idea of the infinitude of scientific knowledge and technical advance that is akin to our own. They are our real spiritual ancestors.

Amid incredible waste, we in America are continuing to pursue the Baconian ideal of power over nature. There are few new industrial and scientific ideas that fail to get an ultimate hearing somewhere—fads, fashions, fakes, and phonies included. This dynamic growth entails an eternal destruction of the old because old knowledge, prized in the traditionalist society, will in and of itself become dead and useless knowledge. The content of our concept of progress has changed from what it was even as recently as the nineteenth century. Progress toward abstract reason, virtue, and moral goodness no longer has any great significance and many of us doubt its validity. We do understand sheer dynamic change at a rate which defies definition in ordinary literate speech. When a popular magazine a few months ago made an effort to describe the transformations of the contemporary American city, it had to resort to such onomatopoeia as "zip" and "zoom."

No society of the past has shown such dynamism, such changeability, and such kaleidoscopic variety of experience. We destroy cities and rebuild them in three decades. No skyscraper standing today can be considered an inviolable monument. We tear up and throw away our clothes; we junk our machines for the slightest damage; our books have become as expendable as newspapers. The book, once revered as a holy object—Jews would not allow a written letter of the alphabet to be discarded—is now tossed away with a shift of lecture topic, as any professor who has seen a littered classroom can testify. Even the past has become for us a vast continent for novelty-seeking. When we conduct historical explorations we are no longer looking to the past as the support of an existing order, its validation in some profound respect, the way Israelite history is conceived in the Bible. We should not be deceived as to the meaning of the proliferation of contemporary historical research. This is merely another form of innovation. We will make a new history every ten years, and thus the past itself is rendered dynamic. Our scientific progress—to turn to our greatest achievement—has become *indéfini* in Condorcet's sense: it is now so immeasurable that you have to climb to a higher level before you can even fantasy what might be in prospect next.

Let me again refer, by way of contrast, to that ideal of social order which dominated the western mind for more than two thousand years, the Platonic model of justice and harmony. Whether one takes Plato's ideal from the *Republic* or from the *Laws*, he comes out with the same result with respect to the idea of change. His guardians would oust anyone who introduced a new tune or a new dance. The slightest modification would bring down upon the culprit Deuteronomic chastisement. The perfect order can only repeat itself or be destroyed. If Plato appeared today, even the most hidebound conservatives among us would cover him with ridicule.

The momentum of our society is its unique character and we must accommodate ourselves to it. The problems this entails are obvious. How can we live with these explosive concepts of knowledge and power when we are aware of their destructive potentialities? At the moment, many intellectuals have a bad conscience about this power. In the past two decades of the atomic age we have been showing some of the same anxieties as did the nineteenth-century Romantics in the face of those minor transformations of the technological landscape that were once grandiloquently labeled the Industrial Revolution. On the other hand, there are American scientists who assure us that only we, of all contemporary societies, have in actuality embarked—and just embarked—upon the great scientific revolution.

In this area, growing self-revelation, even on a superficial level, is a good, lest we recoil before the unknown instead of trying to understand and control it. We have yet to tame ourselves emotionally, so that we can use the instruments of science and technology without fear of their catastrophic effect and without dread that we are toying with the fire of the gods. These new powers, which we try to transform into innocent, familiar, harmless things by sometimes calling them "hardware," are rather recent extensions of our bodies and it will require the passage of time before we are reasonably comfortable with the seven-league boots and magical forces.

There has been nothing comparable to the *internal* dynamism of American society in the twentieth century—and my emphasis is upon the word "internal." There are numerous historical examples of extensive geographic conquest in a brief period—Alexander and Genghis Khan, the Arabs of the seventh century and the Spaniards of the sixteenth, the unification by war of the Andean civilization, and the drive of the Toltecs in Central America. But while our own growth has had its imperialist moments of horizontal extension and we are still enticed by such adventures, in our time the development has been largely within. Our thrust has been vertical. Our energies and aggressions have for the most part been expended upon objects within our midst. The fateful question now is: "Can this same momentum be continued?" And from my vantage point, which deliberately shuts out daily or annual political crises, I see us vacillating.

One type of decision would involve total commitment to the building of a technical-scientific civilization and spreading its benefits as fast as possible to our own people directly, to others indirectly. In this respect everyone is going our way despite verbal noises to the contrary. Even when the voice is the voice of Marx, the technical organization and the artifacts have followed American patterns. It is not less but more science and technology that we should embrace and promote. And by this I do not mean only the physical sciences, where we have been most successful. The whole range of human behavior lies open before us, for probing with a wide variety of methods. Every time a form of knowledge gets into a rut of orthodoxy, like some of our historical and philological sciences, we should try something new. The geographic spread of our universities, the diversity and overlapping of our government agencies, the variety and multiplicity of our private research organizations, despite or perhaps because of the chaos of scientific inquiries, hold a promise of continuous development. Stereotypes may emerge, but the curiosity about novelty seems at least equally strong. In all fields there is a pompous bureaucracy of knowledge, but as long as it does not become hidebound and there is choice and mobility, the dynamism need not be decelerated. If foundations, universities, government agencies, and industries are on the lookout for what is new, even for its own sake, we will not lapse into sameness and we will remain peculiarly ourselves. The Great Society must be prepared to countenance waste. Efficiency can be a grave danger: only those human agencies are most efficient whose purposes are very clearly defined and predetermined, like the Nazi gas chambers. American science and technology should remain flexible and open-ended, and in this respect I need not sidestep the obvious threat of a hypertrophied war science and technology. Thus far, both American universities and American industries have in many instances been willing to encourage creativity irrespective of immediate practical results. If this can continue, we shall be operating in consonance with our historical character, and we may avoid the evils of a mandarin society, a sectarian society, and a warrior society. The role of the individual creative scientist must undergo a transformation. He knows that his discovery will no sooner be published than it will be superseded, and he must feel a certain lack of fulfillment, a certain alienation from the object which he has fashioned. Can we attach his libido to cooperative creative effort without falling into the mire of a stifling scientific bureaucracy? This is an open question.

In the often frenetic quest for novelty we necessarily sacrifice the ideals of durability, permanency, and even beauty, which dominated other societies. Perhaps there remains among us some nostalgia for calm felicity, but I cannot help wondering about its authenticity. Santayana once described the restless Dr. Faustus in heaven serving quietly as a teacher for a while, then impatiently throwing his schoolbooks out of the celestial windows and dashing off to some windier place in the clouds. Spengler was right in choosing Faust as the symbolic figure of western culture, whose dynamic character America has come to embody more than any other sector of the civilization.

COHESION OR LOOSENESS

Great societies of the past often expressed satisfaction with their own cohesiveness, the prevalence among the citizenry of a strong bond of fellow feeling, the warmth of their brotherhood—in a word, their active love for one another.

What happens to these feelings in the fast-moving, sprawling urban agglomerations which are the relentless destiny of our society? That is my next question. Can a society lacking in communal unity be considered great? Of what avail the scientific and technological achievements, if the human beings in these vast urban areas suffer loneliness even though they are well fed and clothed by any historical standards. And by community feeling I do not mean the weak sense of responsibility that manifests itself in sporadic contributions to a community chest or that engages in some charitable activity to drive away boredom. I mean something far stronger.

Ibn Khaldun, the Arab philosopher and historian of the fourteenth century, for example, esteemed fanatical fellow feeling and solidarity, what he called *Assabiya*, above all other qualities of a society. He found it in its most potent form among conquering tribesmen about to overthrow a sedentary urban society that had gone soft and decadent and had lost its own *Assabiya*. Plato's insistence upon absolute unity in the good society is of the same character. It is said by some historians that the citizens of the Greek city-state actually had this *koinonia*, or community feeling. The dominant self-image of Chinese civilization was that of a society initiated to the discipline of life in the first ages of its existence by wise teachers, with the consequence that perfect social cohesion became the guiding principle. In the Chinese Golden Age, a public and common spirit ruled all under the sky. In official orthodox Chinese historiography, there is one recurrent theme—the alternating disintegration and restoration of this unity. The Saint-Simonians of the nineteenth century divided world history into alternating periods which they called organic and critical, and one of the major characteristics of the organic epoch—of which the Middle Ages was for them an example—was the per-

vasiveness of a feeling of cohesion among the people, in contrast
with the isolated, anarchic individualism of the critical epoch.
Something of the same sort may even be involved in the responsibility of the Puritan saints for one another's conduct, though in
their case the mutual love often assumed rather painful forms.
Rousseau is perhaps the greatest modern theorist of this fellow
feeling: in the *Social Contract* the ideal society is defined as one
in which the individual will and the collective or general will
naturally and spontaneously coalesce.

Modern mass movements such as revolutionary nationalism,
communism, and fascism are supposed to provide the libidinal
satisfactions of cohesiveness and social integration. German sociol-
ogists of the late nineteenth century like Tönnies preferred the
virtues of what they called *Gemeinschaft* over those of *Gesellschaft*. There has been much talk of alienation in Western society
since Hegel resurrected the theological term *Entfremdung* and
Marx used it to describe the temper of pre-communist societies—
it being understood that with the dawn of communism alienation
would automatically disappear. There is something of the French
Revolutionary need for *fraternité* in such conceptions. We now
talk popularly of the Atlantic community or the academic community. De Gaulle's constitution called France and its overseas
territories a *communauté*. President Johnson's notion of consensus
appears to border on this idea—rather dangerously. Most of
these emotion-laden phrases are used in our society quite artifi-
cially, with the hope of calling into being what does not exist by
the mere act of naming it.

If we turn to evaluate the possibilities of our society on
this polar scale of strong community feeling at one end and
isolated individualism without cohesiveness at the other, we shall
fortunately find ourselves rather weak on unity and fellow feeling,
as great societies of the past and great utopians of the past conceived this emotion.

It was Aristotle who first attacked the premise of Socrates
that "the greatest possible unity of the whole polis is the supreme
good." But one could go much farther, insisting for our American
society upon the original eighteenth-century conception of social

life based on individual rights, which stressed security *from* the state as Montesquieu did and praised the great virtue of *secrecy*, which meant privacy, as Hume did. One could glorify pluralism, diversity, and variety; and one could accept alienation from the whole as part of the human condition, to be suffered like mortality without recourse to facile verbal palliatives.

We must face the fact that with the urban agglomerations which the Great Society cannot avoid will come urban anonymity. But there are compensations in the vastly expanded range of human relationships. The urban university will not be a tightly knit group of colleagues, and thank the sprawling city for that. But what is lost in intimacy is won in freedom. The "identity" that can express itself only in professional or racial or age-group terms is no identity at all. It is a mask or a badge on the lapel of a professional convention suit. Love will doubtless be diluted in megalopolis, but it will not be as poisoned as it became in the town where Madame Bovary lived. Community is a contradiction in terms in large units of an overwhelmingly urban civilization. Relationships will not be natural—that is, based on geographical proximity. They will require acts of will. The city of the Great Society is dynamic, eclectic, egalitarian, and above all loose and tolerant, not cohesive.

There is no common heroic ancestry in this society. The hardy farmers of Lexington will be relegated to vague legend. The mothers and fathers of the American Revolution simply will not serve as ancestors for the many different nations and peoples who are today becoming effective members of this society. Some ethnic groups will continue to seek and find their own true fathers and they will cease to live on borrowed family portraits and fake genealogies. In time the dynamism of the society may cause us to forget all the founding fathers. In a way the present administration is more forthright in giving recognition to the new ethnic and racial realities than previous ones have been. President Johnson invites Jews, Italians, Irish, Poles, and Negroes into his administration without the self-consciousness from which Roosevelt —who started the trend—was hardly emancipated.

Growing tolerance of all forms of human life is the inevitable characteristic of our great urban society. One simply cannot be as intolerant in the city, no matter how hard one works at it, as residents are naturally in a rural community. Really open, ethnically tolerant societies have been rare in the past. They have usually been highly restrictive even though metics and slaves were occasionally assimilated. I am here standing on its head the value system inherent in most Germanic philosophy of history, which found the high point of a culture in the period when it was most exclusive, integrated, pure in style, uncomplicated racially or ethnically, untainted by the alien.

Our great urban society is demonstrating far greater powers of absorption than either Alexandria or Rome. As each stratum of immigrants or of the racially ostracized enters the society, it is shaken up with new impressions. Only those obsessed with the Germanic fetish of purity will worry about its mongrel quality. As each ghetto finally sends its sons out—and the process is admittedly far slower and more painful than was once imagined— new colors and tones are added to our existence. The picture of a uniform America is shattered; there is religious and ethnic diversity under government. If we can live with this diversity, our example may yet be the salvation of fragmented African and Asian polities. In praise of the pluralism of what he already called the great society in 1929—on the eve of a collapse from which it recuperated rather amazingly—Walter Lippmann wrote: "There is little doubt that in the great metropolitan centers there exists a disposition to live and to let live, to give and take, to agree and to agree to differ, which is not to be found in simple homogeneous communities. In complex communities life quickly becomes intolerable if men are intolerant. . . . The terrible indictments drawn up in a Mississippi village against the Pope in Rome, the Russian nation, the vices of Paris, and the enormities of New York are in the main quite lyrical. The Pope may never even know what the Mississippi preacher thinks of him and New York continues to go to, but never apparently to reach, hell." [8]

The American urban area which I identify with American society, because the rural space is fast losing all but recreational significance, is an inadequately regulated unit which experiences frequent crises. But it is a much more alive and human social form than the tight-knit, intolerant little town of the nineteenth century that de Tocqueville described. The great American city is likely to continue to be formless, the great university eclectic, the architecture of private and public buildings spectacular rather than beautiful. Spontaneity, ease, freedom of movement, immediacy of emotional response—attributes that some psychological historians have identified with the great aristocratic societies— can be found in the democratic American city. The tempo of life will be fast, the painting gaudy, the music loud and brassy; the noise decibels will reach new heights. And let those who do not like it go back to the beastly, cantankerous New England or Midwestern towns whence they came.

The question now is whether this Great Society can preserve its looseness, its often vulgar eclecticism, its tolerance and skepticism, for these are its great glory. It is one-dimensional only to those who see it that way and refuse to plumb its depths. So far, this is not 1984. Our society is uniform only to the lazy, and the secret persuaders are effective only on the unaware. The libraries of the city are large and free, its sidewalks are thronged with persons, its hospitals open to all comers, including staphylococci, its public administration anarchic, its private enterprise aggressive. It is more or less equal. Most automobiles look virtually alike and they are equally unsafe and generally operative. One used to talk about the acquisitive society. I have become impressed with its spendthrift quality, which gives it an expansive character even when it gets junk for its money.

To try to do all things possible and to find out about all things possible is one of the rare attributes of this loose-jointed society. I know of nothing so open to new experiences in modern times since France of the Directorate and Weimar Germany, two great creative moments often maligned by priggish historians. These, too, were great societies, and I would like, in passing, to rehabilitate their image along with our own. In variety of artistic and scientific expression there were no holds barred. Knowledge was pursued into hitherto forbidden areas in the newly founded schools of France in 1795, and the artistic and scientific genius

of Germany of the 1920's is still a seedbed for our contemporary
accomplishments, despite the defamation of the period in the
Germanic world. We today in America are in a similar time of
imaginative expression. The multiplication of universities in our
society has some disadvantages, but the increase in the number of
centers with the intoxicating variety of opportunities they afford
moves one to praise sheer proliferation. I am not dismayed if
vulgar objects win prizes, as long as there are enough rewards
to go around and originality is not officially suffocated. I am not
in sympathy with attacks on the eclecticism of the American
university. This is its grandeur. As we are forced to build urban
universities we will abandon the Ivy League model with its unau-
thentic forms, and transform the university into an intellectual
whirlpool where anything can happen.

Without being cohesive and centripetal, our Great Society
is nevertheless likely to be relatively orderly, as in the age of the
Antonines, of the good Chinese Emperors, and in nineteenth-
century Europe. Those who have watched the American megalopolis in crises have been impressed with its capacity to reorganize
itself under shock. New York during a power blackout or New
York with its major arteries of communication severed has shown
extraordinary recuperative powers and a spirit of mutual helpfulness.

One final word about the lack of cohesiveness in American
society in contrast with other civilizations. We, too, have ceremonials of cohesion in sports arenas, during the funerals of national
heroes, during the filming of dramatic scientific exploits, perhaps
in our elections and inaugurations. But I doubt whether they
have the potency and intensity of mystical communion that took
place between participants and onlookers in dance ceremonials
or during. human sacrifices in as noble a culture as the Mayan.
And maybe that is all to the good—the social bond created among
us is looser and more humane.

THE SACRED AND THE PROFANE

This brings me to religion in American culture. Although
American society is an offspring of European society and until our
own time had remained culturally under the tutelage of the

nourishing mother in most expressions of life and thought, the
declaration of independence is by now quite complete. If anything, it is the parent who has taken to imitating the rather ram-
bunctious child. In the United States, the secularizaion of life
has advanced farther than in many countries of western Europe,
despite the growing number of formal religious affiliations, which
seem to be surpassing population growth. The character of this
Great Society is secular to a degree never reached by other great
societies, not even in the period of their hypersophistication and
decline. The Egyptian, Tigris-Euphrates, Indian, Mayan, Andean
civilizations at their zenith were pervaded by a transcendental
religious feeling, a sentiment that seems quite feeble in ours, at
least in the last half century. This has led some historical commentators to conclude that our society has passed its peak and
is probably on the downgrade. But such jeremiads are the consequence of defining the objectives of our society in spiritual
terms which may have been of paramount importance in other
civilizations but seem to be irrelevant in ours.

The religious establishments in America appear to be essentially political and social institutions whose structure and formal nature may render them useful in binding together groups
of men in civility, even in brotherhood, but which cannot foster,
convey, or interpret religious emotion as it was known, let us
say, in the great moments of Judaism and Christianity. I believe
that the current revival of religion is primarily an aspect and
manifestation of middle-class prosperity in the land, and this
explains its patently dry character, its failure to create either in
the word or in the religious object. Our society is rather Roman
in matters of religion, which means that it is both tolerant and
indifferent. Religion is extrinsic rather than intrinsic to our culture. We are trinitarian in our fashion. There are three formal
establishments—Protestant, Catholic, and Jewish—which in public
ceremonials enjoy virtual equality. A Greek Orthodox establishment may be in the making, but at the moment it has not yet
achieved the same official status as the big three. As long as a
vague, inchoate state civil religion known as Americanism is subscribed to, almost any form of worship is countenanced. We are

somewhat disturbed only by those who in the eyes of the state seem to have no visible gods—as were the ancient Romans when confronted by the Jews and the Christians of the first centuries.

The Judeo-Greco-Christian chain of traditions once significantly fed the scientific experimental spirit, but its values no longer seem to control the life of this society. Their world was for the most part anti-egalitarian, rather rigid, based on communal love and responsibility. It was negative, or at most forbearing, toward the body and its passions. Nevertheless, these principles have endured for more than two thousand years, and in some form they may continue to be part of our civilization. Our problem is: can our present psychic drives, if divorced from these traditions, sustain the momentum of our scientific-technological society? Thus far we have combined this scientific-technological civilization with certain Greek concepts of harmony, Roman concepts of restrictive law, order, and power, and Judeo-Christian concepts of justice, mercy, and perhaps love. Science and technology are now becoming values in themselves and seem emancipated from their cultural origins. There are, of course, those who feel that granted a human science of behavior that is developed enough, we shall come around to the Greco-Roman-Judeo-Christian values in some balanced admixture as the best of all possible regimens for men. At the moment the spiritual foundation of our scientific-technological society is one of the great unknowns.

THE PROBLEM OF GRATIFICATION

Conceding that the Great Society is not likely to give birth to major expressions of religious transcendence, we may then ask: how does it measure up on the sensate level? is it moving to gratify man's desires for food and drink and beauty?

When the tyrants of the sixth century in the Hellenic world, the aristocrats of Magna Graecia, the princes of Pergamon, and the Seleucid kings built monumental cities, outstanding both in esthetic quality and in functional perfection, these cities certainly far surpassed in harmonious beauty anything we seem able to achieve. They were not democratic cities, and with few notable exceptions were meant to reflect the glory of the prince or the aristocracy. The same holds true for the Renaissance city. The aristocratic ideal of Castiglione's Urbino cannot be ours. Leonardo's sketch for a city provided for two architectural planes corresponding to the needs of an upper and a lower class. Our democratic commitment makes their exclusive esthetic ideal virtually impossible. Alberti's conception of beauty was a moral value and his vision implied an eternal order. Beauty and durability were identified. Such lofty moral sensibility will be denied us. Our great urban concentrations seem far too big ever to be harmonious units. To the extent that the city becomes a living landscape it will be as disorganized as nature itself, changing with the vantage point, the moment, and the mood. There may never again be architectural agglomerations comparable to those of the Acropolis, or Florence, or Cambridge, England. Our contemporary monumental structures look alike, and those in New York resemble those in Moscow, London, and, I am told, Peking.

On a lower level, the prospects of gratification are plentiful despite the present realities of mass poverty, which the Great Society aims to eradicate. There is nothing inherent in our situation that excludes an abundance of what Thomas More called "allowable honest pleasures." "To each according to his needs," the second half of the Marxist slogan in the Gotha Program, is a fast-changing concept. Within our own brief lives the definition of minimal needs has been radically transformed and will continue to be altered. I doubt whether we shall ever provide for total freedom from repression, though there is every reason to hope that the traditional chains on instinctual gratification will be loosened. The utopia of a playful rather than a working society seems far off indeed, but the facts are that our museums and theaters and universities can become the popular houses of play which they should be if they are not morgues. In our great urban agglomerations more dancing and feasting and drinking goes on than in Rome. Many are still not invited to the banquet, but more are being asked all the time.

Confucianism, with its emphasis on society as a graded but harmonious organism; the Indian outlook, with its view of the special dharma of each encapsulated social class; the medieval anthropomorphic and organismic conception of society—all have been rejected in the name of a simple egalitarianism which really allows for no rigid class differences. This egalitarianism is naturally suspicious of exclusivity unless it recognizes its immediate utility, and it will not, in the long run, tolerate any significant impediments to equality of opportunity among citizens of the society— which in effect means an equal chance for sensate gratification. Formal differences of rank even now make its members uncomfortable. While most great societies of the past have been elitist and aristocratic, we are irrevocably committed to a democratic society of more or less equals. The only historical analogue I know to what we really are trying to do is Periclean Athens, and it was stained by slavery. The portrait of Athenian democracy in the famous funeral oration as recounted by Thucydides is certainly touched up, but *mutatis mutandis* it still has some relevance to our intentions. "It is true that we are called a democracy," said Pericles, "for the administration is in the hands of the many and not of the few. But while the law secures equal justice to all alike in their private disputes, the claim of excellence is also recognized; and when a citizen is in any way distinguished, he is preferred to the public service, not as a matter of privilege, but as a reward of merit. Neither is poverty a bar, but a man may benefit his country whatever be the obscurity of his condition. There is no exclusiveness in our public life, and in our private intercourse we are not suspicious of one another nor angry with our neighbor if he does what he likes. . . ."[9] An American President might have delivered the same eulogy of his fellow countrymen, and if he, too, would be exaggerating somewhat, as Pericles doubtless did, it would be hyperbole in the same general direction.

MILITARY PROWESS AND OVEREXTENSION

Finally, we come to consider that attribute of societies that has until recent years always earned them the epithet "great." Sometimes it has been attached to the names of their rulers. I refer of course to military grandeur and power. For Plato, prowess in war was the ultimate test of the perfection of a polity and its system of education. Those who sought to provoke war among Hellenes or who maltreated prisoners were condemned, but the heroic virtues were appreciated above all others. The mythic Athens of the age of the Atlantans had, according to the *Critias*, withstood the trial and was the perfect society in action.

Military might is relatively easy to measure. It can be done crudely by counting the square inches of national color on a map. By this criterion, Persians, Macedonians, Romans, Chinese, Mongols, Turks, Spaniards, Englishmen, Russians, Germans, among others, have been great.

But this attribute is a two-edged sword. On the one hand, it has to be admitted that the organizers of great societies have almost always been successful warriors; but on the other hand, there is a strong consensus among philosophers of history from the Renaissance on that the military overextension of societies has ultimately led to their downfall.

The hybris of overextension was Montesquieu's explanation for the decline and fall of Rome. This theory was already a cornerstone of Jean Bodin's system in the sixteenth century, and has been entertained by men as remote from each other as John Adams and Arnold Toynbee. But then again, as Freud has pointed out, men have learned to love one another in the city by killing others, the outsiders. They have killed for a vast complex of verbal reasons and they have buried their dead in grand ceremonials. War has united men in adventurous enterprise and has provided outlets for their aggressiveness. In most ages wars have been brutal and cruel, but on occasion they have been playful, like dancing exercises. For our Great Society, however, maximal war is no longer possible. We must remain unfulfilled and we must sublimate our aggressiveness in other activities. This creates a difficulty: How can we be dynamic and aggressive internally in science and technology while remaining mere holders of the mark on the outside? We know that if we use our colossal strength, we may invite total annihilation; but will not external passivity be impossible to a society that operates in terms of dynamic power? Plato faced the problem of training his guardians to be gentle to the citizens and ferocious to the enemy, like certain types of dogs. We are now called upon to hold the line with no prospect of victory when the nature of our upbringing has made us incorrigible activists. And yet this is our only way, if we are to continue to build a uniquely great society with the many virtues I have presented. For many centuries the Romans fended off the barbarians without advancing beyond the Rhine-Danube boundary that Augustus had established, and we must train ourselves to a similar operation.

As things stand now, the Great Society is still rather burdened with heroic conceptions that are as antiquated as Achilles. We act as though every insult must be requited a thousandfold. Talk of destiny or mission or honor in the tradition of the duello still seems to dominate policy. Such notions belonged to other great societies; they have no place in ours.

"Let the world be destroyed yet justice must prevail" is a heroic posture. But aristocratic punctilio is contrary to the nature of our middle-class sensate society where injuries are adjudicated. It is told of late nineteenth-century soldier hygienists that they could not endure to see certain primitive African tribes die of fever in the swamps they inhabited, and so they drove the savages at the point of the bayonet to migrate to salubrious plateaus that were taboo. One German expedition, however, unable to force compliance, killed all of the natives in order successfully to fulfill their humane mission.

A great society now must exercise restraint even in the face of provocation, and worry less about its image than the reality of its existence. Great societies have faced strange enemies before. Perhaps there is something to be learned from the Confucian Emperor Wen. "The emperor made peace with the Hsiung-nu," we are told, "and, when they violated their agreement and invaded and plundered the borders, he ordered the border guards to stick to their posts, but would not send troops deep into barbarian territory. This was because he hated to bring hardship and suffering to the common people." [10]

Aristophanes, the poet of apolitical individualism and peace and good feeling, is in many ways a better guide for the Great

Society than Christ or Plato. The age of heroes, like the age of the gods, is dead. It is time that the age of men began.

NOTES

1. Plato, *Epistles*, with English trans. by R.G. Bury, Loeb Classical Library (Cambridge, Mass., 1961), Epistle VII, p. 483.
2. Charles Louis de Secondat, Baron de Montesquieu, *The Spirit of the Laws*, trans. Thomas Nugent (New York, 1949), Book XI, pp. 150-151.
3. Arnold Toynbee, *A Study of History* (New York, 1962), I, p. 161.
4. Paul Valéry, "Propos sur le Progrès," in *Regards sur le monde actuel* (Paris, 1931), p. 185.
5. Edmund Burke, *Reflections on the Revolution in France*, ed. T.H.D. Mahoney (New York, 1955), p. 38.
6. Ssŭ-ma Ch'ien, *Records of the Grand Historian of China*, trans. Burton Watson (New York, 1961), I, p. 340.
7. Francis Bacon, *The Advancement of Learning and New Atlantis* (London, 1951), p. 288.
8. Walter Lippmann, *A Preface to Morals* (New York, 1929), pp. 270-271.
9. Thucydides, *The Peloponnesian War*, trans. Benjamin Jowett, Book II, in Francis R.B. Godolphin, ed., *The Greek Historians* (New York, 1942), I, p. 648.
10. Ssŭ-ma Ch'ien, *Records of the Grand Historian of China*, I, p. 362.

INDEX

Achilles, 83, 84, 288
Adam, 72
Adami, Tobias, 97
Adams, John, 287
Adeimantus, 85
Aeschylus, 87
Alberti, Leon Battista, 285
Alcinous, 83
Alexander the Great, 275
Algarotti, Francesco, 187
Alstedt, Johann Heinrich, 89, 91, 95–96, 97, 105, 113
Andreae, Johann Valentin, 89, 96, 97, 98, 100, 104, 105, 109, 116, 120
Anne, Queen of England, 153, 161, 171
Aphrodite, 76
Arago, F., 239
Aratus of Soli, 79–80
Arbuthnot, John, 159, 160, 174
Ares, 76
Ariès, Philippe, 41
Aristophanes, 117, 288
Aristotle, 6, 19, 37, 78, 93, 109, 123, 143, 235, 278
Aron, Raymond, 34
Aston, Francis, 158
Augustin-Thierry, A., 4
Augustus (Gaius Julius Caesar Octavianus), 267, 288
Aumont et Rochebaron, Louis Marie Victor, 172
Axtell, James L., 203

Babeuf, François Noël, 225
Bacchus, 53
Bacon, Francis, Lord Verulam, 89, 90, 91, 92, 93, 95, 96, 97, 99, 100, 103, 104, 105, 106, 107, 108, 109, 116, 122, 124, 125, 172, 207, 224, 247, 252, 272
Baily, Francis, 186
Barnes, Hazel E., 21, 51
Barrow, Isaac, 163

Barth, Karl, 246
Beauvoir, Simone de, 262
Becker, Carl, 57
Beethoven, Ludwig van, 51
Bellamy, Edward, 116, 136
Bellermann, Ludwig, 20
Benedict, Ruth, 143
Bentley, Dr. Richard, 164
Bergin, T. G., 21
Berlin, Sir Isaiah, 65
Bernoulli, Johann, 181
Bernoulli, Nicholas, 163
Besold, Christoph, 89, 91, 96, 97
Bichat, Marie François Xavier, 130, 211, 213, 215, 221, 229–230, 232, 233, 240
Biot, Jean Baptiste, 187
Blair, John, 194
Blake, William, 202
Bodin, Jean, 33, 53, 270, 287
Bolingbroke, Henry St. John, Viscount, 8, 173
Bonald, Louis Gabriel Ambroise, Viscount de, 221, 232, 237
Bonaparte, Marie, 36
Bossuet, Jacques Bénigne, Bishop of Meaux, 111
Bougainville, Jean Pierre de, 126
Bouglé, Célestin Charles Alfred, 263
Bouillé, Françoise Claude Amour, Marquis de, 205
Boulanger, Nicolas Antoine, 59, 78
Bouvard, Alexis, 209
Bovary, Mme. Emma, 279
Boyle, Robert, 164, 195
Brambora, Josef, 113
Brewster, Sir David, 185, 186
Brissot de Warville, Jacques Pierre, 223, 239
Brouncker, William, Lord Viscount of Castle Lyons, 158
Brown, Norman O., 42, 116, 140, 142
Bruno, Giordano, 89, 93, 94, 95, 97, 104, 106, 110, 155

Buckle, Henry Thomas, 54
Buffière, Félix, 81
Bullitt, William C., 37
Bultmann, Rudolf Karl, 55
Bulwer-Lytton, Edward, 117
Burdin, Dr. Jean, 211
Burke, Edmund, 231, 237, 271, 289
Burnet, Thomas, of Kenney, 187
Bury, R. G., 87, 289

Cabanès, Augustin, 37
Cabanis, Dr. Pierre Jean Georges, 207, 211, 221, 227–228, 229, 232, 233, 239
Cabet, Etienne, 128, 133
Cadmus, 84
Calixtus, Georgius, 111
Calypso, 83
Campanella, Tommaso, 89, 94–95, 96, 97, 100, 101, 102, 103, 104, 105, 106, 107, 108, 109, 110, 116
Camus, Albert, 8
Caroline of Anspach, Princess of Wales, 162, 171, 172, 181, 194
Carter, Elizabeth, 187
Cassirer, Ernst, 20
Castiglione, Count Baldassare, 285
Catherine II, Empress of Russia, 53
Cavendish, Margaret, Duchess of Newcastle, 115
Cézanne, Paul, 63
Chamberlayne, John, 153
Charles II, King of England, 173
Cheyne, George, 163, 164
Chiari, Abbate Pietro, 124
Chi'en Lung, Emperor of China, 268
Chilmead, E., 113
Chouêt, Jean Robert, 185
Christ, 93, 103, 176, 235, 289
Chrysippus, 266
Churchill, Thomas, 11, 55, 56
Cicero, 80
Clarke, Edward, 196

Clarke, Samuel, 162, 164, 167, 174, 183
Cole, G. D. H., 239
Collins, John, 163, 180, 187
Comenius, John Amos, 89, 91, 96, 97, 98, 99, 100, 104, 106, 107, 108, 109, 110, 111
Comte, Isidore Auguste Marie François Xavier, 54, 56, 57, 59, 64, 65, 66, 128–129, 130, 134, 138, 215, 243, 245, 246, 249, 250, 251, 253, 254, 258, 260
Condillac, Etienne Bonnot de, 222, 227, 228, 239, 251
Condorcet, Marie Jean Antoine Nicolas de Caritat, Marquis de, 11, 54, 55, 56, 57, 62, 64, 116, 125, 128, 207, 208, 211, 217, 221, 223–224, 227, 228, 230, 232, 233, 238, 240, 243, 247, 247–249, 250, 251, 255, 256, 261, 272, 274
Conduitt, Catherine Barton (niece of Isaac Newton), 154
Conduitt, John, 154, 163, 185, 194
Confucius, 285
Contarini, Cardinal Gasparo, 270
Conti, Abate Antonio, 180, 181, 182
Cotes, Roger, 161, 163, 164, 166, 174
Cousin, Victor, 246
Craig, John, 163, 164
Cranston, Maurice, 203
Crucé, Emeric, 103
Cyrano de Bergerac, Savinien, 86, 103, 145

Daniel, 76, 91
Dante Alighieri, 38
D'Arcy, Father Martin, 55
Darwin, Charles, 135, 136, 137, 139, 238
Davies, D. Seaborne, 186
De Beer, E. S., 186
De Gaulle, Charles, 278
Demeter, 86

Demos, John, 44
Derham, William, 164
Desaguliers, John Theophilus, 164, 166, 168
Descartes, René, 6–7, 35, 37, 38, 43, 63, 91, 96, 103, 155, 156, 194, 209
Des Maizeaux, Pierre, 166, 167, 187
Dewhurst, Kenneth, 203
Dicaearchus of Messana, 78, 79
Diderot, Denis, 126, 208, 210, 224, 245
Diels, H., 87
Dilthey, Wilhelm, 18, 19, 27–30, 34, 48, 58
Dionysius, Tyrant of Syracuse, 265
Donne, John, 90
Dostoevsky, Feodor Mikhailovich, 35
Dunn, John, 203
Dunoyer, Charles, 212
Dupuis, Charles François, 208
Dupuytren, Baron Guillaume, 206
Dury, John, 89, 99, 110
Duveyrier, Charles, 147, 255

Eckstein, F., 50
Edleston, Joseph, 185
Eichthal, Gustave d', 246
Empedocles, 76–77, 78
Engels, Friedrich, 147, 206
Erdman, David V., 203
Erikson, Erik H., 19, 31, 34, 35, 37–40
Eros, 141
Eugene, Prince of Savoy (François Eugène de Savoie-Carignan), 101
Eumolpus, 85
Evelyn, John, 175

Farnell, Lewis Richard, 88
Farrington, Benjamin, 113
Fatio de Duillier, Nicolas, 153, 154, 162, 163–164, 165, 166
Faust (Faustus), 276

Febvre, Lucien Paul Victor, 27, 28, 30–32, 33, 34, 37, 47
Fénelon, François de Salignac de la Mothe, 103, 116
Fichte, Johann Gottlieb, 54, 243
Fisch, Max H., 21
Flamsteed, John, 157, 158, 160, 162, 173, 175–180, 182, 196, 197
Flaubert, Gustave, 41
Floyd, Thomas, 124
Fludd, Robert, 96
Foucault, Michel, 33
Fourier, Charles, 116, 128, 129, 131–132, 133, 134, 135, 138, 140, 141, 142, 210, 231, 234, 235, 243, 254
France, Anatole, 136
Francis, Father Alban, 170
Frazier, T. E., 134
Freud, Anna, 50
Freud, Ernst L., 50
Freud, Sigmund, 5, 11, 18, 19, 28, 30, 31, 33, 34, 35–36, 37, 39, 41, 43, 47, 48, 55, 63, 115, 135–136, 139, 140, 141, 142–143, 244, 252, 287
Fromm, Erich, 116, 140, 141
Fülop-Miller, René, 50
Fyfe, W. Hamilton, 20

Galileo Galilei, 36, 46, 96, 155, 194
Gall, Franz Joseph, 228
Gandhi, 38, 39
Gaquère, François, 113
Garcilaso de la Vega (El Inca), 119
Gay, John, 153, 199
Genghis Khan, 275
George, Prince of Denmark (consort of Queen Anne), 160, 178, 179
George I, King of England, 153, 172, 181, 183
George III, King of England, 268
George, Alexander L., 37

George, Juliette L., 37
Gerhardt, C. J., 186
Geyl, Pieter, 60–61, 62
Gibbon, Edward, 17
Gilbert, Creighton, 51
Glanvill, Joseph, 89, 99, 172
Goclenius, Rudolf, 27
Godolphin, Francis R. B., 21, 289
Godwin, Francis, 86
Goethe, Johann Wolfgang, 27, 230
Goldschmidt, Victor, 87
Graf, Ernestius, 87
Gregory, David, the elder, 174
Gregory, David, the younger, 161,
    162, 163, 164, 166, 174
Groethuysen, Bernhard, 49
Grotius, Hugo, 111

Haldane, J. B. S., 116, 138
Haldane, R. B., 20
Halévy, Elie, 263
Halifax, Lord, see Montague,
    Charles
Hall, A. Rupert, 186
Hall, John, 90
Hall, Marie Boas, 186
Halley, Edmond, 154, 159, 160,
    161–162, 163, 165, 166, 168,
    174, 175, 178, 179, 194
Hamann, Johann Georg, 245
Hamilton, Marian W., 52
Harrington, James, 111, 122
Hartlib, Samuel, 89, 90, 99, 103,
    107, 108, 110, 111, 113
Hartman, Robert S., 21
Hartman, W., 87
Hawes, Nathaniel, 186
Haynes, Hopton, 153
Hearne, Thomas, 161
Hegel, Georg Wilhelm Friedrich, 12,
    13–14, 27, 28, 34, 39, 49, 54, 58,
    64, 65, 141, 200, 217, 243, 245,
    246, 250, 251, 252, 254, 255,
    256, 257, 258–259, 261, 262,
    278
Heidegger, Martin, 28, 30
Held, F. E., 146

Helen of Troy, 82
Helvétius, Jean Claude Adrien, 221,
    222, 227, 228, 229, 239, 240
Heraclitus, 8
Hercules, 141
Herder, Johann Gottfried von, 11,
    18, 27–28, 54, 55, 57, 58, 62,
    63, 230, 243, 245, 246, 247,
    250, 252, 253, 254, 257, 259–
    260, 261, 267
Herlihy, David, 51
Hermes Trismegistus, 110
Herodotus of Halicarnassus, 19
Hertzka, Theodor, 116, 134
Hesiod, 69–76, 77, 80, 81, 82, 83,
    84, 85, 129
Hexter, Jack H., 112
Hiscock, W. G., 185, 186
Hitler, Adolf, 34
Hobbes, Thomas, 198
Hoenig, J., 52
Hofmann, J. E., 187
Holbach, Paul Henri Thiry, Baron
    d', 78
Hölderlin, Friedrich, 29, 30, 257
Homer, 72, 82, 83, 84, 85, 86
Hooke, Robert, 107, 158, 162, 171,
    199
Hughes, H. Stuart, 44
Hui, Emperor of China, 271–272
Huizinga, Johan, 32
Hume, David, 8, 63, 279
Hunter, J., 185
Husserl, Edmund, 30
Hutton, Charles, 186
Huxley, Aldous, 117, 136
Huxley, Julian, 116, 137, 138
Huygens, Christiaan, 182
Hyginus, 80

Ibn Khaldun, 53, 277
Iselin, Isaak, 59

Jackson, John, 183
James II, King of England, 192
Jaspers, Karl, 30, 48, 139

Jeffreys, Lord George, 192
Jensen, W., 50
Joachim of Fiore, 11, 53, 91, 127, 260
John XXIII, Pope, 136
Johnson, Lyndon B., 267, 278, 279
Johnson, Samuel, 57
Jones, Katherine, 50
Jones, William, 163
Jowett, Benjamin, 289

Kant, Immanuel, 54, 64, 140, 243, 245, 246, 250, 251, 252, 254–256, 258, 261
Keill, John Ball, 159, 161, 163, 164, 166, 167, 180
Kemp, J., 20
Keynes, Lord John Maynard, 152
Khrushchev, Nikita, 56, 136
Kierkegaard, Sören, 27
Kneller, Godfrey, 152, 197
Knox, T. M., 263
Kovel, Joel, 50
Kris, Ernst, 36
Kronos, 70, 71, 76, 77, 80, 81, 82, 83, 84
Kudoimos, 77
Kupris, 76, 77

Lafargue, Paul, 134
Lagrange, Joseph Louis, Count, 209
Langer, William L., 44
Laplace, Pierre Simon, Marquis de, 154, 209
Laslett, Peter, 203
Lasswell, Harold, 37
Lattimore, Richmond, 87
Laurenberg, Peter, 98
Lavater, Johann Caspar, 228
Lefort, F., 187
Leibniz, Gottfried Wilhelm von, 90, 101–102, 104, 105, 106, 107, 110, 111–112, 151, 155, 156, 157, 160, 162, 166, 167, 172, 175, 176, 180–184, 196, 200, 201

Lenin, V. I., 192
Leonardo da Vinci, 35, 285
Leroy, Maxim, 50
Lesconvel, Pierre de, 121
Lessing, Gotthold Ephraim, 54, 243, 245, 246, 250–251, 252, 253, 254, 260
Lévi-Strauss, Claude, 15, 16
Levy, Dr. Oscar, 20
Leyden, Wolfgang von, 203
Lichtenberger, André, 239
Liljegren, S. B., 146
Lippmann, Walter, 280
Locke, John, 37, 43, 111, 153, 189–202, 209, 221, 222, 226, 227, 228, 239, 251
Lough, John, 203
Louis XIV, King of France, 101, 102, 106, 166, 267
Louis XV, King of France, 59
Louis XXXVI, 121
Lovejoy, Arthur, 47
Lü, Empress of China, 271–272
Lucian, 86
Lull, Ramón, 99
Luther, Martin, 30, 31, 38, 39, 217, 251, 255
Lyons, Sir Henry, 185

Machiavelli, Niccolò di Bernardo, 270
Maclaurin, Colin, 162, 163, 164
Madison, James, 195
Mahoney, T. H. D., 289
Maier, Michael, 96
Maimonides, Moses, 202
Mair, G. R., 87
Maistre, Joseph Marie, Count de, 232, 237
Malesherbes, Chrétien Guillaume de Lamoignon, 246
Mandrou, Robert, 32–33
Manuel, Frank E., 262
Mao Tse-Tung, 4
Marais, Mathieu, 205
Marcuse, Herbert, 34, 42, 116, 140, 141–142

Mare, Margaret, 186
Maritain, Jacques, 55
Marx, Karl, 18, 27, 34, 40, 41, 43,
    45, 54, 56, 57, 58, 59, 60, 62,
    64, 66, 81, 116, 128, 129, 130,
    133–134, 138, 139, 140, 141,
    142, 143, 172, 200, 244, 257,
    259, 275, 278, 285
Masham, Lady Damaris, 197
Masham, Sir Francis, 197
Maslow, Abraham H., 116, 118,
    143–144
Matthew, Sir Toby, 96
Mazlish, Bruce, 44
Mazon, Paul, 87
Mead, Margaret, 143
Mead, Dr. Richard, 159, 160, 179
Meinecke, Friedrich, 28
Meiss, Millard, 48
Menelaus, 82
Menzicoff, Prince Alexander, 173
Mercier, Louis Sébastien, 121, 124
Mersenne, Father Marin, 102
Metternich, Klemens Wenzel Ne-
    pomuk Lothar, Prince von, 15
Michelet, Jules, 26, 30, 61–62
Miller, Frank Justus, 87
Milton, John, 90
Minerva, 200, 251
Mises, Ludwig von, 59
Moivre, Abraham de, 163, 166
Montague, Charles, Lord Halifax,
    152, 153, 158, 170, 178, 194,
    195
Montesquieu, Charles de Secondat,
    Baron de la Brède et, 247, 252,
    267, 270, 279, 287
More, Louis T., 186
More, Thomas, 90, 91, 92, 97, 106,
    115, 116, 117–119, 120, 121,
    122, 123, 124, 126, 127, 131,
    132, 134, 136, 270, 285
Morelly, 116, 121, 223, 239
Moses, 35, 53, 154
Muller, Herman J., 138
Müller, K., 87
Münzer, Thomas, 91
Musaeus, 85

Napoleon I, 207, 210, 232, 236
Naville, Pierre, 147
Nebuchadnezzar, 76
Necker, Jacques, 231
Newcastle, Duchess of, see Caven-
    dish, Margaret
Newton, Sir Isaac, 91, 135, 151–
    185, 189–202, 206, 207, 209,
    273
Niebuhr, Reinhold, 55
Nietzsche, Friedrich Wilhelm, 7–8,
    23, 29, 128, 136, 143
Nohl, Herman, 50
Nugent, Thomas, 289

O'Brien, James Bronterre, 121
O'Connor, A. Condorcet, 239
Odysseus, 83
Orwell, George, 136
Ovid, 80–81
Owen, Robert, 116, 133

Pandora, 72, 74
Pascal, Blaise, 183
Peleus, 84
Pemberton, Henry, 162, 163, 164
Pepys, Samuel, 158
Pericles, 266, 286
Persephone, 86
Perses (brother of Hesiod), 70, 74,
    75
Peter I, Czar of Russia, 173
Philo Judaeus, 53
Pindar, 83–85
Pinel, Philippe, 38, 228
Plato, 37, 63, 77–78, 85, 90, 91,
    107, 109, 117, 119, 122, 131,
    137, 265, 266, 274, 277, 286,
    287, 289
Plotinus, 85
Plutarch, 85, 86
Poe, Edgar Allan, 36
Poisson, Siméon Denis, 206
Pope, Alexander, 153

Porphyry, 76, 78, 85, 86
Poseidon, 77
Price, Richard, 54
Priestley, Joseph, 54
Prometheus, 74
Proudhon, Pierre Joseph, 134
Prynne, William, 113

Quarrell, W. H., 186
Quintilian, 239

Rabelais, François, 31
Raeff, Marc, 52
Raguet, Abbé Gilles Bernard, 124
Rameau, Jean Philippe, 208
Ramus, Peter, 104
Ranke, Leopold von, 7, 18, 28, 41
Raphson, John, 163
Rawlinson, George, 21
Reade, William Winwood, 129–130
Reich, Wilhelm, 116, 140, 142
Renan, Ernest, 3, 135
Renaudot, Théophraste, 103
Restif de la Bretonne, Nicolas Edme, 116, 120–121, 125–126, 254
Reybaud, Louis, 116
Rhadamanthus, 82, 84
Richelieu, Armand Jean du Plessis, Cardinal de, 102, 103
Rieff, Philip, 143
Rieu, E. V., 87
Robespierre, Maximilien Marie Isidore de, 56
Robson-Scott, Elaine, 50–51
Robson-Scott, William, 50–51
Rolland, Romain, 55
Roosevelt, Franklin D., 279
Rosenkreutz, Christian, 96
Roth, Rudolf von, 87
Rousseau, Jean-Jacques, 7, 26, 78–79, 121, 142, 221, 222, 223, 225, 246–247, 253, 255, 271, 278

Sacheverell, Henry, 153
Sade, Donatien Alphonse François, Count de (Marquis de), 126
Saint Augustine, 10
Saint Jerome, 79
Saint Paul, 176, 253
Saint Thomas Aquinas, 11, 94
Saint-Pierre, Charles Irenée Castel, Abbé de, 112
Saint-Simon, Claude Henri, Count de, 54, 56, 63, 64, 81–82, 116, 128–129, 130, 135, 142, 190, 198, 205–217, 221, 229, 231, 232–238, 243, 245, 246, 247, 249, 250, 251, 255
Saint-Simonians, 54, 64, 128, 129, 131, 132, 133, 134, 136, 140, 243, 246, 249, 250, 251, 255, 258, 277
Santayana, George, 276
Sartre, Jean Paul, 16, 18, 19, 34, 40–41
Saturn, 80
Say, Jean Baptiste, 212
Schaerer, René, 87
Schelling, Friedrich Wilhelm, Joseph von, 54, 243, 252
Schiller, Johann Christoph Friedrich von, 3, 142, 243, 257
Schleiermacher, Friedrich Ernst Daniel, 28, 29
Schopenhauer, Arthur, 7
Scipio Africanus Minor, 268
Sénancour, Etienne Pivert de, 230
Servius, 83
Shaftesbury, Anthony Ashley Cooper, First Earl of, 192
Shorey, Paul, 87, 88
Sibree, J., 262
Sinold, Philipp Balthazar, 123
Skinner, B. F., 134
Sloane, Sir Hans, 159, 165, 169, 179, 180
Smith, Adam, 226
Smith, Preserved, 28
Socrates, 87, 257, 278
Solmsen, Friedrich, 87
Somers, Lord John, 153, 158, 195

Sorokin, Pitirim, 268
Spencer, Herbert, 54
Spengler, Oswald, 28, 54, 57, 58,
    59, 63, 64, 65, 261, 268, 272,
    276
Spinoza, Baruch, 111
Sprat, Thomas, 172
Ssu-ma-Ch'ien, 271
Staël-Holstein, Anne Louise Ger-
    maine, Baroness de, 34
Stapledon, Olaf, 117, 135
Sterba, Editha, 36
Sterba, Richard, 36
Stirling, John, 162
Stobaeus, Joannes, 86
Strachey, James, 50, 146, 148
Strauss, Leo, 203
Strindberg, Johan August, 30
Stukeley, Dr. William, 158, 160,
    169, 173
Sully, Maximilien de Béthune,
    Baron de Rosny and Duke de,
    103
Surtz, Edward, S. J., 112
Swedenborg, Emanuel, 30
Swift, Jonathan, 153, 196

Talleyrand-Périgord, Charles Mau-
    rice, Prince de Bénévent, 226,
    227, 238
Tapley, Roberts, 50
Tax, Sol, 147
Teilhard de Chardin, Pierre, 116,
    137–138, 139
Telesio, Bernardino, 105
Theognis of Megara, 76
Theron, Tyrant of Acragas, 84
Thetis, 83
Thoresby, Ralph, 166
Thucydides, 8, 289
Tillich, Paul, 55
Tocqueville, Alexis de, 281
Tönnies, Ferdinand, 278
Toynbee, Arnold Joseph, 55, 56,
    57, 58, 59, 60, 63, 64, 139, 268,
    287
Trask, Willard R., 51

Trevor-Roper, H. R., 20
Troeltsch, Ernst, 28
Turgot, Anne Robert Jacques,
    Baron de l'Aulne, 54, 58, 62,
    230, 238, 243, 247, 248, 251,
    255, 260, 272
Turnbull, George Henry, 113
Turnbull, H. W., 186

Uffenbach, Zacharias Conrad von,
    186
Utopus, King, 91, 122, 123, 134
Uxkull-Gyllenband, Woldemar, Graf
    von, 87

Vairasse, Denis, 122
Valéry, Paul, 10, 269
Vanderbank, John, 152
Van Gogh, Vincent, 30
Vaux, Clothilde de, 245
Vernant, J. P., 87
Vico, Giambattista, 7, 18, 19, 25–
    26, 27, 54, 55, 56, 58, 61, 62,
    63, 64, 244
Vicq-d'Azyr, Félix, 211
Vincent of Beauvais, 38
Voltaire, François Marie Arouet de,
    11, 54, 60, 176, 190, 193, 223,
    243, 247

Wahl, Jean André, 256
Wallon, Dr. Henri, 32
Watkins, Tobias, 240
Watson, Burton, 289
Weld, Charles Richard, 186
Wells, H. G., 116, 128, 129
Wen, Emperor of China, 288
Wense, Wenceslaus, 96, 97
Whiston, William, 153, 161, 162,
    164, 165, 174, 183, 186
White, A. Hastings, 185
Whitehead, Alfred North, 23
Wilkins, John, 89, 99, 105
William of Orange (later William
    III, King of England), 192

Willoughby, Francis, 167
Wilson, Woodrow, 37
Winckelmann, Johann Joachim, 243, 257, 260
Woodward, Dr. John, 169–170
Wotton, Sir Henry, 90
Wren, Sir Christopher, 158, 182

Yates, Frances Amelia, 91, 113
Yolton, John W., 203
Young, Robert Fitzgibbon, 113

Zamiatin, Yevgeny, 117, 136
Zeus, 70, 74, 77, 82, 84
Zweig, Arnold, 50–51